DATE DUE

91/10/12	
~~DEC 2 0 1989~~	
6/30/90	
SEP 1 5 2010	

IMPORT / EXPORT
CAN MAKE YOU RICH

IMPORT / EXPORT
CAN MAKE YOU RICH

L.B. Lanze

PRENTICE HALL
Englewood Cliffs, New Jersey 07632

Library of Congress Cataloging-in-Publication Data

Lanze, L. B. (date)
   Import/export can make you rich / L. B. Lanze.
     p.   cm.
   Bibliography: p.
   Includes index.
   ISBN 0-13-451857-8:
   1. Imports. 2. Exports. 3. International trade. I. Title.
HF1419.L36 1988
658.8'48—dc19   88-9802
                                        CIP

Editorial/production supervision and interior design: Denise Gannon
Cover design: Ben Santora
Manufacturing buyer: Mary Anne Gloriande

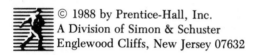 © 1988 by Prentice-Hall, Inc.
A Division of Simon & Schuster
Englewood Cliffs, New Jersey 07632

The publisher offers discounts on this book when ordered in bulk quantities.
For more information, write:

Special Sales/College Marketing
College Technical and Reference Division
Prentice-Hall, Inc.
Englewood Cliffs, New Jersey 07632

Printed in the United States of America
10 9 8 7 6 5 4 3 2 1

ISBN 0-13-451857-8

PRENTICE-HALL INTERNATIONAL (UK) LIMITED, *London*
PRENTICE-HALL OF AUSTRALIA PTY. LIMITED, *Sydney*
PRENTICE-HALL CANADA INC., *Toronto*
PRENTICE-HALL HISPANOAMERICANA, S.A., *Mexico*
PRENTICE-HALL OF INDIA PRIVATE LIMITED, *New Delhi*
PRENTICE-HALL OF JAPAN, INC., *Tokyo*
SIMON & SCHUSTER ASIA PTE. LTD., *Singapore*
EDITORA PRENTICE-HALL DO BRASIL, LTDA., *Rio de Janeiro*

To Dr. James E. McConnell

CONTENTS

Contents

PREFACE

This book is designed as a step-by-step guide to exporting and importing. While most international trade texts focus on more theoretical concepts drawn from economics and business, this book answers the practical questions most commonly asked by individuals who wish to export and import goods and services. The material discussed contains the information an export or import manager knows and handles routinely—the knowledge gained from years of experience in the field.

The book is appropriate for college courses in international trade and international business at both the undergraduate and graduate levels. In such courses, the college instructor may also find this book to be a useful supplement to a standard text. In an operations/methods course, the book should be used as a primary text. Laymen interested in exporting and importing will benefit from the design and contents of this book as well. Terms and concepts are explained thoroughly. Unnecessarily technical language is avoided. This book can also assist individuals interested in starting their own export/import businesses.

The book is divided into three sections: Section I develops an overview of the process of international trade and its effect on the firm's marketing strategy, Section II dissects the export process, importing is detailed in Section III. The appendices include a glossary of international trade terms, revised foreign trade definitions, a guide to selecting publications for a personal international trade library, and a resource guide.

ACKNOWLEDGMENTS

My first, and foremost, debt is to Dr. James E. McConnell, Professor and Chairman of the Department of Geography, and Coordinator of the International Trade Concentration at the State University of New York at Buffalo. Dr. McConnell is an extraordinary teacher and inspiring advisor who taught me much of what I know about international trade. The manuscript also benefited from his reading and comments.

This book would not have been possible without the generous assistance of Mary T. Conrad, Trade Specialist at the Baltimore District Office, U.S. Foreign and Commercial Service, U.S. Department of Commerce, International Trade Administration, who gave the manuscript a thorough reading. I have profited enormously from her suggestions.

I would also like to thank Jeffrey A. Krames, Business Editor at Prentice Hall for getting this book off the ground, and Denise Gannon for guid-

Acknowledgments

ing the manuscript through production. In addition, I would like to thank my family for their support of this project and especially my husband, Mark, for his helpful comments on the first draft.

Buffalo, New York   LAURA BUONANNO LANZE

Section One

International Trade:
The Global View

1

THE 17 "INGS"
OF EXPORT/IMPORT

Trade, as Adam Smith pointed out in *Wealth of Nations,* is a propensity found in man alone. "Nobody ever saw a dog make a fair and deliberate exchange of one bone for another with another dog" he writes, perhaps with tongue in cheek, but his observation encapsulates the purpose of our discussion. "Fair and deliberate exchange" is an elusive enough goal in our own country, but the uncertainty associated with international trade supersedes the perplexities of domestic trade.

International trade—the export and import of goods and services—seems discouragingly complex to many beginners. This text simplifies every aspect of the import/export process. The information presented is for the novice, whether a college student, a person who contemplates setting up an import/export company, or a marketing manager of an industrial concern attempting to expand his or her company's market. Retailers interested in obtaining lower costs and better quality products without a middleman, and wholesalers interested in adding imported products to their lines will find this book to be an invaluable asset for expanding profits as well. One may equally benefit as a purveyor of services. Perhaps a technical consulting firm wants to expand its client base. Why not investigate foreign markets eager to obtain and willing to pay top dollar for American know-how?

If there are infinite opportunities in trade, one might ask, why isn't everyone making a fortune in the import/export business? The answer is quite simple—lack of knowledge. Opportunities literally pop out at people once they get started. Former students of our "how to" courses have brought success stories about exporting and importing such diverse products as dental floss, shoes, candy, antique cars, jewelry, soaps, and highly engineered equipment. At the beginning of each course, they filled the room with enthusiasm, a restlessness to get started, and ingenuity, but lacked the catalyst for success—*information*. The major deficiency that characterizes much of the currently published material on the import/export trade is its lack of detail. A cursory treatment of marketing, finance, and documentation is inadequate given the extra costs and potential profits associated with international trade.

The successful company begins by drawing up a strategic plan. Let's go over the major points using the checklist "The 17 "ings" of Export/Import."[1]

Estimating and Assessing

Consulting and Selecting

Organizing

Locating

Evaluating the Market

Pricing

Advertising

Communicating

Agreeing

Producing

Packaging

Financing

Insuring

Documenting

Shipping

Collecting

Evaluating Performance

One task in this model tends to follow directly after another. It reminds us that the logical place to begin is with an assessment of a company's goals. When one is "Estimating and Assessing" he or she asks, how risky is the venture? Is the expected return on the venture commensurate with the risk? In the next step, "Consulting and Selecting," one solicits the advice of experts such as Commerce Department trade specialists, freight forwarders, bankers, customhouse brokers, and members of local international trade groups. The company shops around for the best services for

---

[1]Based on a model developed by James E. McConnell, Department of Geography, State University of New York at Buffalo.

its product line, carefully selecting the right banker, brokers, and distributors. As a company is "Organizing" for international trade it sets up the appropriate facilities, such as an in-house export or import department or a foreign sales branch.

The "Locating" decision is concluded by investigating and targeting potential export markets. An importer identifies foreign products to import and locates American customers. "Evaluating" the potential market requires data collection that describes markets in terms of crucial economic, social, and geographic variables.

When a company develops a "Pricing" strategy it must estimate the product life in that market. Is there a large market available for exploitation or is it a small market with little potential for steadily increasing sales? How can a company price its product to protect itself from foreign exchange fluctuations? Costs of transportation, insurance, documentation, and financing must be carefully estimated before delivering a price quotation to a potential customer. Language and other cultural differences affect a company's plan for "Promoting and Advertising." For instance, a product may be advertised primarily in magazines in the U.S., but such a strategy may not be appropriate in a country where approximately 85 percent of its citizens are illiterate. "Communicating" is yet another important piece in our strategic model. What is the procedure for contacting a foreign buyer? Do marketing managers simply pick up the telephone and dial up potential customers or make sales calls to distant markets? When companies operate in different languages and cultures, business customs may imply disparate obligations. "Agreeing" considers such issues as responsibility for payment when a product disappears in shipment, which party to the sales contract will incur such costs as insurance, ocean freight, and bank charges.

When "Producing" for export, the production department must be aware of extreme temperature differences. If the product doesn't hold up well in a tropical or Arctic climate, what is the chance of the company developing a "quality" reputation in those markets? Is the export manager certain the deal has been confirmed before ordering production on that $200,000 order? The product is loaded on a truck at the company's loading dock, carried 35 miles, loaded on a train, shipped to the Port of Baltimore, trucked to the dock, and loaded on a steamship at the bottom of a stack of crates in the hold, with a final destination of a small city located in the foothills of the Andean Mountains in South America. The production department did order special "packaging" from an experienced export packaging house, didn't it?

"Financing" is another essential element in our model. A foreign customer may insist that he or she will take the company's business elsewhere if the American company doesn't offer them a payment term of 90 days after receipt of shipment. How can the American company arrange this financing when it can't even afford to produce the product without cash in advance? What arrangement can the American importer make with his or her overseas suppliers to obtain financing? International shipments must be insured. Hence the "insuring" decision evaluates the chance an import or export will be confiscated by foreign authorities. Which party is responsible if the goods arrive damaged? Was insurance obtained? By whom? How willing is one's insurance company to settle claims?

"Documenting" is one of the more difficult processes to master in the import/export trade because of its technical nature. What documents are required to clear cargo through the U.S. Customs Service? The export department learns that the negotiating bank refuses to clear payment under a letter of credit, citing a "stale" bill of lading. Proper attention to documentation could have averted such a crisis.

Is the export or import manager "shipping" the product via a reliable carrier? Can the manager obtain a better rate if he or she arranges to consolidate the shipment with other importers or exporters? How can a forwarder or broker assist the manager? "Collecting" is another area that must be considered in developing a trade strategy. It is more difficult to collect payment from a delinquent overseas account. Are there alternatives to legal action? Could this situation have been averted? Finally, the company must have a means of "evaluating" its success. How would the company's long-run profit projections appear without importing or exporting? Are there discernable trends in the sales volume? Is there adequate feedback from the end-user regarding problems with the product?

This book covers each element of the strategic model considered above. Hence we open the book with an overview of economics: how budget deficits and the price of the dollar affect international trade. In Chapter Three we analyze the connection among sales revenue, expenses, and profitability and discuss how to employ knowledge of these variables to build a long-run marketing strategy. A short survey of industrial policy provides the reader with a general understanding of why governments concern themselves with protecting domestic industry from foreign competition while promoting exports. Chapter Five discusses the basic forms of business organization available for engaging in the import/export trade.

Section II of this text contains detailed information that heretofore has been unavailable to the novice interested in entering the export trade. We take the process chapter by chapter: from whom the exporter can receive assistance; finding a market for one's product: pricing, promoting, and distributing the export; financial support; the requisite documentation; and the procedures for export license application through the Commerce Department.

Our final section is written for the novice importer. We outline strategies for finding products to import and discuss how to pay for imports, and, perhaps most important, how to avoid shipment delays with Customs.

The reader should find our appendices important additions to the text. We have included a glossary of international trade terms, Revised American Foreign Trade Definitions, a guide to selecting publications for a small trade library, and a resource guide that contains addresses of major support groups.

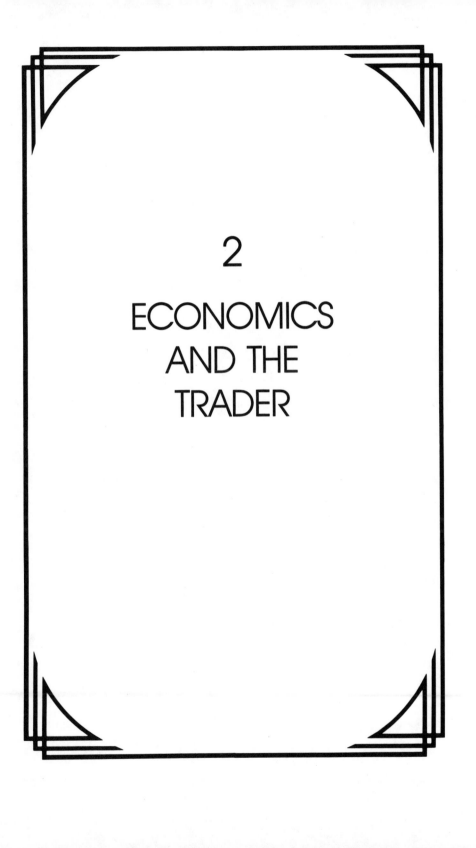

2

ECONOMICS
AND THE
TRADER

The United States was once its own common market, self-sufficient in raw materials with large, expanding domestic consumption. Today's statistics, in contrast, attest to the importance of international trade in America's economy. U.S. merchandise exports reached $217.3 billion in 1986 while merchandise imports totaled $387.1 billion, seven percent above the 1985 level of $361.6 billion. Business services (other than transportation and tourism and fees and royalties from sale of proprietary rights) produced a surplus of nearly $7.4 billion. Fees and royalties for proprietary rights produced another surplus of about $5.7 billion. A $10 billion deficit in tourism and transportation eroded the size of the surplus down to $3 billion. Major U.S. markets for service exports continue to be Canada, Mexico, Western Europe, and Japan.[1]

When the United States exports more than it imports over the course of a year, it is said that the U.S. enjoys a balance of trade "surplus." Every year from 1891 through 1970 the U.S. experienced trade surpluses. Since 1970, however, the U.S. has recorded just two trade surpluses. The U.S. routinely posts balance of trade "deficits," that is, imports exceed exports.

The 1973 and 1977 oil crises only masked the long-term changes that threaten American world economic hegemony. In the 1950s Western Europe and Japan, having rebuilt their manufacturing plants, began to challenge U.S. supremacy in their own markets, in other markets, and on U.S. soil as well. In 1983 the U.S. exported 5.9 percent of its GNP, while West Germany exported 25.9 percent of its GNP, Great Britain 20.1 percent, and Japan 12.7 percent. Newly industrializing countries (such as Taiwan, Brazil, Mexico, South Korea, and Hong Kong) compete with the U.S. and the other advanced industrial democracies of Western Europe and Japan.

---

[1]*Business America*, March 30, 1987, p. 5.

Economics and the Trader

A major factor exacerbating American trade deficits in the early to mid-1980s was an overvalued dollar. A strong dollar, next to other major currencies, drives up the price of exports. American exports become more expensive to importers who must exchange their less valuable currency for dollars in order to pay the American exporter for his or her goods. Hence a rising dollar reduces exporters' sales volume abroad. Conversely, sales pick up for importers. A low dollar, on the other hand, tends to favor export sales, as evidenced by the increase in exports which began to show up in 1987 trade statistics after the dollar began to fall next to many currencies in the latter half of 1986.

Which factors cause the dollar to fluctuate and whether its appreciation is beneficial or harmful to American buyers depends on your point of view. Yet economists and businesspeople generally agree that the strong dollar of the 1980s was linked to the American federal budget deficit. A budget deficit occurs when a government collects insufficient revenues to pay for its obligations, whether the commitments are for national defense, social entitlements, federal employee salaries, or highway reconstruction. If a private citizen can't meet his or her expenses, the individual might borrow money from a friend or a bank, but the government borrows money from the public. The government can't simply print dollars because that causes inflation. By inflation we mean "too much money chasing too few goods." Inflation occurs when the demand for goods and services increases without a companion increase in production. Increasing plant capacity can take months, and is risky for business. What if this increase in demand is just temporary? Business will be burdened with underutilized plant capacity—machines and buildings sitting around unused. The Treasury proceeds with its only possible course of action; issuing more bonds and notes. The increase in government issues wouldn't present a problem if no other groups competed for investors' dollars, but business depends on investment capital for expansion.

An increase in demand causes an increase in price. U.S. Treasury bonds and notes increase the cost of investment money, which is measured by interest rates. Therefore, interest rates go up. When interest rates rise, not only do loans become more costly, bank accounts such as money markets and certificates of deposit carry higher interest rates. Both business and government bonds reflect these higher rates. Given such high payouts, many foreign investors prefer to hold their money in American bank accounts and bonds rather than in accounts denominated in their own currency. As a consequence, foreigners begin to buy dollars.

The currency market is like any other competitive market: supply and demand affect price. An increase in the demand for the dollar causes an increase in the price of the dollar. When the dollar appreciates, the price of American exports rise and foreign products become cheaper.

The trade deficits of the 1980s are also tied to the international debt crisis. Many Latin American countries represent crucial import markets for American traders. But the austerity measures imposed on most of these importing countries by the International Monetary Fund as a condition of loan rescheduling greatly reduced their imports. Another factor exacerbating trade deficits may simply be that the economic recovery the U.S. began to experience in the early 1980s was stronger than that of Western Europe. If our economy is healthy we have the money to import products, while other countries don't have a comparable amount of money to purchase our exports.

Government policy and economic conditions will affect a business whether it trades in goods or services or is indirectly linked to a trader through shipping or by supplying services or products. The best way to stay abreast of changes is to read *The New York Times*, *The Wall Street Journal*, and *The Journal of Commerce*. In addition, there are many excellent business magazines such as *Business America* and *The Economist*.

The value of the dollar and the budget deficit are not the only things that affect the trader. Chapter Three introduces the connection among revenues, expenses, and profits and explains why international competition must be included as a variable in the development of a long-run business strategy.

SUGGESTED READINGS

Heilbroner, Robert L. and Lester C. Thurow. *Understanding Macroeconomics* Eighth Edition. Englewood Cliffs, N.J.: Prentice Hall.

———. *Understanding Microeconomics* eighth edition. Englewood Cliffs, N.J.: Prentice Hall.

Heilbroner, Robert L. *The Worldly Philosophers: The Lives, Times, and Ideas of the Great Economic Thinkers*. Fifth edition. New York: Touchtone Books, 1980.

Okun, Arthur. *Equality and Efficiency: The Big Tradeoff* Washington, D.C.: The Brookings Institution, 1975.

Vernon, Raymond and Louis T. Wells. *Economic Environment of International Business*. Englewood Cliffs, N.J.: Prentice Hall, 1976.

3

SPEAKING
THE LANGUAGE
OF TRADE

*Revenues, Expenses,
and Profits*

International trade is the export and import of goods and services, yet there are other ways in which international business is transacted. A U.S. company may allow a foreign company to produce its products under LICENSING agreements. The U.S. company may hold a patent and receive royalties for the sales of its product. A company might provide critical inputs such as soft drink syrup or specially trained engineering consultants.

Closely paralleling the licensing agreement is the franchising agreement, which involves an ongoing business relationship between the franchisor and franchisee. Foreign franchising includes a broad range of computerized services, professional services, temporary help, ice cream shops, video equipment sales, food markets, restaurants, automotive products and services, weight control centers, and printing and copying stores. In 1985 the ten areas in the world with the most American franchises were Canada (239), followed by the Caribbean (88), Australia (75), Asia, other than Japan and the Middle East, (74), Continental Europe (73), the United Kingdom (68), Japan (66), the Middle East (41), Mexico (36), and South America (35).[1]

When companies from different countries combine capital and human resources in specific ventures it is called a *joint venture*. The GM-Toyota joint production of the Chevrolet Nova in California is a recent highly publicized example of a joint venture.

When a company buys or builds production facilities in a foreign country it creates a *wholly owned subsidiary*. To have a wholly owned subsidiary, the parent company must hold 100 percent of the equity (the

---

[1]*Business America*, March 16, 1987, p. 19.

shares) in the subsidiary. The foreign country is referred to as the "host" country and the country of origin is called the "home" country.

International business is the collective term for international trade, licensing, joint ventures, and wholly owned subsidiaries. These different modes of engaging in business are not mutually exclusive. An American company may export to Canada, license in England, engage in a joint venture in Brazil with a Brazilian-owned company, and maintain a wholly owned subsidiary in Nigeria. The choice of any one of these methods depends on many variables including the long-range market potential of the product, local government laws that may prohibit wholly owned subsidiaries, the level of skills in the host country, political risk such as expropriation of facilities, and the financial ability of one company to provide the necessary capital investment. This book focuses on the practice of international trade, but the connection among the structures of trade, licensing, joint venture, and wholly owned subsidiary must be considered in the development of long-run strategy by any American company that faces foreign competition.

A manager's primary goal is to increase profits through increasing sales revenues and decreasing expenses. Among the many planning strategies available to international managers, the most widely used models are the *product life cycle* (PLC), which charts the revenue side of the profit equation, and the ECONOMIES OF SCALE curve, a tool for studying costs.

Figure 3.1 demonstrates the PLC, which illustrates the growth of products in terms of sales.

As we move from the zero point or the origin, the values of both time and sales increase. The movement from point A to point C represents an increase in both sales and time. At point C the curve levels off. This PLC curve shows us that when a product is new its sales increase, but at some point (C), sales begin to decline. Point A is associated with the innovation or invention of the product. Early growth is identified by the region of the curve around point B. Maturation of the product occurs at point C. Sales of the product begin to decline in the range between points C and D.

All products face this cycle of growth, maturation, and decline. How fast the cycle progresses depends on the ability of competitors to imitate the product and how quickly the domestic market absorbs the product. For instance, a consumer nondurable such as a household detergent profits from a large domestic market, but the ability of competitors to imitate or surpass innovations makes it virtually impossible for such a product to increase its sales without eventually facing competitive innovations. A durable good, such as a personal computer, on the other hand, may reach

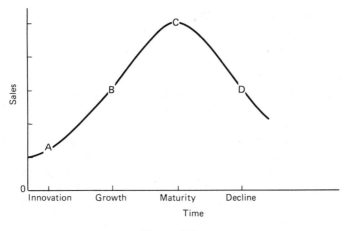

Figure 3.1

market "saturation" earlier (shorter product cycle) because the product is infrequently replaced and may not be demanded by significant portions of the domestic market.

Many businesses become interested in international trade when they find that exporting can extend the life of a product. Figure 3.2 illustrates the extension of the PLC through trade. By exporting to countries A, B, and C, the company arrests the product's decline.

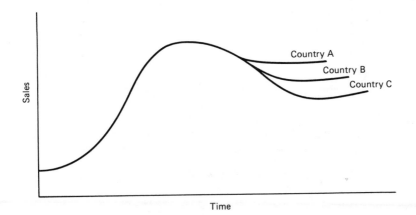

Figure 3.2

Another application of the PLC to trade links exporting with investment and global competition. Figure 3.3 illustrates how Raymond Vernon used the PLC to explain the movement from exporting to investment.[2]

As with the domestic PLC, sales are plotted against time. As the product passes through maturation in the domestic PLC, Vernon's trade/investment formulation becomes applicable. The U.S. company extends a product's cycle through exports, but in time, faces competition in the country of importation as technology ages and foreign-based companies learn how to produce the product. The American exporter may experience a decline in export sales for many reasons. Manufacturers in foreign countries have a natural transportation cost advantage. Labor in the foreign country may be cheaper. The plant in the foreign country is newer and

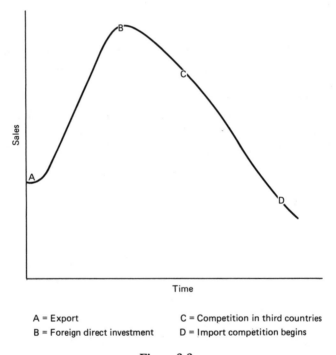

A = Export   C = Competition in third countries
B = Foreign direct investment   D = Import competition begins

Figure 3.3

[2]Raymond Vernon, "International Investment and International Trade in the Product Cycle," *Quarterly Journal of Economics*, May 1966, pp. 191–207.

may utilize more efficient, cost-saving technologies. The foreign government may have placed import tariffs or non-tariff barriers on the product. The American exporter must build or buy a plant in that market in order to maintain its presence.

At point C, however, the American exporter faces competition in third markets from companies in the original country of importation. For instance, an American company may have originally exported highly specialized machine tools to Brazil. For any or a combination of the reasons listed above, the American company builds a tool plant in Brazil to service its South American customers. Yet it continues to service most countries from its American plants. Its Brazilian competitors begin to export machine tools to Nigeria where the American manufacturer had once enjoyed a near-monopoly. Cheaper labor and a more efficient plant may combine to edge the American company out of the Nigerian market.

Finally, at point D, import competition begins. The Brazilian machine tool manufacturers begin to export machine tools to the U.S. Again, Brazilian cheaper labor and more efficient plant may obliterate the American manufacturer's transportation advantage. The American manufacturer's market share declines dramatically and American production may even cease.

The implications of this cycle provide the strategical groundwork of an exporter's marketing plan. A profitable exporter will handle products on all stages of the PLC. As some products approach the decline phase, the manufacturer must consider licensing or foreign direct investment as well as the introduction of new products. The PLC provides the exporter with a handy, theoretical construct for ordering his or her export marketing strategy.

Expenses tied to "economies of scale" production are especially important for the foreign trader. Figure 3.4 illustrates an economies of scale curve.

The economies of scale curve slopes downward, which implies that as output increases, per-unit costs decrease. Per-unit costs decrease because of a concept called "spreading the fixed costs." In business, two major types of costs exist: fixed and variable. Typical fixed costs include plant, equipment, land, basic utility costs, marketing budgets for advertisements, and administrative and clerical salaries. Variable costs, on the other hand, include such expenses as laborers' wages, raw materials, utility costs of running machinery, and commissions.

Let's suppose that an American company, Mohawk Ballpoint Pen Company, only sells ballpoint pens in the United States. Plant capacity is 250,000 pens per quarter. Yet Mohawk has found that the American demand for its product is only 150,000 pens at a price of $1.00. Mohawk

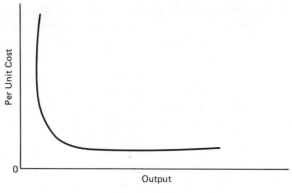

Figure 3.4

can cut the pen's price to increase its sales, but by so doing it will face retaliation by its competitors and is not in a strong enough financial position vis à vis the market leader to withstand a price war. Further assume that Mohawk has found it will run most efficiently (lower costs) at 90 percent capacity. At greater than 90 percent it experiences machinery breakdowns, higher worker absenteeism, and lower worker productivity. Mohawk would like to sell 225,000 pens per quarter (250,000 × 0.9). By selling more pens Mohawk will increase its profit per pen. This per-pen profit margin increase is realized through economies of scale. It is helpful

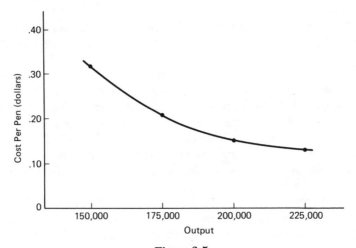

Figure 3.5

to refer to the economies of the scale curve shown in Figure 3.5 to explain this concept:

Note that at a production of 150,000 pens, the cost per pen is $.30. At 175,000 pens, the cost per pen is about $.20. But at 225,000 pens, the cost per pen is only about $.12.

How does the per-pen cost decrease as the output of pens increases? The answer lies in the distinction between fixed and variable costs. Mohawk must pay mortgage payments for its land and plant. Banks must be paid for loans on capital equipment. The building must be heated whether 10,000 pens or 225,000 pens are produced and sold. The fixed salaries of the president of Mohawk, the secretaries, the accountants must be paid regardless of the number of pens sold per quarter.

Let's assume Mohawk's quarterly fixed payments total $100,000 and that each pen continues to sell at $1. If 150,000 pens are sold per quarter the total revenue will be $150,000 and the profit (based on fixed costs only) will be $50,000 (sales of $150,000—fixed costs of $100,000). But if 225,000 pens were produced and sold, the profit based on fixed costs would be $125,000 (sales of $225,000—fixed costs of $100,000).[3] The greater profit came from no additional fixed costs. Only variable costs will increase. *The fixed costs were spread out over higher sales revenues.*

In this example, the Mohawk Ballpoint Pen Company has an excess capacity of 75,000 pens. It is assumed that Mohawk can't increase its sales in the American market. But it *could operate* at 90 percent capacity by selling its additional pens in a foreign market. These extra sales will lower the cost of doing business in the United States as well as increase sales through export markets.

Extending the PLC will increase sales revenues. Making the most of plant capacity reduces the expense of doing business in both the domestic and foreign market. By including both of these tools into decision-making routines, you have a sound working model for developing a long-run strategy.

---

[3]Of course from this profit must be subtracted the variable costs (e.g. materials, labor) associated with this increased production of 225,000 pens.

4

INDUSTRIAL POLICY AND TRADE

All exchange, whether in capitalist or socialist economies, is based on "factors of production." The price of a product can be reduced to four factors: labor, entrepreneurship, capital, and land. By *labor*, we mean sheer numbers, not skill level. A country with a large labor supply relative to another country will enjoy cheaper labor costs. *Entrepreneurship* refers to the actual level of skills among workers, management ingenuity, and technological know-how. Countries with high educational levels hold an entrepreneurial advantage. *Capital* generally refers to the amount of money spent on the factory, buildings, and machinery. Service industries tend to be more "labor intensive" than manufacturing, because people perform most of the work in the former, while machines execute the bulk of the work in the latter. *Land* as a factor of production is defined as the amount of arable land for farming as well as products mined from the land such as petroleum, salt, gold, and uranium.

People work in four major sectors: agriculture, manufacturing, service, and research. Today's low-technology industries were yesterday's high-technology groups. Textiles, furniture, leather goods, and paper products are industries characterized by old, relatively stable technologies with low value-added. "Value-added" is the amount of capital added from the processing of raw material to the product itself. Let's take a bolt of wool fabric as an example. The sheep are shorn, and machines spin, weave, and cut. Not much was added to that original wool. It was reconstituted. The cost of the machinery and labor would be added, but *compare* this process to the building of an automobile with its hundreds of separate, sophisticated parts.

The second major type of production is characterized by the "heavy industries." These industries encounter high "economies of scale," a concept we introduced in the previous chapter. In the production of chemicals, steel, and automobiles, the product gathers substantial value through labor, materials, transportation, and energy costs, but principally from the capitalization of plant and equipment. Substantial start-up costs are incurred. Whenever start-up costs are high, economies of scale will be important because only large production volumes can spread the fixed costs. These industries are "capital-intensive."

The newest stage of production is not as easy to categorize. High technology industries are more labor-intensive (as measured in engineers and technicians) than heavy industries. They are more flexible because they don't have as much capital invested in machines that can only perform one type of operation.

Governments are subjected to enormous pressure from industries in the development of industrial policy, under which trade policy falls. They simultaneously protect domestic industry while promoting exports. Protectionism in advanced industrial economies like that in the United States is usually extended to lower-technology industries such as textile, garment, shoes, steel, and automobile. By virtue of their market entrenchment, these older industries employ more labor than younger industries. The low value-added industries tend to be labor-intensive and can't compete with cheap labor from overseas. Although the economies of scale industries face higher labor costs than developing countries, the cost of labor is not the only reason American business faces competition from foreign imports.

To stay competitive, businesses must continually invest capital to modernize their plants. In the postwar era, while Europe and Japan built new manufacturing facilities out of the rubble left by World War II, American manufacturers preferred to invest profits in acquisitions of other corporations rather than modernize existing production facilities, a practice termed "paper entrepreneuralism" by one commentator.[1] Yet no business can remain a market leader when its competitors in other countries are working with more modern, efficient equipment.

As one moves out along the product life cycle, the product becomes more standardized, that is, capital replaces labor.[2] Given the profit equation of Revenues − Expenses = Profits, you can conclude that if revenues are decreasing due to market saturation, to maintain the high profit margins of the PLC's maturity stage, a firm must reduce expenses. In so doing, capital (machinery) replaces labor. Yet by engaging in such massive capital investments a firm is making its production inflexible, or more simply,

---

[1]Robert Reich, *The Next American Frontier.* New York: Penguin Books, 1983.

[2]From Robert H. Hayes and Steven G. Wheelwright, "The Dynamics of Process-Product Life Cycle." *Harvard Business Review*, March–April 1979.

people can be retrained, machines cannot. As technology diffuses, the product innovator—in our case, the United States—will face import competition. Despite its distance advantage, as manifested in transportation costs, the commodity will still be cheaper to import from a less advanced economy due to lower labor costs in that particular industry, combined with lower cost output from newer, more efficient plants.

In the 1970s the industrialized world's markets experienced an emerging technological revolution. Entrepreneurship, manifested in engineering and scientific directed research and development (R&D), replaced scale production as the critical input into the profit function of these new industries. New technologies sprouted in university laboratories and in the basements and garages of private homes, and in corporate labs as well. Product life cycles are shorter than any time in history as producers around the world fiercely compete, wanting to become the first to introduce a product to market and sail up the product life cycle curve and down the learning curve.[3] The presence of three distinct production sectors (low-technology, low value-added; economies of scale-high value-added; high-technology) makes a simple choice between *laissez faire* and government intervention difficult.[4] Table 4.1, developed by the Boston Consulting Group, illustrates this dilemma.

TABLE 4.1   Market Share Potential

		High	Low
Growth Potential	High	*	?
	Low	Cow	Dog

Question marks represent those goods (or industries) for which the overall growth potential is high, but the development of the product for a firm will require large research and development expenditures. In the PLC model the question mark corresponds with the innovation stage. The star coincides with the growth phase of the PLC. A star enjoys both high market share potential and high growth potential with commercial success

---

[3]The Boston Consulting Group first reported that a learning/experience curve measures costs against time, whereas the economies of scale curve measures costs against output. This curve recognizes the cost advantages a company has simply as an outcome of learning better ways of producing, selling, and distributing its products.

[4]When a government adopts a laissez faire policy it tends to limit its involvement in economic affairs.

virtually guaranteed. The cow stage is one in which the product is milked because although it approaches maturity (through the combination of competition and market saturation) the initial costs of R&D, factory, and machinery are spread over ever more sales. The dog product dies in the PLC's decline phase. Little growth is expected from the product unless substantial innovations can transform the product back into a star.

But at each phase—?, *, cow, and dog—industries have different needs. By fitting the three major industrial stages discussed above into the Boston Consulting Group Model, one might hypothesize the arrangement illustrated in Table 4.2.

TABLE 4.2 Market Potential

Growth Potential	Telecommunications	Biogenetics, Space
	Auto, Steel	Textiles, Clothing, Shoes

What are the needs of each of these industries? The dog industries are characterized by labor-intensive rather than capital-intensive production. Unless there is some radical change in the nature of American production, such as a mass movement into workers' cooperatives, it is impossible for such producers to compete on commonly purchased goods under conditions of free trade. They must create specialty fabrics and designs that can bear the higher associated labor costs.

Question marks often need public support such as grants to universities, low-interest financing, and tax breaks. For instance, the basic research associated with the Strategic Defense Initiative and the space shuttle is considered vital for the eventual commercialization of space.

In the cow phase a dilemma associated with democratic pluralism surfaces.[5] Failing industries lobby governments for protection. But protectionism, although perhaps satisfactory as a short-term, temporary solution, engenders a redistribution of incomes, away from household and industrial consumers and foreign producers, toward domestic producers and their labor force. The maintenance of sinking cows through protec-

---

[5]Theodore Lowi, *The End of Liberalism*. Second Edition. (New York: W W. Norton, 1979.)

tionism is the most politically expedient solution, in that refusing to protect these industries creates mass structural unemployment.

One expert on industrial policy suggests that the U.S. government should develop policies to promote the production of sophisticated products—specialty steel and chemicals, computer-controlled machine tools, advanced automobile components, semi-conductors, fiber optics, lasers, biotechnology, and robotics.[6] Another approach is espoused by Don Gervirtz who argues that politicians have not recognized that an entrepreneurial constituency exists. He opposes government-directed industrial policy, preferring that the government take steps to stimulate the entrepreneurial process through fiscal and monetary incentives.[7]

No company is safe from international competition. One must stay abreast of international developments and search for ways to innovate the product itself and the way in which it is produced. New products must be continuously added to a company's product line. A recent study questions just how much long-term protection American industry has received from Congress, the President, and the International Trade Commission.[8] The guiding principles of American policymakers have been "fair and free" trade, rather than protection. Protectionism simply magnifies the inability to compete by making the industry of a failing product even more flabby than it was before protection. As the shake-up in the 1970s and 1980s of the American steel and automobile giants demonstrated, the trade protection the federal government does award certain industries is merely a bandaid to the problem of aging production facilities and ideas.

SUGGESTED READINGS

Drucker, Peter. *Innovation and Entrepreneurship.* New York: Harper & Row, 1985.

Etzioni, Amitai. *An Immodest Agenda: Rebuilding America before the Twenty-First Century.* New York: McGraw-Hill, 1983.

Galbraith, John K. *The New Industrial State* Fourth Edition. Boston: Houghton Mifflin, 1985.

---

[6]Robert Reich, *The Next American Frontier.* (New York: Penguin, 1983), p. 13.

[7]Don L. Gervirtz, *Business Plan for America: An Entrepreneur's Manifesto.* (New York: G. P. Putnam's Sons, 1984).

[8]Judith Goldstein, "The Political Economy of Trade: Institutions of Protection," *American Political Science Review*, March 1986.

Lowi, Theodore J. *The End of Liberalism*. Second Edition, New York: W. W. Norton & Co., 1979.

Reich, Robert. *The Next American Frontier*. New York: Penguin, 1983.

Thurow, Lester. *The Zero-Sum Society*. New York: Basic Books, 1980.

Toffler, Alvin. *The Third Wave*. New York: William Morrow & Co., 1980.

5

ORGANIZING
FOR TRADE

This chapter begins with a brief review of the standard forms of business organization. Intended as an introduction for readers with little knowledge of business, we discuss both the advantages and drawbacks of sole proprietorships, partnerships, and corporations.

Sole Proprietorship

A sole proprietorship is owned by one person. Proprietorships are the most common form of business organization in the United States. The primary advantage of the proprietorship is its sheer simplicity: you only have to register the company's name. An attorney isn't necessary to draw up papers nor to suspend operations. Federal income tax filing is straightforward, business income or loss goes right on a Federal 1040 with the attached Schedule C.

Yet the proprietorship does have important limitations. It's difficult to raise capital; a proprietorship can't issue bonds. Capital can only be raised through loans. Another disadvantage is possible management deficiencies.

By far the biggest concern of a business is its ability to stay solvent. The owner of a proprietorship is personally responsible for judgments against his or her business. Let's say a worker is delivering a product to a railroad terminal and runs over a pedestrian. If the proprietorship's insurance doesn't cover the claim, the plaintiff can sue for the proprietorship's assets. If those assets don't cover the claim, they can tap into your personal assets—your savings, car, house. If the business goes bankrupt and the sale of assets doesn't cover creditors' claims, creditors can sue for personal assets.

Partnerships

Partnerships are taxed the same way as proprietorships, subject to the formula laid out in the partnership agreement. Like the proprietorship, there is no "corporate shield," that is, financial liability is unlimited.

There are two extra advantages: the complementary management skills of the partners and the expanded financial capability of more than one owner. But unlike the proprietorship, the partnership is not easy to form because agreements must be very specific about exactly who performs what duties, how profits are shared, and how business assets will be divided if and when the business is dissolved.

Corporations

The corporate shield is that of limited financial liability. If liability insurance doesn't cover a claim or the corporation goes bankrupt, claimants cannot collect beyond the corporate assets. Neither the officers of the corporation nor the stockholders are personally liable for corporate debts. Starting a corporation is more complex than starting a proprietorship or partnership. You can draw up your own papers to start a corporation, but it's best to hire an accountant or attorney to handle the paperwork.

The corporation's financial capability is greatly expanded by its ability to sell shares of stock. New corporations sell stock in the venture capital market. But raising capital from investors isn't an easy process. Investors demand a track record. They need to see that the corporation has the potential for making the kind of profit that would make the risk worth it. (The higher the risk, the higher the expected rate of return.)

Although the corporation sounds ideal, there are cases when it is not the optimal form of business organization. A bank may be more willing to make loans to a small business if the owner doesn't hide behind a corporate shield. Let's say the business doesn't have much in the way of assets. If the business can't meet its debt obligations, the bank wants to have recourse to a collaterized item, often the owner's house. Even if a small business is incorporated, the bank might require that the owner put his or her house as collateral for a loan. In some kinds of businesses limited liability is not even necessary because liability insurance covers risks.

Another disadvantage of the corporation is its extra tax burden or "double taxation." Corporations are subject to federal and state income taxes. In addition, profits distributed as dividends are taxed. The "subchapter S corporation," in which businesses enjoy the corporate shield but are taxed as proprietorships or partnerships, is an important combination of business forms. An attorney can explain the qualifying criteria.

Organizing for Export

If research shows that there is a big export market for a product, it is more profitable over the long-run to incur the costs of setting up an export department. On the other hand, if the company sees a marginal market, it's more cost effective to sell products through agents and merchants and not incur the costs of a built-in export department. (In the section entitled "Distribution" in Chapter Eight, the many alternatives the manufacturer can choose to reach foreign buyers are considered.)

Let's say research indicates that there is an adequate export market. A rule of thumb is that when a firm's export sales fall between $200,000 and $500,000 annually, a company should build its own export department.[1] If there is no one employed by the company who is capable of carrying out such research, an international consultant can provide business references. The in-house export department will also need an experienced export manager and clerk. There may be someone within the company who can rise to the challenge. Commerce Department district offices regularly hold seminars and assist companies in learning how to export. Because it is generally more expensive to hire someone good from the outside, consider a current marketing manager who is enthusiastic and has a solid track record.

Unlike domestic sales, exporting does require special licensing. Chapter Twelve contains an explanation of export licensing. In Chapter Ten we examine documentation requirements.

Countries attempt to promote export sales without violating the unfair subsidy agreements made in multilateral negotiations under the General Agreement on Tariffs and Trade. The United States has three special types of legislation that pertain to exporting companies: Webb-Pomerene Associations, Foreign Sales Corporations, and Export Trading Companies.

Webb-Pomerene Associations (WPAs) were authorized by the Webb-Pomerene Act of 1918, which provided an exemption from antitrust laws for associations formed exclusively for export sales. Some of the ways that a WPA can cut costs and open markets is through shared production facilities, larger shipments (which obtain cheaper rates), shared sales offices and agents, shared warehousing, and pooled expertise.

There are two major acts that prohibit trusts (monopoly formation or behavior): The Sherman Antitrust Act of 1890 and the Clayton Antitrust Act of 1914. The Federal Trade Commission was authorized under the Sherman Act to monitor trusts and break them up. The Clayton Act

---

[1]Warren J. Keegan, *Multinational Marketing Management*. Second Edition. (Englewood Cliffs, N.J.: Prentice Hall, 1980), p. 435.

was passed later to correct deficiencies and clarify congressional intent in the Sherman Act, especially to spell out in Section 6 that labor unions were not to be construed as trusts by the courts. Essentially antitrust legislation grew out of the threat to free enterprise and the market system posed by the control over many basic industries such as tobacco, oil, whiskey, and sugar exercised by big trusts. Contracts, combinations, or conspiracies in restraint of interstate trade or commerce is illegal. If a competitor takes a company to court and wins a case based on these acts the plaintiff is entitled to treble damages.

Competing manufacturers can form a Webb-Pomerene Association by filing with the Federal Trade Commission. However, there aren't many WPAs, perhaps between thirty and forty in all.[2] The major problem with the Webb-Pomerene Act is that it does not provide preclearance with the FTC. Hence the manufacturers participating in a WPA are still subject to an antitrust suit filed against them by a competitor and the risk of treble damages. Furthermore, the Webb-Pomerene Act only included manufactured goods, but today the export of services is an important portion of American trade.

Export Trading Companies

Legislation signed in October 1982 attempts to correct some of the deficiencies of the WPA as well as emulate the successful Japanese trading companies that are said to handle two-thirds of Japanese exports. The basic philosophy behind the Export Trading Company (ETC) is to encourage businesses to join together to export or offer export services. The Act's two major features are the institution of an antitrust certification and the ability of banks to own an interest in the ETC. These provisions were written with an eye toward a major problem encountered by small- and medium-sized companies: they might have a good export product, but they just don't have the kind of financing available to develop an overseas market.

To qualify for ETC status the company must do business in the United States, principally for the purpose of exporting goods and services. It can also assist unrelated companies to export their products. The ETC can either export goods and services or it can provide services for exports or other companies. The ETC can also engage in countertrade between two other countries. The Commerce Department's International Trade Administration operates the Office of Export Trading Company Affairs. To learn if a company qualifies, contact your district office of the U.S. Com-

---

[2]Keegan, p. 434.

merce Department. Some publications of interest are listed at the end of this chapter.

Foreign Sales Corporation

The Foreign Sales Corporation (FSC) Act of 1984 replaced the tax deferral advantages of the now defunct Domestic International Sales Corporation (DISC) with a reduction of tax liabilities on sales originating from exports made to a company's subsidiary operating as a sales office in a foreign country which is registered with the IRS as a FSC. The tax benefit can be as much as a 32 percent reduction in income reported by FSCs for individuals and partnerships and 30 percent for corporations. The law provides for three types of FSCs.

1. **Small FSC**—tax benefits are limited to export sales of $5 million or less annually. The FSC must be incorporated in an approved jurisdiction (outside of U.S. Customs territory). Areas certified by the Treasury Department through 1986 are the U.S. Virgin Islands, American Samoa, Guam, the Northern Marianas, Australia, Austria, Barbados, Belgium, Canada, Denmark, Egypt, Finland, France, Germany, Iceland, Ireland, Jamaica, Korea, Malta, Morocco, The Netherlands, New Zealand, Norway, Pakistan, Philippines, South Africa, Sweden, Trinidad, and Tobago.

Other requirements include having one member on the board of directors reside outside of the U.S. Customs territory, maintain a set of books and records at the FSC office outside the U.S., and create the proper legal arrangements for the FSC to act for the exporter, and for the exporter to act as the FSC's agent to carry out the required business activities.

2. **Regular FSC**—the requirements are the same as with the small FSC except that export sales are unlimited. Additional requirements include incurring some business expenses outside of the United States and engaging in certain business activities outside of the United States as well.

3. **Interest Charge DISC**—a small exporter is permitted to use a modification of the old DISC rules to defer U.S. tax on export income attributable to $10 million or less of qualified export receipts annually. The shareholder of a DISC must pay interest on the deferred tax at a rate determined annually by the Treasury based on the average investment yield of 52-week Treasury bills.

For more information write or call the "Office of Trade Finance," Room 1211, Washington, D.C. 20230, (202) 377-4471 or check with your district Commerce office.

Organizing for Import

In one sense it's much easier to import than to export because you work in a market with which you are familiar. Entrance into the import trade is a two-step process. You must find and obtain exclusive distributing rights to foreign products. Second, domestic wholesalers, retailers, and manufacturers must be willing to purchase the imported products. Whether you set yourself up as an agent (commission) or merchant (buy and sell) depends on the amount of risk you are able to assume as well as the suppliers' terms. Techniques for the development of import markets are discussed in Chapter Fifteen.

SUGGESTED READINGS

Goldsmith, Howard. *How to Make a Fortune in Import/Export*. Reston: Reston Publishing Company, 1980.

U.S. Department of Commerce. *A Basic Guide to Exporting*. Washington, D.C.: U.S. Government Printing Office, 1986.

———. *Business America*. Commerce bi-weekly magazine.

———. *Contact Facilitation Service Directory*. Directory of names and addresses of banks, ETCs, EMCs, manufacturers, exporters of services, foreign freight forwarders etc. About 4800 entries. Spring 1987.*

———. "Export Trading Companies: A Competitive Edge for U.S. Exports" Brochure, 1985.*

———. "ETC Guidebook." Detailed description of the Export Trading Act. 1987.*

---

*To obtain Commerce Department publications, you can call your district office or write to the U.S. Department of Commerce, International Trade Administration, Washington, D.C. 20230

6

MAJOR PRIVATE AND GOVERNMENT ACTORS

In Chapter One we presented a model to assist us in developing a strategic export plan. Each component is discussed more fully in each of the chapters below:

The 17-ings of Exporting

Estimating and Assessing—Chapters 2, 3, 7

Consulting and Selecting—Chapters 6, 8

Organizing—Chapters 5, 6, 8

Locating—Chapter 7

Marketing Evaluation—Chapters 7, 8

Pricing—Chapter 8

Promoting, Advertising—Chapter 8

Communicating—Chapter 8

Agreeing—Chapter 8

Producing—Chapter 8

Packaging—Chapter 13

Financing—Chapter 10

Insuring—Chapters 6, 8

Shipping—Chapter 13

Documenting—Chapter 11

Collecting—Chapter 9

Evaluating—Chapter 7

Foreign Freight Forwarder

The foreign freight forwarder, under license of the Federal Maritime Commission, acts as the exporter's agent in moving his or her products to their overseas destination. The freight forwarder books steamer or air cargo space after checking vessel availability, sailing dates, and estimated time of arrival at the foreign port. If steamship containers are required, he or she arranges for their use. He or she works with truckers to ensure timely pier deliveries. On receipt, shipping documents are checked to make sure they are proper, complete, and correct and that they conform to any letter of credit stipulations. The forwarder prepares the necessary shipping documents. Clearance of export shipments through U.S. Customs is handled by the forwarder.

The forwarder gathers all the shipping documents and distributes them to the bank and/or customer as instructed. She or he files claims for overcharges and missing packages. The forwarder can assist with quotations by determining in advance freight costs, port charges, consular fees, cost of special documentation, insurance costs, and handling fees. The packaging of merchandise, warehousing, and trucking services can also be recommended by the forwarder.

Export consolidating offers cost savings over individual shipment by the exporter. Forwarders may handle shipments for several exporters to the same port of destination. A forwarder can frequently combine several shipments (for which he or she secures a single bill of lading) enabling the forwarder to make shipments for less than the sum of the individual shipments. The forwarder can offer the exporter economies of scale in shipping and in so doing, can prorate the fixed costs.

The forwarder's services are more important to some exporters than others. If the manufacturer wants to build up a foreign market the export department can devote its efforts to selling rather than the clerical technicalities of exporting. Shipping cost can be reduced through economies of scale shipping as well as the better knowledge the forwarder has of steamship and air cargo rates. A forwarder will make fewer errors in documentation. A forwarder's services are practically indispensable to an inland shipper.

Freight forwarding fees are quite variable. You must shop around and obtain a fee break-down for each service requested. For instance there is a basic charge for each bill of lading prepared as well as for other documents. The reservation of steamship or air cargo space is cost-free to the exporter. A freight commission is paid by the steamship company or airline to the forwarder the same way a travel agent receives commissions from the airline.

Forwarders also carry open insurance policies. Unless the exporter frequently exports, the forwarder can get marine insurance cheaper. Insurance companies offer better rates for frequent shippers because their risks are spread out over many shipments. For a fee, the forwarder will insure a commodity under his or her policy. But make sure the terms of the policy are satisfactory for product needs and risk ability.

When choosing a forwarder, evaluate the forwarder carefully. The forwarder should be willing to supply client names for references. Is the forwarder experienced in shipping your type of cargo to the place of destination? It's important that the forwarder have a good credit rating. In addition, be certain that the forwarder has facilities for securing expensive or fragile cargo.

Export Packers

Export packers box, crate, warehouse, unitize, consolidate, and deliver goods for export. These companies can offer the exporter expertise. The packaging for domestic shipment will not suffice for transnational shipment. The climate, length of voyage, conditions of roads in the country of destination, and durability of the product must be considered in the packaging of the goods for export.

Ocean and Air Shippers

There are many types of arrangements available for ocean transportation. "Liner" service is characterized by a regular schedule of service to ports. Dates of arrival and sailing are assured. They are common carriers and ship a variety of cargo.

Many liners belong to a "Conference" system. Steamship conferences regulate freight rates and standardize shipping practices. Schedule reliability and rate stability are important services the conference offers to the exporter. The Federal Maritime Commission regulates the practices and rate setting of steamship conferences. Conference carriers offer contracts to exporters that guarantee them reduced freight rates if they agree to utilize conference liners for all shipments.

"Non-conference" steamships offer a cheaper rate than conference vessels (approximately 10 percent lower), but schedules, sailing, transit, and ports of call are not as precise as those published by steamship conferences. "Tramp" vessels are unlike liners in that they wander the world from port to port offering no regular service and schedule their sailings based on the requirements of the cargo they carry. Their rates are determined by bargaining between the shipper's broker (freight forwarder) and the tramp's agents rather than being a fixed freight rate. "Chartered" vessels are usually tramps—the charterer leases or hires the ship either for a single or round trip, or for a definite period of time. Tramps are primarily used for bulk shipments.

Air transportation represents the biggest change taking place in international shipping. Shipments can be containerized or palletized—important ways of shipping that reduce transportation costs, pilferage, and damage. Air cargo companies offer much tighter control of the shipment and a more consistent service in terms of delivery date and time than can ocean carriers.

Banks

Major U.S. banks have international departments staffed with specialists who are familiar with specific foreign countries and various types of commodities and transactions. These large banks, located in major cities, maintain correspondent relationships with smaller banks throughout the country. Banks also maintain correspondent relationships with banks in most foreign countries or operate their own overseas branches. Interbank electronic networks enable banks to transmit financial messages and to transfer funds electronically. The Society for Worldwide Interbank Financial Telecommunications (SWIFT) is a nonprofit corporation that transmits financial information in English. Funds are transferred via settlement systems such as the New York Clearing House Payment System.

Banks provide credit information, transfer funds, exchange foreign currency, offer a means of hedging against currency fluctuations, collect funds, handle documents, provide financing, supply credit information on potential overseas buyers, and guarantee payments through letters of credit.

Insurance Companies

Insurance in trade is needed to cover three risks: shipping, political, and credit. Export shipments are usually insured against loss or damage in transit by ocean marine cargo insurance. It also covers air shipments, foreign parcel post, as well as rail and truck shipments to foreign destinations. Coverage is effective while goods are in transit from the seller's warehouse to the buyer's warehouse. It is available in two basic forms: a special cargo policy that insures a single specified cargo movement and an open cargo policy that remains in continuous effect and automatically insures all cargo moving at the seller's risk.

The special policy is more expensive because the risk can't be spread over a number of different shipments. The standard method for computing the amount of coverage needed is to allow for the cost of the goods, freight, and insurance itself plus ten percent of the total to cover incidental and unexpected costs.

In addition to marine insurance, forms of political risk can be added to the policy. Insurance for strikes, riots, and civil commotions can be added by endorsement to an all risks policy. Loss or damage arising from acts of war can be covered under a separate policy.

The third major risk is that of not receiving payment. Exporters accustomed to selling for cash or confirmed letters of credit are finding it increasingly necessary to offer terms ranging from cash against documents to time drafts, open accounts, and even installment payments spread over several years. (These terms will be discussed in Chapter Nine.) Since 1961, the Foreign Credit Insurance Association (FCIA) has administered U.S. export credit insurance on behalf of its member insurance companies and the Export-Import Bank (EXIMBANK), an independent agency of the U.S. government. The private insurers cover the normal commercial credit risks. EXIMBANK assumes all liability of political risks. The Overseas Private Investment Corporation (OPIC) insures against medium- to long-term political risks including war, revolution, and insurrection.

MAJOR PUBLIC ACTORS

The U.S. Department of Commerce

Exporters frequently work with their district offices of the Commerce Department's International Trade Administration. District offices are listed in the appendix. Throughout this book the reader will be directed to the many Commerce publications and services designed to assist exporters in developing export businesses.

Small Business Administration

You should contact your local SBA office for information on seminars, publications, and counseling. It is a federal agency and can be found in the phone book in the government pages.

State and Local Export Agencies/
International Trade Clubs

Many states, counties, and cities have set up their own export offices. There may be an international trade club in the exporter's city as well. Commerce Department district offices and local Chambers of Commerce will be able to direct petitioners to such groups.

The GATT

Some economists attribute much of the global tension that built up prior to World War II to the high tariff barriers imposed by countries to protect their domestic markets, sometimes called "beggar-thy-neighbor" policies. Territorial expansionism, they suggest, provided the only alternative for economic recovery under capitalism. The General Agreement on Tariffs and Trade (GATT) is a multilateral organization that grew out of an attempt to create a more stable world order in the aftermath of World War II. The GATT's member nations have achieved dramatic success in eliminating many tariffs on goods among its some 150 nations. The GATT has had less success in combating non-tariff barriers and tariffs on services.

As an American exporter, non-tariff barriers can make the difference between a large market or no market at all. The distribution of import licenses is often based on a country's policy of protecting domestic producers. Measurement, health, and safety standards for particular products are sometimes designed to keep the foreign product out rather than protect the local citizenry. These non-tariff barriers, many of which grew up to circumvent the GATT's tariff negotiations, are often much more damaging to the exporter. Tariff information is readily available and the exporter can calculate his or her ability to offer the product at a competitive price. Non-tariff barriers are often difficult to identify. Exporters complain they can be buried in the foreign country's bureaucracy.

The United States is a signatory to GATT and negotiates with other countries on both a multilateral and bilateral basis. The current GATT negotiations, called the "Uruguay Round" centers on agricultural protectionism and subsidies, intellectual property, product counterfeiting, and trade in services.

The International Monetary Fund

Tariffs and quotas exacerbate world depressions. The short-run fix to declining exports is a depreciation of the nation's currency. For example, in the 1930s the German government's decision to depreciate the mark next to other major currencies made German exports cheaper for other countries. The depreciation also raised the price of imports necessary for the German economy. Rampant inflation ensued.

The International Monetary Fund (IMF), founded in 1947, helps to maintain discipline in the international monetary system. If a country has a balance of payments difficulty, the IMF will assist the country in regaining financial health. In this capacity, it is sometimes termed the international bank of last resort.

The current debt crisis and the IMF's efforts to restore financial discipline in debtor nations is of supreme importance to exporters. Mexico, for example, one of the two largest debtor nations, is a major American trading partner. Its financial predicament and its inability to generate enough hard currency contributed to a decline in Mexican imports from the United States. The IMF's success in helping Mexico and other Latin American nations will very much affect the ability of these countries to resume importing American goods at the pre-debt crisis rates.

Another important service the IMF maintains is its action as an international bank. Often lesser developed countries (LDCs) are short of certain hard currencies. The IMF allows the LDC to deposit its own currency in exchange for a hard currency. The hard currency obtained can then be applied to imports. The ability to borrow is gradated, that is, as a country continues to borrow a particular hard currency, it becomes difficult to obtain more of that currency.

The World Bank

The International Bank of Reconstruction and Development (IBRD) or the World Bank is an autonomous United Nations agency. The World Bank will lend money directly to governments who are members of the IMF. Capital is lent for very large projects abroad such as power generation and highway construction. Although originally the World Bank's lending activities focused on reconstructing Europe after World War II, today it primarily lends capital to developing countries, and only when loans can't be obtained from other sources at reasonable rates. The International Development Association is a member of the World Bank Group, lending capital to the poorest countries at even better rates than can be obtained through the World Bank. The International Finance Corporation (IFC) also falls under the auspices of the World Bank. The IFC, unlike the IBRD and the IDA, makes loans directly to private companies. The IFC finances projects that expand or modernize companies and industries.

Regional Development Banks

Regional banks limit their loans to the particular region they serve. The Inter-American Development Bank serves developing countries in Latin America and the Caribbean. Other regional banks are the Asian Development Bank and the African Development Bank.

The Export-Import Bank

The Export-Import Bank (EXIMBANK) is an independent government agency. Its purpose is to aid in financing and facilitating the export of U.S. goods and services. To fulfill this purpose, it provides financing and credit risk protection (through the FCIA). EXIMBANK programs assist many types of exporters from small inexperienced firms to multinational corporations. Chapter Ten details the financing activities of EXIMBANK.

7

FOREIGN MARKET EVALUATION

Marketing is based on four principles: product, price, promotion, and distribution. Marketers call these elements the "marketing mix." Although finding and assessing export markets is more complex and costly than the research associated with domestic market evaluation, the marketing mix is the optimal framework to begin any research project. Much can be learned by consulting sources available at the library of one's local university or the main branch of a public library. Research is the cost-saving prerequisite to a visit overseas. What at first glance may have seemed a lucrative export market may turn out to be a dead end once enough data are collected. The quality of one's research will provide the foundation for export success.

The way to initiate research very much depends on our circumstances. A manufacturer with a product to sell will take a different approach from a distributor. Or as a manufacturer you may find that there is a market for a product that you aren't manufacturing, but have the capacity to produce. With the many needs of our readers in mind, we'll look at the process one step at a time.

FINDING A MARKET FOR THE PRODUCT

Working with Trade Statistics

The first step for the company looking for an export market for its product is to sit down and assess the market profile of the home market. Warren Keegan calls these the "six W's":[1]

---

[1] Warren J. Keegan, *Multinational Marketing Management* Second Edition. (Englewood Cliffs: Prentice-Hall, 1980) p. 427.

Foreign Market Evaluation

1. What need or function does our product serve?
2. Who buys our product?
3. Why is our product purchased?
4. When is our product purchased?
5. Where is our product purchased?
6. What are the critical factors determining sales and profitability of our product?

Once the company takes a hard look at its domestic market it is ready to replicate its success in foreign markets. America's top 25 merchandise markets in 1986 are listed in Table 7.1, followed by pie charts (Figure 7.1)

TABLE 7.1   U.S. Trade Statistics, 1986

Top 25 U.S. Markets *U.S. Domestic and Foreign Merchandise Exports, 1986* *f.a.s. Value*		*Leading U.S. Suppliers* *U.S. General Merchandise Imports, 1986* *c.i.f. Value*	
	$ Billions		*$ Billions*
World Total	217.3	World Total	387.1
1. Canada	45.3	1. Japan	85.5
2. Japan	26.9	2. Canada	68.7
3. Mexico	12.4	3. West Germany	26.1
4. United Kingdom	11.4	4. Taiwan	21.3
5. West Germany	10.6	5. Mexico	17.6
6. Netherlands	7.8	6. United Kingdom	16.0
7. France	7.2	7. South Korea	13.5
8. South Korea	6.4	8. Italy	11.3
9. Australia	5.6	9. France	10.6
10. Taiwan	5.5	10. Hong Kong	9.5
11. Belgium & Luxembourg	5.4	11. Brazil	7.3
12. Italy	4.8	12. Venezuela	5.4
13. Brazil	3.9	13. Switzerland	5.4
14. Saudi Arabia	3.4	14. China	5.2
15. Singapore	3.4	15. Singapore	4.9
16. Venezuela	3.1	16. Sweden	4.6
17. China	3.1	17. Netherlands	4.4
18. Hong Kong	3.0	18. Belgium & Luxembourg	4.2
19. Switzerland	3.0	19. Saudi Arabia	4.1
20. Spain	2.6	20. Indonesia	3.7
21. Israel	2.2	21. Spain	3.0
22. Egypt	2.0	22. Australia	2.9
23. Sweden	1.9	23. Nigeria	2.5
24. Malaysia	1.7	24. Malaysia	2.5
25. India	1.5	25. Israel	2.5

TABLE 7.1 *(continued)*

U.S. Trade Balances

Listing of U.S. Merchandise Trade Balances

General Imports, c.i.f. Value; Domestic and Foreign Exports, f.a.s. Value

U.S. Surplus Positions		U.S. Deficit Positions	
	$ Billions		*$ Billions*
		World Total	−169.8
1. Netherlands	+3.5	1. Japan	−58.6
2. Australia	+2.7	2. Canada	−23.3
3. Egypt	+1.9	3. Taiwan	−15.7
4. Belgium & Luxembourg	+1.2	4. West Germany	−15.6
5. U.S.S.R.	+0.6	5. South Korea	−7.1
6. Pakistan	+0.5	6. Italy	−6.5
7. Turkey	+0.5	7. Hong Kong	−6.4
8. Morocco	+0.4	8. Mexico	−5.2
9. Ireland	+0.4	9. United Kingdom	−4.6
10. Kuwait	+0.3	10. Brazil	−3.5
11. Jordan	+0.3	11. France	−3.4
12. Panama	+0.3	12. Sweden	−2.8
13. Bahamas	+0.3	13. Indonesia	−2.7
14. Bermuda	+0.2	14. Switzerland	−2.4
15. Tunisia	+0.2	15. Venezuela	−2.3
16. Paraguay	+0.1	16. Nigeria	−2.3
17. Brunei	+0.1	17. China	−2.1
18. Leeward & Windward Islands	+0.1	18. Algeria	−1.5
19. Jamaica	+0.1	19. Singapore	−1.5
20. Oman	+0.1	20. South Africa	−1.3
21. El Salvador	+0.1	21. Denmark	−1.1
22. Bahrain	+0.1	22. Ecuador	−1.0
23. United Arab Emirates	+0.1	23. Thailand	−0.9
24. Yemen, North (Sana)	+0.1	24. India	−0.9
25. Lebanon	+0.1	25. Malaysia	−0.8

Source: Business America, March 20, 1987, p. 6.

that summarize the data presented in Table 7.1 and indicate the composition of U.S. merchandise trade. There are many reasons to consider the markets of America's major trading partners. First, it suggests that in those countries political factors aren't blocking exports, that is, the foreign government does not discriminate against American products in such areas as tariffs, buying practices, and the awarding of import licenses. For instance, the American and Soviet governments discriminate against each other's products through U.S. tariff schedules and Soviet buying practices. If the United States is actively trading with another country it probably indicates that there are no strong cultural objections to buying American

COMPOSITION OF U.S. MERCHANDISE TRADE WITH THE WORLD 1986

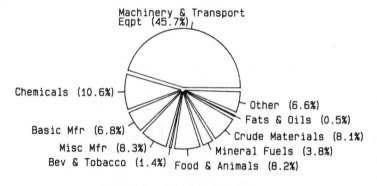

EXPORTS: $217.3 Billion

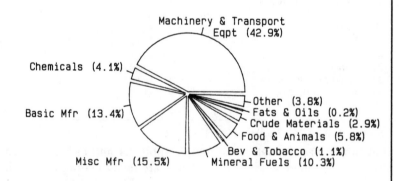

IMPORTS: $387.1 Billion

Figure 7.1

goods. Anti-American sentiment is so strong in many countries that American multinationals often attempt to disguise the product's origin. Heavy trade indicates that the country has modern and efficient transportation facilities that are capable of handling the volume of American trade. In a highly modern society like ours we often take for granted the many people we depend on to ensure a smooth transaction: banks, customhouse brokers, distributors. If we're trading heavily with a country it is fairly certain that the kind of support we take for granted in the United States can also be expected in the export market.

Aggregate statistics don't tell us anything about just what is being sold in foreign markets. Fortunately, the Commerce Department and the Census Bureau publish detailed statistics about American domestic and international trade. Even if you can't obtain these statistics you may be able to locate statistics published by the United Nations.

Each year over 10,000 different kinds of products leave and enter the United States. To facilitate data collection about these exports and imports, the Bureau of Census groups similar kinds of items into a number of broad categories. These broad categories are subdivided into a series of increasingly more detailed classifications. Each category at each level of detail is assigned a code number. United States classification numbers range from one digit at the broadest classification level to seven digits at the maximum level of detail.

The United States uses six classification schedules (see Figure 7.2). The following explains the schedules used for compiling export statistics:

1. Schedule B is a detailed (4,500 seven-digit items) system of export categorization in which U.S. export data are originally recorded. (The product's Schedule B number is required on the "Shipper's Export Declaration.")
2. Schedule E is a rearrangement of Schedule B export data to a form closely resembling the SITC international data format developed by the United Nations. Schedule E data first became available in 1978.
3. SIC (Standard Industrial Classification) foreign trade data classification system was developed by the Bureau of Census to rearrange import statistics collected (TSUSA, see Chapter 13) and Schedule B Statistics into a format used for the classification of U.S. domestic trade. Publications using SIC statistics provide information pertaining to domestic, export, and import trade.

Every export valued at over $1000 ($500 for postal shipments) must be accompanied by an official U.S. document issued by the Department of Commerce's Bureau of the Census and International Trade Adminis-

Foreign Market Evaluation

U.S. Data Classification Systems

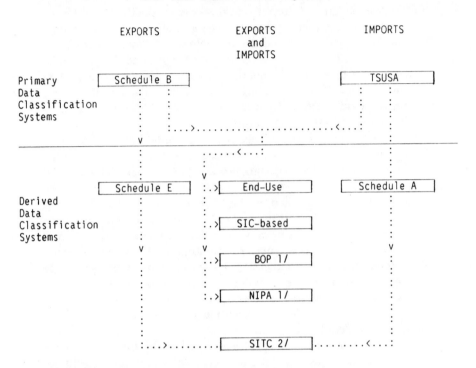

1/ Produced by the Bureau of Economic Analysis from Census Bureau Schedule
B and TSUSA data.
2/ Produced for the United Nations by Census from Schedule E and Schedule A
data.

Figure 7.2
(*Source: Understanding United States Foreign Trade Data.* U.S. Department of Commerce, International Trade Administration, August, 1985.)

tration which is called a "Shipper's Export Declaration." (More detailed information on the SED will be provided in Chapter Eleven.) The exporter should check with the Commerce Department to be sure he or she uses the correct Schedule B number. To illustrate the organization of trade statistics, a classification of grapefruit juice in airtight containers, not frozen, according to the seven-digit Schedule B classification system is shown in Table 7.2:[2]

---

[2]U.S. Department of Commerce, ITA, *Understanding Foreign Trade Data*, August 1985, p. 14.

TABLE 7.2   Schedule B Classification

Level of Detail	Schedule B Number	Commodity Description
7	0535010	Grapefruit juice, single strength, in airtight containers, not frozen
6	053501	Citrus juice, single strength, in airtight containers, not frozen
5	05350	Fruit and vegetable juices
4	0535	Fruit and vegetable juices
3	053	Fruits and nuts, prepared or preserved
2	05	Fruits and vegetables
1	0	Food and live animals

Schedule B data are raw numbers. They are converted into "Schedule E" numbers for publication purposes. Schedule E numbers have the advantage of being easily converted into the Standard International Trade Classification (SITC) numbers used by the United Nations.

Schedule E has nine categories:

Section 0: Food and live animals

Section 1: Beverages and tobacco

Section 2: Crude materials, inedible, except fuels

Section 3: Mineral fuels, lubricants, and related products

Section 4: Fats and oils—animal and vegetable

Section 5: Chemicals and related products

Section 6: Manufactures classified chiefly by material

Section 7: Machinery and transport equipment

Section 8: Miscellaneous manufactures

Section 9: Items not classified elsewhere

When Schedule B data are converted to SIC numbers the researcher can compare American domestic commerce to American international trade data. The kind of information one requires will determine which schedule to select.

The exporter should stay abreast of talks to develop a new coding system that may be adopted on January 1, 1988 called the "Harmonized Commodity Description and Coding System" (HC). The HC will be used by manufacturers, exporters, importers, Customs Service, Census, Commerce, statisticians, and anyone classifying goods moving in international trade in the 60 countries, 14 government-sponsored international organizations, nine private international organizations, and two national trade facilitation organizations. It will be set up in a fashion similar to classi-fication systems currently used in the United States.

Let's say we want to compare total French exports of farm equip-ment to American total exports of farm equipment for a certain year. One could find this information in the appropriate year of the *Yearbook of International Trade Statistics* published by the United Nations. These vol-umes are large compilations of statistics shelved in either the reference section of the library or in government documents. Schedule E statistics provide the greatest detail on American exports. You can find out which countries are importing American farm equipment with Schedule E and UN statistics. In sum, the most complete statistics about American trade can be found in Commerce/Census publications, while trade between countries other than the United States is better documented in UN statis-tics.

At least five years of data collection are needed to obtain a reliable trend. One can chart a trend through graphs. The simple method is to represent the amount exported against the year. If we were to graph such figures on "semi-log" paper we would observe the rate of change over time. The graphed line would represent the proportional change between any or all points in the time series. A line that is increasing offers diverse inter-pretations according to its position in relation to the origin. A straight line radiating out at a 45 degree angle from the origin indicates constant change. A line shifted to the left of the 45 degree reference line indicates exports increasing at an increasing rate. A line shifted to the right of the reference line indicates exports increasing at a decreasing rate.

A third method, which is commonly used in government reporting, is that of "percentage change." One selects as a base a year that he or she believes was a normal one for the company: neither a business slump nor a rally. To calculate the percentage change each year, use the following formula:

$$\frac{\text{Value of the Year Under Consideration}}{\text{Base Year}}$$

Multiply the result by 100. Subtract 100 from the product. The an-swer will be the percentage change from the base year.

Collecting Demographic, Economic, and Policy Data

Let's assume you have studied trade statistics and found that there is a brisk export market for the company's product. The next step is to study the market itself. By "demographics" we really mean "charting the people." How do they live? How much money do they earn? "Psychographics," as well, has become very important in marketing in recent years. Psychographic customer profiles chart the way people live and think. Constructing psychographics on international customers requires in-depth reading of current events as well as a knowledge of their literature and history. Table 7.3 contains a checklist of the statistics one may wish to collect.

Discounting other factors, the greater the population in a country, the better the market. This maxim is especially true with necessity goods such as ethical drugs, health care items, certain food products, educational supplies, and clothing. It also works for low ticket items such as soft drinks, candy, or ballpoint pens. High population will usually indicate a good market for the "universals," products such as bicycles and sewing machines that are demanded by people throughout the world, rich or poor, hot or cold climate. Beyond the universals, aggregate population statistics provide the exporter with little information. The exporter must look at the population of a region. For instance, Europe is a small land area but is densely populated, while most of Canada's population is concentrated in a narrow band along its border with the United States. Latin America's population is highly coastal. Brazil is heavily concentrated at its southeastern corner. Egypt's population is almost entirely located along the Nile. It's much cheaper to service customers clumped together. One saves on transportation costs, advertising (reach more people with a single advertisement), and brokers' fees.

Population growth rates are also important. Growth rates are slow

TABLE 7.3

Demographic	*Economic*
Total Population and Density	Gross National Product
Population Growth Rates	Per Capita Income
Population Distribution	Economic Policy
— Age	Inflation Rate
— Urbanization	Unemployment Rate
— Ethnic and Language	Labor Force Participation
— Religion	Rates
Climate	Energy Consumption
	Infrastructure

Government Regulations
Customs Tariffs
Other Taxes
Nontariff Barriers
Intellectual Property Rights

in the advanced industrial democracies, but still out of control in most underdeveloped countries. Latin America has the highest growth rates (with the exception of Argentina and Uruguay). South Asia is the next highest area, followed by Africa. While population growth rates boost the demand for goods, cash poor countries end up spending their limited capital on basic goods instead of modernization.

The population can be segmented into categories. *Age* helps the exporter chart the demand for products that are associated with the human life cycle. A young population (under 20) purchases hedonistic products, those that will give pleasure. Young adults purchase automobiles, furniture, and household appliances. The "full nest I" describes the young family that purchases baby and children items. "Full nest II" families purchase products associated with teenagers. And the "empty nest" couple spends more money on recreational activities and health care.

A country's level of *urbanization* provides us with information about consumer dependency on manufactured goods. Urban dwellers rely on manufacturers for almost all of their material needs, while rural people are largely self-sufficient. Urbanites tend to be sophisticated consumers, willing to try new products, receptive to new ideas. Rural inhabitants slowly change their buying habits.

Many American businesses have failed to realize their full profit potential due to insensitivity to the *ethnicity* and *language* of their market. Products won't sell as well if French labeling is used to the exclusion of Dutch in the Dutch speaking regions of Belgium. It's expensive to print multiple labels. Will multilingual labels do? Does the product name translate into the foreign language? Be sure to consult a language expert familiar with the use of the language in the specific locality, for example Spanish as spoken in Mexico.

Religious beliefs of a region can also influence product demand. For example alcohol and tobacco are forbidden in Moslem countries. The Hindu religion forbids the consumption of beef or the use of beef products such as hides.

The exporter must consider *climate* as well. An equatorial country isn't going to have a raging demand for automobile heaters, but may require air conditioners as standard equipment. Product construction, as well, may require modification to withstand extreme climate conditions.

W. W. Rostow divided economic development into five stages: Traditional society, Preconditions for take-off, Take-off, Drive to maturity, and Age of high mass consumption. Rostow's model can be used by exporters as a rough sketch in which to insert countries. That is, the products demanded are somewhat dependent on the stage of development. Although no stage is completely exclusive of the other, different social tensions, government policies, and consumer needs are evident at each of these stages. Rostow's model is quite useful to the exporter because it provides a framework for selecting the best marketing strategy.[3]

Psychographics are very important in American marketing. Toothpaste marketing is an interesting example of how psychographics and demographics are combined. Consider the many features on which toothpaste is advertised—fresh breath, protection (fluoride), taste, white teeth, ease of use (pump), and color. Then carefully watch some television commercials. Toothpastes that emphasize fresh breath and white teeth target the psyche of young, single people who are anxious to attract members of the opposite sex. Mothers and fathers worry about protecting their children's teeth. Another example of American psychographic work centers on the "Yuppie." Today's major challenge is to identify a life style that distinguishes the Yuppie from other psychographic profiles.

As international traders we must chart feelings and needs in foreign markets and read sources (fiction, country profiles, magazines) to gain an understanding of cultural idiosyncracies.

There is a host of *economic* statistics that the exporter should consider. A country's Gross National Product is a general indicator of its market size. A more specific measure of a market's buying power is *per capita income*, which is calculated by dividing population into GNP.

Don't place too much reliance on per capita income as a measure of buying power unless the country has a large middle class and no profound regional disparities. A large middle class is the foundation of a thriving economy in that there are many people with the ability to buy. Some historical examples might illuminate this concept. Most of the people who lived under the rule of the Roman Empire were slaves or landless peasants, and as such they didn't have the capacity to consume. Some economic historians argue that the industrial revolution arose in England through centuries of evolution which fostered a middle income level of people—yeomen farmer, merchant, guildsman, shopkeeper. America's North-South income disparity can also be traced to the historical absence of a large middle class in the South vis à vis its northern neighbors. Slave societies or societies in which there is a huge disparity between rich and poor and but a small layer between can never become thriving markets until some kind of redistribution begins to take place.

Published studies of the country inform us about the size of the middle class and regional disparities. Brazil and Italy, for example, suffer pro-

---

[3]W. W. Rostow, *The Stages of Economic Growth*. (Cambridge: Cambridge University Press, 1960).

found regional disparities. Brazil's southeast region is quite prosperous, while its Amazon region is poor. Italy's south, despite postwar inroads, remains poor next to the northern provinces. India and Mexico are held back by the indigent masses, a relatively small privileged class, and a small middle class. But countries recognize these problems and strive to eliminate them. Brazil and Italy have done much to correct these regional inequities. India and Mexico, too, work toward building a solid middle class. A rule of thumb when using GNP and per capita income figures is that with goods requiring high consumer incomes, the exporter is better off concentrating his or her effort on countries with higher per capita incomes.

Knowledge about a country's *economic policy* will save the exporter research time if he or she finds that the product line is in an industry that the government protects. The government may be trying to stimulate exports and limit imports. The *inflation rate* should be considered because if it is high in a particular country (as has been the case in many countries especially in Latin America and Israel) that country may impose strict controls over foreign exchange. In turn, the importer may not be allotted the dollars he or she needs to purchase exports. Furthermore, if incomes aren't keeping pace with inflation, the demand for your product will plummet.

High *unemployment* rates will suppress demand for all products, domestic or foreign. *Labor force participation rates* show us who is earning and spending the money and in which sectors. For statistical purposes sectors are normally separated into the categories of fishing, mining, agriculture, manufacturing, and service. Workers in these sectors are classified according to sex and age. Do women work outside of the household? What is the percent of women in clerical? In professional? These facts will not only help determine their buying power, but what products they will purchase. How much of the population is employed in manufacturing? In agriculture? A largely agrarian population will not purchase as much as a country that is industrialized.

Knowing a country's *energy consumption* is very important for exporters of electrical machinery as well as consumer durables such as refrigerators, stoves, dishwashers, and vacuum cleaners. When countries report low per capita figures on energy consumption it probably means the countryside is not electrified.

Infrastructure is defined as the country's system of bridges, paved roads, railroad tracks, seaports and airports, transportation terminals, and commercial and financial services. Americans are accustomed to a well-developed, regulated, and efficient infrastructure. But to expect such a highly developed infrastructure in lesser developed countries will only create frustration.

The exporter's access to the market may be hindered by customs tariffs. Import duties fall into two basic categories: general and preferential. In addition, an exporter may encounter three types of duties. *Ad valorem* duties are percentage calculations, based on the value of the good, which is usually the price the importer paid for the goods. For example, to figure a 20 percent "ad val" duty on an imported machine for which the importer paid $10,000, the duty would be $2,000. A *specific* duty is assessed according to the weight of the shipment or number of pieces. A combination of ad val and specific duties is called a *compound* duty.

Preferential tariffs are designed to promote trade with countries for reasons of foreign policy. For instance the European Economic Community has free trade among its members and discriminates in favor of countries that were once European colonies. (The U.S. Generalized System of Preferences will be discussed in Chapter Fifteen.) The exporter should be aware of the trade diversion effects of regional associations. A *free trade area* removes internal tariffs. The now defunct Latin American Free Trade Association tried, but failed to create a free trade area in Latin America. A *customs union* not only eliminates tariffs between member nations, but also surrounds itself with a *common external tariff*. The CET creates a single tariff schedule for the entire customs union. Actually a CET makes the job easier for the exporter. He or she need only be conversant with the CET instead of each country's tariff schedule. The success of "Benelux," a customs union of Belgium, Netherlands, and Luxembourg, provided the model on which the European Economic Community (EEC) was created. The next level of regional integration is that with which we are most familiar, *common market*. The EEC is a common market. In addition to the removal of internal tariffs and a CET, it also has free movement of capital and labor across borders.

The EEC was created by the Treaty of Rome in 1957. Its original signatories were Belgium, Luxembourg, the Netherlands, France, Italy, and West Germany. The first expansion of the EEC, (termed "accession") took place in 1972 when Great Britain, Ireland, and Denmark joined. A second accession occurred in 1980 with Greece. And the latest accession took place in 1986 when Portugal and Spain were made full members.

Over the past few years we have seen the EEC referred to as simply the "EC," which stands for the "European Community." This change reflects the stated goal of harmonization of economic policy (which is already evident in the European Steel and Coal Community and the European Atomic Energy Commission) as well as political integration. The

European Parliament, headquartered in Brussels, consists of members of the EC chosen through direct elections in the member countries and is considered a vital step toward political integration.

In addition to the customs tariff levied on imports, the exporter needs to know if there is an internal tax imposed on his or her product. Alcohol, tobacco, and petroleum products are prime targets for extra taxes.

A *quota* is set as a specific quantitative limit to the import of a product or class of products for each year. Quotas are more effective in limiting imports than tariffs because once the quota has been reached no imports can be legally obtained.

Nontariff barriers are often just a sneaky way of keeping a foreign product out of the market while abiding by multilateral agreements that the country has signed through the GATT. (See Chapter Six for more on the GATT.) To learn about such country-specific regulations, contact the Commerce Department's International Trade Administration, Office of Country Marketing.

Many countries require an *import license* which is used by the government to limit imports. Cash poor governments may be trying to limit the outflow of foreign currency or they may be protecting an infant industry.

Protecting Intellectual Property

Intellectual property refers to rights relating to such objects as books, films, inventions, trademarks, and designs. The three types of protection available are patents for inventions, trademarks for a product or service, and copyrights for literary, dramatic, musical, artistic, and computer programs.

There are no international treaties that protect all types of intellectual property, but the United States is a participant in international conventions that offer some protection. The oldest patent treaty, "The Paris Convention," provides the right of national treatment and the right of priority; an application for a patent in the foreign country that is a signatory of the Paris Convention (there are 96 signatories) will not be discriminated against on the basis of nationality. Rights will be the same as those of the country's own citizens. The right of priority allows the applicant a year (six months for a design or trademark) in which to file for protection in another member country.

The United States is also a party to the "Patent Cooperation Treaty" which provides procedures for filing patent applications in its member countries. With the filing of one international application, several countries can be designated. But trademarks must be registered in each country in which protection is desired. United States international copyright relations are governed by the "Universal Copyright Convention" administered by the United Nations Educational, Scientific, and Cultural Organization (UNESCO).

Many developing nations insist that technology and the like should be shared with all countries. They may require that the product be produced locally in order to receive patent or trademark protection. It is a good idea to consult an attorney experienced in international business practices for assistance in obtaining the necessary protection.

Sizing Up the Competition

Assessment of the competition is similar to monitoring the competition at home. Begin with a search of foreign magazines (for a consumer product), trade journals (for an industrial product), and foreign newspapers for advertisements. Maintain a record of advertisements, including the dates on which these advertisements appear. The timing of the advertisements may indicate seasonality that is slightly different from the seasonality your company is accustomed to in the United States. Advertising strategies should be evaluated. The competitor's product can be compared in terms of price, features, promotion, and distribution. Who is distributing the competitor's product? Perhaps distributors have complaints about the product or about post-sales servicing of technical products. There may be features consumers want but are not getting. Check credit terms and discount allowances. Can your company offer the distributor better credit terms and more generous allowances for high volume purchases? If the product is being manufactured in the foreign country be certain that the product is differentiated enough to sell at a price that will probably be higher than the domestic product due to the added costs associated with exports.

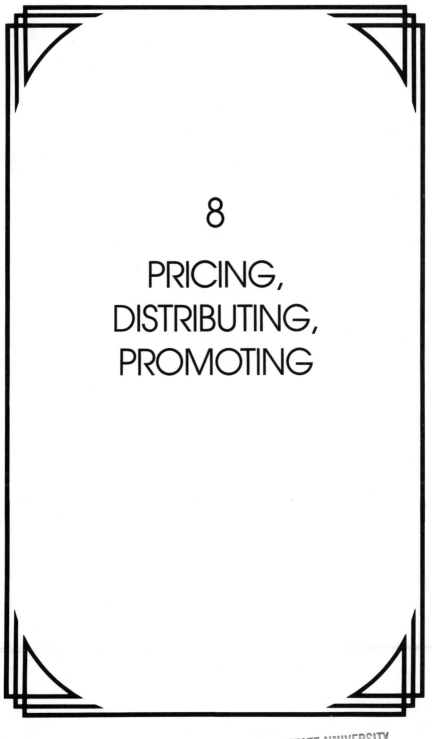

8

PRICING,
DISTRIBUTING,
PROMOTING

Pricing the Product for Export

The company's strategic plan for entering the market will largely determine the price range selected. If a company is operating below capacity and its goal is to get back up to capacity to decrease unit costs, it might be a good idea to set a low price for exports. According to multilateral trade agreements the American government has made through the GATT, however, it is illegal to "dump" American products overseas, that is, you can't legally sell a product for a lower price overseas than it is currently selling for in the United States. An overseas producer can initiate litigation against the foreign competitor.

If the company's goal is to obtain the highest price possible, it should *skim*. This strategy should be used with caution, only when the export market is quite small and isn't expected to grow or if local or foreign competition will soon be able to match your product at a lower price. Skimming is a short-run strategy for a small or ephemeral market.

Penetration pricing involves offering one's product at a low enough price to create a mass market. The product must be one of mass appeal and with potential for developing a large share of the market. If no long-run market exists, undercutting is foolish. In general charge a high price if any of the following conditions apply to the company: first, the product is unique and protected by an international patent or trademark (consult an attorney); second, the product is complex, which implies that market acceptance requires a great deal of promotion and training of sales representatives; third, the size of the market is never expected to be very large; fourth, the company doesn't expect competition to be attracted into the market because of the high price; and fifth, the company lacks the production capacity to meet the demand of international markets.

A low price is charged if any of the following conditions applies: first, the product isn't well known overseas; second, excessive unused production capacity is available; and third, the foreign competition is charging low prices. With today's aggressive global competition and a high dollar, American exporters have to sharpen their pencils and find ways to shave costs. You must shop around for the best bargains in insurance, transportation, and banking services. There may be expenses you can deduct from the export price that are strictly domestic in nature.

There are other reasons for getting into international markets and roughing it out in an era of high dollars. First, the dollar won't be so high against other currencies forever. As it falls, companies will still have a network in foreign markets, a great advantage over competitors who dropped out of foreign competition because of currency difficulties. Second, a company must fight it out for market share all over the world, surrendering learning curve and economies of scale gains to competitors, foreign and domestic alike. This can spell future difficulties for competition on your own turf.

Let's say that a buyer writes or telexes a company asking for information about its product. The first rule is to give him or her all the facts and right away to lessen the risk of giving a competitor the sale. A quote or catalog should always be accompanied by a friendly letter. This letter should tell a little bit about the company as well as point out the availability of other products that are compatible with the one about which he or she is inquiring. When applicable, a discount sheet should be enclosed. Slang is never used in business correspondence; apart from its unprofessional nature, there's a good chance the correspondent won't understand idiomatic English, and he or she will have to hire a translator. Form letters are rude. Didn't the potential customer take the time to write a personal letter? Letters help the customer learn more about the exporter. If the company contacts the exporter in his or her native language, the exporter should answer in the same language. If the letter is in English, the response should be in English, even if the grammar or vocabulary in the letter is weak. Letter # 1 is a sample of the type of letter to send as a reply to a tentative inquiry into a product.

Let's assume that a company is interested in a product and asks for a quotation. The appropriate response is to send a letter and a *pro forma invoice*. Table 8.1 contains a checklist of cost factors to consider when determining an export price.[1]

The pro forma invoice is a document that contains the quotation to

---

[1]U.S. Department of Commerce, *A Basic Guide to Exporting*, 1986.

M & L Machines
2156 Seneca Street
Buffalo, New York 14201 U.S.A.
Phone 716 822-1903

December 12, 1986

Mr. Giancarlo Benditti
Guerra Products
Via Madaloni
Benevento, Italy

Dear Mr. Benditti:

We appreciate your interest in our line of industrial machines.

M & L Machines has been making quality machines since 1927. As we are a member of our local Chamber of Commerce, Chamber officials will verify our record as reliable, responsible suppliers. Our bank, Buffalo National, can verify our excellent business standing as well.

Our machines are shipped in special export packaging to ensure that they arrive in good condition.

We have enclosed descriptive literature for your examination. If you find a machine that meets your needs, we will be happy to prepare a pro forma invoice giving your cost including export packing, inland freight, insurance, forwarding fees, pier costs, and ocean freight.

Please send your response via airmail. We look forward to hearing from you very soon.

Sincerely yours,

Angela Symanski,
Export Marketing Manager

enclosure:
descriptive literature

Exporter's Reply to Potential Importer's Product Query

TABLE 8.1   Export Costs

---

*Personnel and equipment needed to establish and maintain export operation
*Market research and credit checks
*Shipping and insurance costs
*Business travel
*International postage, cable, and telephone rates
*Product modification and special packaging
*Overseas advertising and promotion efforts
*Translation costs
*Fees charged by consultants and freight forwarders
*Commissions, training charges, and other costs involving your foreign representatives

---

the foreign buyer. Figure 8.1 contains a sample pro forma invoice. The pro forma invoice is a binding document, that is, the quote remains valid for the period specified (unless otherwise stated). Although the exporter can insert a clause that makes it clear the quote is subject to change, many importers will not accept the risk it implies. The pro forma must also be precise because the importer often uses this invoice to arrange for an import license and/or to secure a letter of credit.

The exporter is more assured of getting the sale if he or she delivers a firm quote. If the buyer asks for a quote in his or her currency, don't quote in dollars unless you are willing to take the risk of losing the sale. Metric measurements should be used if the buyer so specifies. Don't seek credit information in this letter. The sale is not assured; nothing should be done to irritate the prospective buyer. Credit data can be obtained through other means. If it's going to take a few days to work up a quote, respond immediately, acknowledging receipt of the inquiry and stating that a quote will follow.

The pro forma invoice also enables the buyer to obtain an import license (if required) and his or her foreign exchange allotment. Table 8.2 contains a checklist of items that should be included in the pro forma invoice.

Terms of trade is a crucial shorthand language that has two functions. First, it determines at what point responsibility for the shipment passes to the importer; second, it defines who is responsible for payment of the many portions of the shipment. Although we will go over the main points of terms of trade, for an in-depth treatment of terms, refer to the American Foreign Trade Definitions included in Appendix II. Another term of payment system is called *Incoterms*, which is a classification by the International Chamber of Commerce aimed at standardizing payment terms used by all countries. For a copy of Incoterms, call (212) 206-1150, Telex 661519, or write ICC Publishing Corporation, 156 Fifth Avenue,

PRO FORMA INVOICE

Shipper:

Sold to:

Via:

NO. **P-**

DATE:

REFERENCE NO:

CUSTOMER P.O. NO.

TERMS OF PAYMENT:

ESTIMATED DATE OF SHIPMENT:

Ship to:

ITEM	QUANTITY	FULL DESCRIPTION OF MERCHANDISE	PRICE	TOTAL PRICE

Authorized Signature/Title

The above offering is based on current prices and is valid for _____ days from invoice date.

Form No. 10-010   Printed and Sold by Unz & Co., Division of Scott Printing Corp., 190 Baldwin Ave., Jersey City, N.J. 07306 — N.J. (201) 795-5400/Toll Free (800) 631-3098

Figure 8.1 (*Source:* UNZ & Company, Jersey City, New Jersey.)

Suite 820, New York, N.Y. 10010. Because most American exports use terms of payment based on American Foreign Trade Definitions, we will examine that system. Figure 8.2 is provided as a schematic aid to understanding American Foreign Trade Definitions.

TABLE 8.2

Name and address of seller
Date of invoice
Buyer and Seller's Order Number
Name and address of importer
Form of transportation
Terms of payment (Chapter Seven)
Insurance reference
Customs declaration
Shipping marks (Chapter Eleven)
Number of packages
Quantity and description of commodity
Unit price and extended price
Currency quoted
Gross, legal, and net weight (defined in glossary)
Terms of sale (based either on American Foreign Trade Definitions or Incoterms)
Export Packing
Commissions to forwarders
Consular invoice
Marine insurance
Ocean freight

With "EX-FACTORY" the buyer pays all costs once the good is brought out to the factory's loading dock. Even special export packaging and crating must be paid by the importer. Once the product leaves the factory, the buyer is responsible for its shipment—that is, the seller is relieved of all responsibility such as theft, damage, or loss. With "F.O.B. PLANT" (Free on Board) the seller pays for export packing. The buyer pays all other costs. In "F.O.B. PORT" the seller pays forwarder's fees, consular fees, and inland freight. When the seller quotes "F.A.S. VESSEL" (free alongside), he or she is quoting a price that includes all costs of delivering the goods alongside the overseas vessel (or plane) and within reach of its loading tackle. When quoting an "F.O.B. VESSEL" price the seller pays for all delivery costs up to and including the loading of the goods on the vessel or aircraft. A "C&F PORT OF IMPORT" quote makes the seller responsible for all previous costs and ocean (or air) freight. "C.I.F. PORT OF IMPORT" makes the seller responsible for paying all those delivery costs named under C&F, as well as marine or air insurance. Figure 8.2 indicates that all other costs associated with export trade—unloading the vessel or aircraft, import duties, inland freight, and import brokers fees—are covered by the seller in an "EX-DOCK" quote.

The terms you quote are important. For instance, imagine being a foreign buyer and receiving a quote stating "Ex-Plant Rochester, New

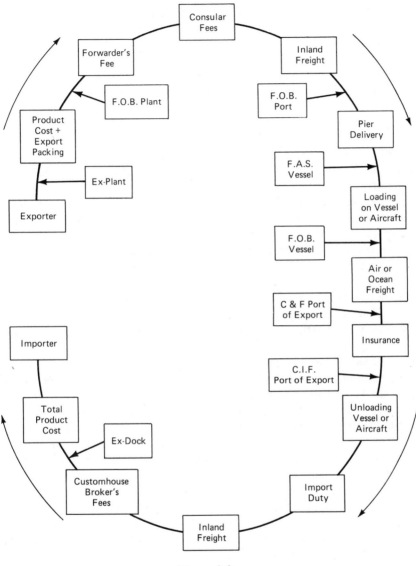

Figure 8.2

York." The inexperienced importer wouldn't have any idea of the final import cost of the product.

Exporters are normally expected to quote C.I.F. prices. This quote will tell the foreign buyer exactly how much it's going to cost him or her to get the product to the port of importation. The rest of the costs the importer can handle because they are incurred at home. Another advantage of a C.I.F. quote to the importer is that responsibility for keeping track of the shipment remains with the seller until it reaches the importer's country. But C.I.F. does have its risks. Freight charges, insurance rates, wharfage—all may rise in between the quote and the actual time of shipment. The exporter must be certain the figures he or she uses to work up the quote are precise. If not, he or she may end up *losing* money on the transaction. The exporter should *never* quote "ex-dock." There are too many costs subject to change that the exporter cannot keep track of from overseas. The buyer should also be familiar with the costs and reliability of inland carriers.

The most efficient method of working up a quotation is through the use of a cost worksheet. (See the costing sheet shown.) There are many other specific costs that the exporter may need to include when developing his or her own costing sheets, such as an unloading charge, terminal charge, notification charge, and heavy lift charge.

This costing sheet is designed to illustrate how some of the different shipping terms fit in as we move closer to the buyer.

There are four ways to weigh a shipment: *gross, tare, legal,* and *net.* The tare weight is the weight of packing and containers without the goods to be shipped. The net weight is the weight of the goods alone without any immediate wrappings, for example, the weight of the tuna from a tin can, without the weight of the can. The legal weight is the net weight plus the tare. The gross weight, the weight on which the freight charge is assessed, is the legal weight plus the export packing or crating. *Wharfage* is the charge assessed by pier personnel for the handling of incoming or outgoing cargo. *Consular* fees may be incurred if special forms such as the "consular invoice" (See Chapter Eleven) are required by the importer's country.

Freight rates can be obtained from the steamship line, steamship conference, or freight forwarder. If you are new to the business, don't try to schedule a shipment on your own. Employ a foreign freight forwarder.

Ask the forwarder to advise on listing ocean freight as "estimated" because ocean freights (non-conference) have been known to make unexpected rate jumps. (Conference liners give advance notice of freight rate changes.) When the quote is accepted with "estimated ocean freight" the buyer will make allowances for a rate increase. Ocean rates are set according to characteristics of the commodity—insurance claims against damages of the type of product in the past, value of the export, costs of loading/unloading, the area to service, packaging, storage, and handling. Distance is the least important factor in rate determination.

COST WORK SHEET

Product Unit Price   *Number of Units*

                                        (Ex-Plant) _____
Export Packing.. _____
                                        (F.O.B. Plant) _____
Type of Packing:
# of Containers:
WEIGHTS   Gross: Tare: Legal:
DIMENSIONS: Length: Width: Height:
Total Cubic Feet:

Forwarder's Fees.. _____
Consular Fees.. _____
Inland Freight .... _____
                                        (F.O.B. Port)
Pier Delivery .... _____
                                        (F.A.S. Vessel)
Wharfage .... _____
Other Pier Charges.. _____
                                        (F.O.B. Vessel)
ESTIMATED OCEAN FREIGHT
$ per metric/short/long/measurement ton
WM   tons at $ ton................................. _____
                                        (C & F Port of Import)
INSURANCE: Insured value $
Marine $ per $100 insured value
   War $ per $100 insured value
                        Total Insurance .... _____

C.I.F. PORT OF IMPORT.. _____

The exporter should also be prepared to provide measurements to the forwarder of the product. The ocean carrier has the option of choosing the method of calculating revenue to his or her greatest advantage, unless the tariff schedule calls for revenue on a weight or measurement basis. Table 8.3 contains the values one needs to compute ocean freight costs.

TABLE 8.3

By weight:
METRIC TON 2204.68 pounds
SHORT TON 2000 lbs.
LONG (gross) TON 2240 lbs.

By measurement:
MEASUREMENT (or freight) TON 40 cubic feet of space or one cubic meter (reckons the space that the export will take up in the ship)
To calculate:

$$\frac{\text{Width} \times \text{Height} \times \text{Length}}{1728 \text{ (number of cubic inches per foot)}}$$

W/M: Weight/Measurement ton Cargo is rated per weight or measurement ton. Carrier's option.

Like steamships, airplanes are cube-limited. Exports are charged for either the dimensional weight or actual weight, at the air cargo service's option.

Insurance is another area in which a freight forwarder can be employed with a cost advantage to the exporter. The large volume dealings of the forwarder usually earn him or her better rates on insurance than the exporter can hope to find on his or her own. Through the use of an *open policy* the forwarder can obtain protection for your exports. Insurance must cover the cost of the goods, export packing, inland freight, ocean freight, forwarding fees, wharfage—the price of the product and all the charges associated with its exportation. If the product gets lost or damaged, all the extra costs cannot be refunded without insurance. The general practice is to insure 110 percent of the value just in case of unexpected costs and also to allow for the appreciation in the value of the commodity at the port of import.

Marine insurance covers the loss or damage of goods at sea that can't be legally recovered from the carrier, such as losses sustained by fire, shipwreck, piracy, acts of God, quarantine restrictions, arrest or seizure under legal process, and insufficient packing or marking. The particular coverage the exporter seeks depends on the amount he or she is willing to pay the insuror. For instance, in the popular "all risks" form of marine insurance, the exporter doesn't have to prove what peril caused the loss. He or she need only show that the commodity was in good condition when shipped, that the loss resulted from a risk, and that the cause of the loss was not a peril that was specifically excluded from the all risks policy. The all risks policy has four primary exclusions: first, the loss of a customer or market or the good itself (such as perishables) because of delay; second, a loss from an imperfection in the export (inherent vice); third, loss or damage arising from wars, strikes, riots, and civil commotions (special endorsement is required); and fourth, losses arising from acts of war. (*War risk insurance must be obtained.*) The glossary contains more information on specific marine insurance terms and perils policies under the heading "marine insurance."

Note that in the costing sheet the insurance rate is applied per $100 of insured value. For example, marine insurance that was $.85 per $100 on a C&F shipment valued at $20,000 would be found by multiplying $.85 × 200 = $170.

If there is a loss, the exporter doesn't have to handle its claim if the title has already passed to the importer. The insurance certificate is passed along with the title (the certificate is transferable). Some importers will ask the exporter to deliver F.A.S. or C&F quotes so that they can choose their own insuror and policy. Furthermore, some countries require that the marine insurance on imports be written by local insurance companies.

DISTRIBUTING THE PRODUCT

Marketing channels include four distinct types of members: manufacturer, wholesaler, retailer, and customer. These actors may be organized in a number of ways, but the more common international channels are diagrammed in Figure 8.3. As Figure 8.3 indicates, there are two major ways to develop distribution channels: *direct* or *indirect*. Exporting through direct channels requires that a manufacturer erect overseas sales offices and/or sell directly to wholesalers or retailers in a foreign country. Products move through U.S. agents when a company chooses indirect exporting.

Indirect Exporting Agents

The export agent, export merchant, commission agents (export commission house), country-controlled buying agents, export management company (EMC), and export trading company (ETC) are the major types of organizations in the United States that purchase or represent American products for export.

The *export agent*, like the manufacturers' rep, doesn't take title to the goods, earning a commission for finding a foreign market for the exporters' product. An *export merchant* purchases products directly from the manufacturer and markets them to overseas buyers. *Commission agents* represent foreign customers by acting as their buying agents. They fill spe-

Pricing, Distributing, Promoting

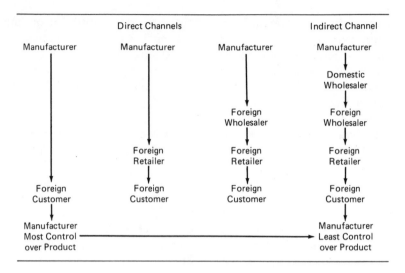

Figure 8.3

cific orders or regularly purchase a certain quantity of the product. *EMCs* act as the export department for several manufacturers of complementary, but noncompetitive, products. Rather than hire an export manager for let's say $35,000, an export sales rep for $25,000, and an export clerk for about $12,000, the EMC will provide the services of these full-time employees without the fixed costs.

Some EMCs work on commission, while others purchase products. They will expect a price that is lower than the domestic wholesale price to cover the many extra costs associated with selling a product overseas. The EMC conducts market research for the exporter, travels overseas to seek contacts, appoints foreign distributors, exhibits products at international trade fairs, manages the documentation, extends financing, works up the advertising and promotional devices, corresponds in the appropriate foreign language, and combines manufacturers' shipments to take advantage of the lower costs of high volume shipping that the small exporter can't achieve on his or her own.

There are about 1,100 EMCs in the United States, most of which are located at seaports and Great Lakes ports.[2] The "Sources" section lists readily available publications that will help you choose the EMC that is best for your company. In addition to published guides, local international

[2]"The Export Management Company: Your Export Department," U.S. Department of Commerce, International Trade Administration, August 1981.

trade associations, Commerce Department district offices, Small Business Administration offices, and local and state export offices can assist you in the proper selection.

Export Trading Companies (ETCs) are relatively new organizations in the United States, but certainly aren't new to trade. The British monarchy gave trading monopolies to the Hudson Bay Company and the East India Company. The modern type of trading company is associated with Japanese imports and exports. Japanese trading companies are praised for their ability to mobilize credit, scan world markets for information about product prices and market needs, and for finding small-scale producers in Japan to fill market needs.[3]

America's Export Trading Act was signed into law by President Reagan on October 8, 1982. The Act is an attempt to emulate the success of the Japanese trading company, ETCs export, import, and engage in "countertrade," (buying products in one country in order to sell one's own products). The ETC then takes the traded products and finds markets for them. The ETC purchases the product, acting as a merchant rather than an agent. A group of manufacturers may operate an ETC, a bank, a trade association, and even a local community can set up an ETC. Chapter Five contains additional information about Export Trading Companies.

You can also contact the Commerce Department's Office of Export Trading Company Affairs, Room 5618, U.S. Department of Commerce, Washington, D.C. 20230 (202) 377-5131.

Direct Exporting Agents

Direct exporting transactions utilize sales reps or agents, foreign distributors, foreign retailers, direct sales to consumer, and state-controlled trading companies. The *sales rep* works on a commission. He or she doesn't take title to the goods, thereby leaving the risk with the manufacturer. *Foreign distributors* purchase exports at a deep discount. They carry spare parts and provide servicing and technical training. Consumer products can be marketed directly to *foreign retailers*. It's only cost effective to deal with big foreign retailers who purchase high ticket items or in large volume. Smaller retailers should be serviced through distributors. *Selling direct to consumer* is more appropriate for high-ticket industrial products when the market is quite small. *State-controlled trading companies* or government purchasing agencies may be an option. Government markets are

---

[3]Raymond Vernon, *The Economic Environment of International Business.* Second Edition. (Englewood Cliffs: Prentice-Hall, Inc. 1976), p. 20.

large. They purchase items as small as pens and pencils as well as complex high-tech equipment such as computers. Unlike most private purchasers, government demand is quite stable, largely unaffected by recessionary slumps. When dealing with government buyers, be sure the person has proper authorization to order your product.

Many government markets have been more accessible to American exporters since implementation of the 1979 Government Procurement Code, a nontariff measure adopted through multilateral trade negotiations. The current list of signatories includes the United States, the European Community, Japan, Canada, Sweden, Norway, Finland, Austria, Switzerland, Hong Kong, Singapore, and Israel. Signatory countries agree not to discriminate against or among products from other signatory countries in many government purchases. All purchases must be advertised in advance and bid conditions must be nondiscriminatory. The announcement must permit at least 30 days to bid. If the exporter's bid is unsuccessful, the company must be informed why the government didn't take its bid.

The Commerce Department provides trade leads covering foreign government procurement through its computerized "Trade Opportunities Program" (TOP) and through *Commerce Business Daily,* the Department's daily publication. The Agency for International Development (AID) maintains a mailing list for specific export opportunities created by its programs as well. If an exporter thinks his or her company faced unfair competition, either in cases where rules were discriminatory or where other governments were intervening aggressively on behalf of their exporters, the exporter can contact a Commerce district office for help in reporting any violation of the Code rules.

Finding a Distributor

The Commerce Department offers an "Agent/Distributor Service," which is a custom search for qualified agents and distributors for the company's products. The search will identify up to six qualified, interested agents and distributors. Commerce Department specialists also assist in making initial contact and arrangements with the foreign agent or distributor. The fee is $90 for each country in which the search is conducted. For more information, one should contact your district office or write to Export Communications Section, Room 3056, Office of Export Marketing Assistance, U.S. Department of Commerce, International Trade Administration, Washington, D.C. 20230.

Commercial banks also assist its customers in finding reputable foreign agents and distributors. It is in the bank's interest to help its customers develop export markets because the exporter will need the bank's services for extending credit to the export customers, in getting paid, and in foreign exchange transactions. Foreign freight forwarders, airlines, local port officials, and chambers of commerce may also provide leads.

Once you select a foreign distributor or company, you should check the foreign buyer's reputation before drawing up a contract. The Commerce Department recommends that the exporter obtain at least two business and credit reports. For a fee of $75, the Commerce Department provides reputation, payment history, and trade and credit references of a company through its World Traders Data Reports (WTDRs) service. Private commercial credit reporting can provide an exporter with similar information. A banker is also a valuable source for credit information.

Choosing the Right Channel

The exporter doesn't have to select indirect over direct exporting or vice versa. One product line may be more profitably handled through indirect exporting, while another is easily managed through direct exporting. For instance, if you are familiar with the credit of the importers, know the market customs of the country, and have the appropriate or potential sales volume, direct exporting is the profitable choice.

Begin by reviewing the rationale behind the domestic channel. Is it short? Is the company selling directly to its end-users or retailers in the United States? It may be necessary to retain control over the product even if it means higher costs of maintaining a sales force. The longer the channel, the less control the exporter has over all aspects of the marketing process—price, distribution, promotion, and servicing. And, the greater the distance between customer and manufacturer, the more difficult it is for the manufacturer to obtain feedback about the product and the quality of servicing. Just as in any marketing decision, channel decisions must evaluate the customer, the product itself, the middlemen, and the goals and restraints on the company. Let's review some general guidelines.

Customer

If the exporter services a mass market, he or she must depend on many channel members. Foreign distributors have channel relations with many wholesalers and retailers. A pack of chewing gum is a mass purchased item which needs many middlemen to place the product with the tens of thousands of retailers who sell it. The presence of large volume retailers, such as department store chains, may make it cost effective for the manufacturer to deal directly with the retailer, bypassing wholesaler costs.

Product

The more complex the product, the higher its price, and the better it can handle the higher price attached to it for the commissions paid out to the sales force. Perishable products, whether produce, flowers, or fashion items, need short channels. It wouldn't do to have the upcoming season's dress line shifting from warehouse to warehouse when it should be out on the retailer's floor. Bulky products need a direct channel because it is too expensive to ship them from middleman to middleman.

Middleman

The manufacturer always enters into a contract with the distributor. The contract protects both the distributor and the manufacturer. The manufacturer receives assurance that the distributor won't handle competing lines, will provide the service the manufacturer requires, and will promote the product. In turn, the distributor is assured exclusive territory and is also protected from the manufacturer trying to cut him out of the channel by going directly to the customers, a market which the distributor may have developed by spending much of his own capital. Be careful about granting liberal exclusive distributorships. Distributors often request a territory much too large for their market knowledge, personnel, and contacts.

When an exporter engages a distributor he or she should hire an attorney experienced in international contracts. The contract should be drawn up for two to three years, with a right to renew for one year after that period. After that time the exporter may be dissatisfied with the distributor or he or she may wish to revise the contract. Just as the manufacturer can drop the distributor, the distributor can drop the manufacturer. A competitor might be offering deeper discounts, more liberal credit, better promotional devices; these are the competitive weapons that the manufacturer can artfully employ. The middleman is a member of the exporter's channel, therefore the exporter should work (within capital limits) to make the distributor's job easier.

Warren Keegan points out that middlemen are notorious for their "cherry picking," that is they are order takers for products in demand, but don't bother to push new products with which customers aren't familiar.[4] Professor Keegan suggests that one method of averting such neglect is to pay for those members of the sales staff employed by the distributor who are assigned to sell the manufacturer's products. In this way the manufacturer will still be receiving the advantages of the distributor's channel networking while ensuring that its own product line receives adequate attention.

The exporter will need to consider what types of middlemen are available. Are there distributors willing to handle or capable of handling the product, especially if it is technically complex and requires support and servicing? The manufacturer may have to set up a sales and service branch in the country.

The overriding advantage for choosing channel members to distribute your products is that it involves minimal capital outlay and operating expenses compared to operating one's own sales branches and warehouses. The international middleman is also an expert in his or her market. He or she already knows the customers. Middlemen carry complementary products that, by association, boost sales of the exporter's products, benefits accrue to unknown products when they are marketed alongside products with many loyal consumers.

Many countries (especially lesser developed countries) have contract termination laws that penalize the exporter who terminates business relations with the foreign distributor. Some laws require the exporter to compensate the agent for the goodwill generated by the agent. Another feature of many of such laws is that the agent is permitted to contest a termination notice by submitting it to arbitration. Some agents are even considered employees under the law and as such are entitled to pensions, payable by the exporter, if the exporter terminates the contract.

To protect the position in the agency agreement, the exporter should hire an experienced international lawyer and consider the following guidelines:

1. The agency agreement should be in writing.
2. The agreement should set forth the benefit to both parties.
3. A clear definition and meaning must be given to all contract terms. Use "Revised American Foreign Trade Definitions" or "Incoterms."

---

[4]Warren J. Keegan, *Multinational Marketing*. Second Edition. (Englewood Cliffs: Prentice-Hall, Inc., 1980), p. 334.

An English version of the agreement should be written into the contract to *prevail* in cases of doubt as to the meaning of contractual terms.

4. The rights and obligations of the parties should be written into the contract, for instance, which party bears responsibility for returns, rejects, and product liability. The degree of responsibility for advertising and promotion, as well as periodic review of the program, should be included. The contract also must include specifics about service, training, and inventory. Specify delivery and payment practices.

5. A jurisdictional clause should specify the jurisdiction to handle legal disputes if local law allows that the case be adjudicated in a court other than in the foreign country.

6. Basic arbitration rules and principles are generally the same throughout the world. A clause should identify the arbitration body or forum as well as the arbitration rules and procedures. It is less time-consuming and cheaper to solve disputes through arbitration than litigation.

7. Consider the impact of foreign laws on the contract.

8. Any right to terminate or not to extend the contract should require written notice to be provided enough in advance to permit the distributor to make other business arrangements.

Manufacturer's Restraints and Goals

A small manufacturer won't have the kind of money to handle the costs of promoting, advertising, and servicing that the foreign distributor would expect. The company is then forced to export through domestic middlemen. But if the manufacturer seeks to build up a large export market, then selling through distributors may be counterproductive because distributors often market the product under their own name, and as a consequence, goodwill accrues to the distributor.

As the market develops, the manufacturer should consider expanding its profits by bypassing channel members. The manufacturer obtains more knowledge of the market when he or she engages in direct exporting. The marketing department may be able to bring out new products or find more effective ways of promoting existing products. Generally, the more experienced a company becomes in international markets, the more it should begin taking over the distribution function. A large, steady, or increasing demand for the product reduces the financial risks associated with building up a direct export channel. If export sales are concentrated, rather than spread thinly throughout the country, it will be less costly to maintain a direct sales force.

PROMOTING THE PRODUCT

Whether you sell the product domestically or internationally, there are four distinct ways to communicate information about a product to the consumer. Direct mail, including personal correspondence, is an important method of communicating with the overseas customer. Another method of reaching markets is through promotional devices such as catalogs, samples, motion pictures, slide films, window displays, and exhibits. Advertising in print media, on the radio, and television is used by exporters as well. And direct selling—the use of sales representatives—is another very important method of reaching customers. Which mode of communication or combination of modes to use is determined by the product itself and characteristics of the market.

Professor Keegan presented a model for developing a product-promotion strategy for international markets.[5] He identified five strategies:

Product-communication extension

Product extension-communication adaption

Product adaptation-communication extension

Dual adaptation

Product invention

If the product is used the same way overseas and satisfies the same needs, you can export the identical product and market it in a similar fashion. But if the product is used somewhat differently, you need a different marketing strategy. For instance in countries where bicycles are used as an important means of transportation rather than recreation, the reliability and durability of the bicycle may be emphasized over other features. This strategy would be one of "product extension-communication adaption."

---

[5]Warren J. Keegan, "Multinational Product Planning: Strategic Alternatives," *Journal of Marketing* 33. January 1969.

If consumer tastes and needs are somewhat different from those in the United States, but the product is used the same way, the "product adaptation-communication extension" strategy is suitable. Dual adaptation would become necessary if the product needs to be altered and its use is somewhat different. Product invention is often required for marketing to poorer countries that can't afford to purchase sophisticated American products. Keegan suggests "inventing backwards," that is, marketing a product that has become obsolete in the American market, but suitable for underdeveloped economies.

Direct Mail

The potential customer should be contacted in his or her own language. You don't need a language expert on staff. Local Chambers of Commerce or District Offices of the Commerce Department supply lists of local translators. Colleges also have many foreign nationals eager to make some money at translating, as well as Americans majoring in foreign languages.

If the customer replies in English, the exporter should respond in English. Some foreigners prefer to correspond in English. Once a business relationship is established, it is appropriate to invite members of the importer's company to visit your company. The export manager should learn the customs of customers' holidays. Something as simple as a greeting card can build up goodwill for the exporter with foreign customers.

Remember the name of each contact. All of the amenities that are natural for trade with domestic customers should be applied to international customers. Remember that each letter you send is a sales instrument.

Sales Promotional Devices

The Commerce Department assists exporters in sales promotion through its Export Development Offices (EDOs). These offices are located worldwide in major commercial cities and in many developing markets as well. For products that require inspection by the prospective buyer, EDOs organize "trade fairs." Thousands of companies from many countries display their products at trade fairs. The Commerce Department will provide exhibit space, design and construct the exhibit, advise on shipment of products to the site, unpack and position displays, supply basic utilities and housekeeping services, provide a lounge or meeting room for exhibitor-customer conferences, and provide appropriate show hospitality and market counseling. As a participant at the commerce-sponsored exhibition, the exporter must provide U.S. products for display, supply technical and promotional handout literature, ship products to the exhibition site, and assign a representative qualified to staff the booth, transact business, make a specified participation contribution.[6]

Opportunities for companies to come together with foreign buyers, agents, and distributors are provided by "trade missions." The Commerce Department sponsors missions as do associations, chambers of commerce, and state development agencies.

In addition to trade fairs and missions, the Commerce Department sponsors "Catalog and Video/Catalog Exhibitions." These types of exhibitions may be the exporter's best way to reach small markets.

Advertising

It is best to hire a reputable advertising agency that has an office or correspondent overseas. If the product is a mass item, you might assume that television advertising will reach customers, but you may learn, however, that the television stations are publically owned and do not permit commercial advertising. You could then restructure your advertising strategy toward print media and radio. If the potential market tends to be illiterate, then radio and television are more effective than print media. Some magazines are more appropriate for the product. The product should be readily available so that when the advertising campaign begins, foreign customers won't have any trouble finding it.

It's unwise to depend on American translators for developing an advertising campaign because they may be unaware of idiomatic changes in the language of the foreign country. Just as there are many idiomatic differences between British English and American English, there are differences in the Spanish spoken in Spain and Latin America. In many cases, the *last* thing an advertising campaign needs is a direct translation of the wording used in American advertisements. Ads are filled with idioms and cultural connotations. Besides wording, pictorial constructs differ from one culture to the next. For instance, it's not a good idea to show a girl and boy with their arms wrapped around each other in a conservative culture no matter how intent the advertiser is on showing that their chewing gum freshens breath.

---

[6]*A Basic Guide to Exporting.* (Washington, D.C.: U.S. Department of Commerce, International Trade Administration, November 1981) p. 74.

Direct Sales Force

Although this method is the most expensive type of promotion, complex products such as ethical drugs and computers will need salespeople who know the language and customs of the export market. The exporter will need to establish branch offices that act as both distributorships and post-sales service centers.

SUGGESTED READINGS

Publishers That Print Serial Information

"Business Latin America" publishes business information relevant to Latin America.

"Business International" publications.

"Price Waterhouse" publishes business studies of countries.

"Touche Ross International" publishes business studies of countries.

Directories

American Export Register.
 Thomas International Publishing Company
 One Penn Plaza
 New York, N.Y. 10001
 (212) 695–0500
 Directory of American manufacturers selling to world markets. Annual. $112.

Directory of Leading U.S. Export Management Companies,
 Bergamo Book Company, 15 Ketchum St., Westport, CT 06881. 1984. $37.50

Europe's 15,000 Largest Companies.
 Dun's Marketing Services

——. *Principal International Businesses.*

——. *Dun's Latin America's Top 25,000.*

Export Directory: Buying Guide, biennial, *Journal of Commerce,* 110 Wall St., New York, N.Y. 10005. $225

International Register of Department Stores.
International Publications Service, 1979.
Tamborrino, F. and P. Gulizia, eds.

Local Chambers of Commerce which Maintain Foreign Trade Services.
International Division, Chamber of Commerce of the U.S., 1615 H
Street, NW, Washington, D.C. 20062. 1983. Free.

Mail Order Business Directory
B. Klein Publications, Inc.
P.O. Box 8503
Coral Springs, Florida 33065
(305) 752-1708
U.S. and throughout world

Stores of the World Directory.
Heineman, Inc. Publishers
Biennial. Two volumes.

General Reading

Copeland, Lennie and Lewis Griggs. *Going International: How to Make
Friends and Deal Effectively in the Global Marketplace.* New York:
Random House, 1985.

Keegan, Warren J. *Multinational Marketing Management.* Latest Edition. Englewood Cliffs: Prentice-Hall, Inc.

Root, Franklin, R. *Entry Strategies for Foreign Markets.* American Management Association, 1977, $10.

Rostow, W. W. *The Stages of Economic Growth.* Second Edition. Cambridge: Cambridge University Press, 1971.

Terpstra, Vern. *The Cultural Environment of International Business.* Latest Edition. Cincinatti: South-Western Publishing Co., 1978.

Government Publications

Area Handbooks for particular countries. See, for example, Weil, Thomas
E. *Area Handbook for Argentina.* Washington, D.C.: U.S. Government
Printing Office, 1974.

ORGANIZATION FOR ECONOMIC COOPERATION AND DEVELOPMENT (OECD) publishes statistical profiles of member countries as
well as special reports. Suite 1207, 1750 Pennsylvania Ave., NW, Washington, D.C. 20062-4582, (202) 724-4582.

U.S. DEPARTMENT OF COMMERCE PUBLICATIONS: Check the last issue for each year of *Business America* for list of available government pamphlets.

Commerce Business Daily—daily list of government procurement invitations, contract awards, subcontracting leads, sales or surplus property, and foreign business opportunities. $160 annual 1985 subscription.

Country Market Surveys. Summary of in-depth "International Market Research" reports listed below. $10 each. Export Promotion Services, U.S. DOC P.O. Box 14207, Washington, D.C., 20044 (202) 377-2432

Foreign Economic Trends. Presents business and economic developments and the latest economic indicators in more than 100 countries. They are prepared on an annual or semiannual basis by the U.S. Foreign Commercial Service. $70 annual, single copies, $1.00.

International Market Research. Is an in-depth analysis for those who want the complete picture for one industry in one country. A report includes information such as behavior characteristics, trade barriers, market share figures, end-user analysis, and trade contacts. Price range $50–$200.

Overseas Business Reports. Include current and detailed marketing information, trade outlooks, statistics, regulations, and marketing profiles. $26 annual.

Market Share Reports. Provide exporters and market analysts with data on imports of manufactured products into foreign countries' markets and the shares supplied by the United States and eight leading suppliers. Thirty-five additional reports in the Country Series, and 1500 Commodity Series Reports. Country Reports, $11 each.

TOP Bulletin. A weekly publication of all the leads received the previous weeks for all products from all countries. $175 annual.

TOP Notice. Searches daily the TOP computer and automatically sends the customer only the leads for those products and services requested. $25 to set-up file, $37.50 for each block of 50 leads (1985).

Trade Lists. These are published directories of overseas customers for U.S. exports in selected industries and countries. They contain the names and product lines of foreign distributors, agents, manufacturers, wholesalers, and address, other information is provided on each contract including the name and title of a key official, telex and cable numbers, and company size data.

Customized Export Mailing Lists. Custom tailored service—lists of foreign companies of the particular industries, countries or types of business requested by the client. Provides gummed mailing labels for each listed firm.

Statistics

U.S. Department of Commerce. Custom Statistical Service. Individually tailored tables of U.S. exports and imports. Range from $50–$100.

——. Country Trade Statistics. Export Promotion Services. Set of four key tables that indicate which U.S. products are in the greatest demand in a specific country over the most recent five-year period. $25 for first country, $10 for each additional country

——. *Export Statistics Profiles.* Tables of U.S. exports for a specific industry that are designed to help you locate the best export markets. They analyze the industry's export products and byproducts, country-by-country over each of the last five years. Data are rank-ordered by dollar value to quickly identify the leading products and countries. Each ESP includes competitive growth and future trends information, as well as brief narrative highlighting the industry's performance. $70 per ESP, 1985.

——.FT 410: *Foreign Trade Report.* A monthly report that provides a statistical record of shipments of all merchandise from the U.S. to some 160 countries in both quantity and dollar-value terms.

——. FT-900. *Summary of U.S. Export and Import Merchandise Trade.* Arranged by 1- through 4-digit. Monthly and Year-to-date data.

——. FT-610: *U.S. Exports of Domestic Merchandise.* SIC-based 8-digit product code and area. Annual data.

——. EA-676: *U.S. Exports.* By country of destination. Annual data.

——. FT-990: *Highlights of U.S. Export and Import Trade.* Customs and CIF value. 2-digit level. Annual and monthly.

United Nations. *Yearbook of International Trade* in two volumes New York: UN Statistical Office, Annual.

——. *Commodity Trade Statistics.* New York: UN Statistical Office, Annual.

——. *Demographic Yearbook.* New York: UN Statistical Office, Annual.

——. *National Accounts Statistics.* New York: UN Statistical Office, Annual.

9

MONEY AND BANKING—
GETTING PAID

The handling of foreign currency and alternate payment methods confuses and frightens many new exporters. The goal of this chapter is to familiarize the exporter with the logic behind payment arrangements in international trade.

Not all export sales are transacted in dollars. Clinching a sale may very well depend on your willingness to accept a currency other than American dollars for payment. But even if the importer pays in dollars, the exporter should understand some of the elements that affect the international price of the dollar.

Foreign currencies have disparate levels of convertibility. Exchange controls limit the amount a country allows to be exchanged as well as the direction of that change. *External convertibility* is the policy that allows nonresidents of a country unlimited convertibility of the foreign country's currency into another currency. The residents of that country, however, are by law, limited in exchange allowances. Most countries, including Western European nations, are characterized by external convertibility. *Full convertibility* allows both residents and nonresidents to purchase unlimited amounts of foreign currency. The United States, the United Kingdom, West Germany, and Switzerland are nations in which full convertibility is permitted.

Another important foreign exchange concept is that of *fixed* exchange versus *floating* exchange. In the Bretton Woods (1944) agreements, which formed the International Monetary Fund (IMF), the United States agreed that the American dollar would be the only currency directly convertible into gold for official monetary purposes. The relationship was fixed at $35 per ounce of gold. Other currencies were assigned "par" values in relationship to the U.S dollar. The dwindling supply of gold in American reserves prompted President Nixon, in August 1971, to abandon the U.S.

Treasury's commitment to buy and sell gold at $35 per ounce in transactions with central banks and governments. This action sent shock waves through European money markets. The U.S. Treasury attempted to maintain the dollar at a fixed rate through market operations (buying and selling dollars) but by 1973 officially abandoned its commitment to a fixed dollar and allowed it to float.

The rate for fixed exchanges is set by the central bank or treasury of a country. The market determines the rate on floating exchanges. Tied to this concept of fixed versus floating exchange is the concept of hard versus soft currencies. Hard currencies are easily convertible, enjoy heavy demand, and represent strong economies. In the foreign exchange market, hard currencies are those of the advanced industrial economies whereas soft currencies are of the lesser developed countries (LDCs) as well as communist (command) economies. Hard currencies are allowed to float. Soft currencies are subject to frequent government interference. If the importer in the LDC or command economy is unable to obtain hard currency, the exporter may have to forfeit the sale because the importer's currency may not be convertible by an American bank. The American exporter must be wary of such transactions. To avoid losing the sale, the exporter could ask for payment in hard currencies other than American dollars such as French francs, British pounds, German marks, or Japanese yen. These currencies can be readily exchanged for dollars at an American bank. Bartering, a traditional means of trade in the Soviet Bloc, has become more popular in trade between the advanced industrial economies and the LDCs that are hard currency poor. The American exporter will trade his products for goods manufactured in the LDC and in turn find a market for those goods in the United States or in another country. Countertrade (reciprocal trading arrangements based on the barter system) often arises from foreign exchange difficulties.

The exporter who sells to an LDC may find that an import license is required. This license allows the importer to obtain the necessary allotment of dollars. No contract should be made with importers in LDCs until exchange restrictions are verified with the U.S. Commerce Department's ITA or with a banker. A shortage of dollars in the LDC will decrease the issuance of import licenses. Many exporters have assumed a contract was made only to find after the equipment went into production that an import license was required. In that hard currency is scarce, the LDC will allot the import license according to need, for example, it will give priority to necessity and high-technology goods over luxury goods and goods that compete with an industry the LDC's government is trying to foster. On the other hand, the issuance of these licenses has been subject to much corruption. In very poor countries that report hard currency shortages and consequent difficulties in importing adequate quantities of foodstuffs, import licenses have been obtained for luxury goods. These luxury goods, in turn, are then sold for tremendous mark-ups to privileged classes. Another corrupt, but common, practice is for an importer to ask the exporter to deliver an inflated, but fictitious quote. In this way, the importer will be able to obtain extra dollars, which he or she can sell on the black market or use to import additional goods.

If foreign exchange rates were fixed, trade would be less complicated and less subject to risk. This tenet brought about the Bretton Woods fixed exchange system. But as the Bretton Woods system became unmanageable and began to break down, the risk of losing money in exchange transactions was exacerbated. There really isn't a problem for the American exporter if he or she can insist on payment in dollars, but getting the sale may require a quote in the buyer's currency.

Forward Exchange Contract

The following problem illustrates the effects of appreciating and depreciating currencies on an international sale. Let us assume that an Italian buyer wishes to import an American machine. The cost of the American machine is $10,000, which includes the selling price, insurance, and freight. Further assume that the Italian importer specifies the payment will be made in lire, which automatically shifts the exchange risk to the exporter. But if the American exporter refuses to accept payment in lire rather than dollars, he or she may lose the sale. If at the date of the quote 1600 lire equal $1, then the American exporter will need 16 million lire (1600 lire × $10,000). Let us also assume that the terms are stated so that sixty days after shipment of the machine, the American exporter can cash the draft of 16 million lire at his bank or perhaps a bank specified by the importer. Now we are ready to consider the effects of appreciation and depreciation on the 16 million lire.

If the American exporter presented the 16 million lire draft at the bank in sixty days and the exchange rate had changed to 1800 lire: $1, the American exporter would receive $8888.89 (16 million lire/1800), which represents a loss of $1111.11 ($10,000 – $8888.89). It had cost 1600 lire to purchase one dollar, but now it costs 200 lire *more* for every dollar. Thus, the lire has depreciated next to the dollar.

Next, suppose that after sixty days the exporter presents his or her draft and the rate has changed to 1200 lire:$1. In this case the exporter will receive $13,333.33 (16 million lire/1200), which represents a profit of $3333.33. Before it had cost 1600 lire to purchase one dollar, but now it costs 400 lire *less* to purchase one dollar. Thus the lira has appreciated next to the dollar. If the lira appreciates, the exporter will earn extra revenues, but if it depreciates, the exporter will lose money.

The forward exchange system was developed to circumvent the risk associated with foreign exchange. The exporter will sell 16 million lire to the bank that will equal $10,000 in sixty days. It also becomes a means of short-term financing in that the exporter does not actually sell 16 million lire to the bank at that time. The exporter makes a contract that will allow him or her to sell 16 million lire for $10,000 once the exporter presents the draft to the bank. The bank is willing to assume the risk for two reasons; first, it takes a fee for its service and, second, banks have enough capital reserves to speculate in foreign exchange markets. If the lira depreciates, they can hang onto their lire until the market changes in the lira's favor.

The forward exchange contract provides one-way insurance against foreign exchange fluctuations. In shifting the risk to the bank, the exporter forfeits an opportunity to gain from an appreciation of the lira. Currency options represent a recent innovation, which allows exporters to take advantage of the speculative aspects of foreign exchange while continuing to provide the insurance of a forward exchange contract.

Currency Options

Foreign currency options provide the right to buy or sell a set amount of a currency during a specified time period. The Philadelphia Stock Exchange specializes in currency options and is currently the market leader. Let us consider the benefits of a currency option using the previous example.

Suppose the American exporter buys a currency option that gives him or her the right, but not the obligation, to buy 16 million lire at 1600 lire:$1. The premium paid averages 1 to 5 percent of the current spot rate and is the insurance for currency risk. Currency options have standard times for expiring: March, June, September, and December. If the lira has depreciated to 1800 lire:$1 when the option comes due, the American exporter would exercise the option without occurring any loss except the premium paid for the option. If, however, the lira had appreciated to 1200 lire:$1, the American exporter would simply allow the option to go unexercised and exchange the lire for dollars at the more advantageous rate. The difference between the forward exchange contract and the currency option is that the forward exchange contract *must* be exercised. No matter what the exchange rate is, the American exporter is required to exchange

16 million lire to $10,000 by the specified date. The currency option is flexible. It can be exercised or not. In either case, a fee is charged.

To decide which is the cheaper method for each transaction, the exporter should discuss the currency options available and the appropriate fees with his or her stockbroker. Because options are traded on stock exchanges, a brokerage firm must have a seat on the exchange and act as the exporter's agent in the option's purchase. The brokerage firm takes a commission for its service. The exporter will need to compare the fees incurred for the forward contract with that of the currency option.

Uncertainty in the transaction itself may be another basis for choosing an option over a contract. According to international law, as soon as a quote is sent to the Italian importer, the American exporter is bound to honor that quote for the time period noted in the pro forma invoice. In effect, the American exporter does not know whether the importer will accept the 16 million lire quote when he or she telexs or mails the pro forma invoice. What happens if the lira depreciates in the time period for which the quote is valid but has not yet been accepted by the importer? To prevent this potential loss, the exporter can take out a forward contract at the time the quote is delivered. But what will happen if the Italian importer decides against purchasing the machine? The American exporter must deliver 16 million lire to the bank at the date of the contract even if *no sale has occurred*. If the American exporter had bought a currency option, he or she would be responsible only for the fee because he or she would not be required to exercise the option.

GETTING PAID

If a Nigerian company (M) wished to purchase $150,000 worth of machinery from an American manufacturer (X), the easiest transaction would be that shown in Figure 9.1.

This transaction is improbable, however, for several reasons. First, the exporter and importer may not know one another. The importer may not wish to send the cash because he does not trust the manufacturer to

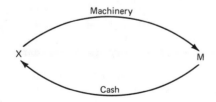

Figure 9.1

send the machinery. The exporter may not trust the importer to send the cash once the machinery is shipped. Second, the importer may not be able to afford to pay for the machinery until later. Perhaps he or she plans to produce goods using the machinery and can't pay until some of the goods produced with the imported machinery are sold.

The terms of payment offered is a function of type of merchandise (for example, components, engineered equipment, or construction machinery), the sum of money involved, the market custom, the country in which the buyer is located, the buyer's credit standing, whether there are exchange restrictions or controls in the country of destination as well as the strength of the importer's local currency in international money markets, the terms granted by competitors, the political and economic stability of the foreign market or market region, and the past payment experience the exporter has had with the customer. It is also very important to assess the competitive nature of the market when making this decision. Exporters are often forced to offer certain terms of payment because the importer can take his or her business to a company offering more liberal terms. Competitive markets require generous terms. The knowledgeable exporter can select terms that satisfy the importer's financial constraints while ensuring payment. Experienced exporters understand that cash in advance is rarely a viable term of payment in today's marketplace.

There are many terms of payment. These terms are presented in order, from least risk to highest risk for the exporter. Table 9.1 contains a summary of the terms of payment.

Cash in Advance

Payment is made prior to shipment—that is, the goods are available to the buyer after payment. Provided payment is made in U.S. funds, cash in advance involves no risk to the exporter. Yet the importer completely relies on the exporter to ship the goods as ordered. Cash itself should not be handled, other payment instruments such as checks, money orders, or drafts should be issued by and drawn on a reputable international bank. Generally, an exporter should not accept personal checks. If a personal check is expedient, the exporter should postpone the product's shipment until the collecting U.S. bank reports that the check has been honored.

Cash in advance should be used when both the political and economic conditions of the importer's country are unstable. In such cases, cash in advance should be used with all customers, regardless of their credit rating. This method is rarely used because it is a hardship on the buyer.

TABLE 9.1 International Terms of Payment

Method	Usual Time of Payment	Goods Available to Buyer	Risk to Exporter	Risk to Importer
1. Cash in advance	Before shipment	After payment	None	Completely relies on exporter to ship goods as ordered
2. Letter of Credit Unconfirmed	After shipment is made and documents are presented to bank	After payment	Very little depending on status of opening bank	Assures shipment is made but relies on exporter to ship the goods described in the documents
Confirmed	Same as above	Same as above	Depends on terms of letter of credit	Same as above
3. Documentary Collection				
Sight draft with documents against payment (D/P)	On presentation of draft to buyer	After payment to importer's bank	If draft is not honored, goods must be returned	Same as above, unless importer can inspect goods before payment
Time draft with documents against acceptance (D/A)	On maturity of the draft	Before payment after acceptance	Relies on buyer to honor draft upon presentation	Same as above
4. Open Account	As agreed, usually by invoice	Before payment	Relies completely on buyer to pay his account as agreed upon	None
5. Consignment	Upon sale	Before payment	Same as above	None

Note: Terms ranked from least risk to most risk for the exporter.

105

The fierce competition in today's global marketplace usually requires the exporter to offer more liberal terms.

A variation of cash in advance can be found in "Contract Terms." This type of transaction is more commonly found in medium-term transactions, which are from 181 days to five years. Credit risk insurance through the Foreign Credit Insurance Association (FCIA) should be obtained. The FCIA cooperates with the Export-Import Bank (Eximbank), an independent government agency charged with financing and facilitating American exports. Examples of medium-term exports that qualify for credit risk insurance include equipment for mining, refining, construction, agriculture, service contracts, planning/feasibility studies, and general aviation aircraft. These policies are written on a case-by-case, seller-to-buyer basis. Certain conditions must be met on all exports covered by medium-term insurance, for instance, the importer must make a cash payment of at least 15 percent of the contract price on or before delivery. Furthermore, the U.S. exporter must retain for its commercial account and risk at least 10 percent of the financed portion of each transaction. Chapter Ten details other Eximbank programs.

Letter of Credit

The Letter of Credit (L/C) is a document in which a bank undertakes to pay a party named in the document (beneficiary) a sum of money, provided certain conditions described in the L/C are met. The money is paid when the beneficiary submits documents that prove the beneficiary has met the conditions stated in the L/C. The importer opens the L/C at his bank (issuing bank) and names the exporter as the beneficiary. A distinction is usually made between import letters of credit and export letters of credit; actually the distinction between the two is that of perspective— that is, whether you view the process as an importer or exporter.

The L/C comes in two forms: *revocable* and *irrevocable*. The issuing bank does not guarantee the revocable L/C. It can withdraw credit without advance notice. The issuing bank may also amend the L/C without the beneficiary's consent. In sum, the revocable L/C provides no guarantee of payment for the exporter. The revocable L/C is rarely used in today's international transactions except between parent and subsidiary companies.

The irrevocable L/C legally binds the issuing bank to pay the exporter if he or she presents the appropriate documents to the American bank (advising/negotiating bank) in exact accordance with the L/C's specifications. The documents always include an "Order" Bill of Lading, stamped "On Board," which verifies that the goods have been loaded on the ship. Such a document ensures the buyer that the goods have been loaded on the conveyance and are moving toward their point of destination before payment is released. An "Order" Bill of Lading is usually required because its negotiability allows the exporter to transfer title to the advising (if confirmed) or issuing bank. If the buyer doesn't pay, the bank can protect its financial interest by exercising its control over the title. At the same time, the exporter is guaranteed payment. Hence, the L/C provides protection for both importer and exporter. As the irrevocable L/C is a legally binding document, any changes desired by the importer or exporter must be made as an amendment to the L/C. Amendments must be approved by all parties.

The irrevocable L/C constitutes a commitment by only one bank; the issuing bank. The U.S. bank merely acts as an agent of the foreign bank. It has no commitment to pay the exporter if the foreign bank does not pay the credit. In some instances importers have been involved in scams involving phony offices, printed dummy stationery with phony bank letterhead, and phony telex numbers. In such scandals, the bank used is known as a reputable financial institution, but the importer may have forged documents and channeled bank inquiries to its own offices.

Such deception is less likely with today's more security-conscious communications networks. Yet, there is still a risk that the foreign bank itself is experiencing financial difficulties. When the exporter's bank (advising bank) adds its guarantee to the L/C, it becomes a *confirmed irrevocable L/C*. The confirmed irrevocable L/C is the only L/C that virtually assures that the exporter will receive payment if he or she complies exactly with the terms of the L/C. It is important for the importer to remember that banks deal in documents and not in merchandise. A bank can't ensure that goods shipped conform to document specifications. The bank sees to it that the merchandise is on the vessel and the required documents have been delivered. The importer must rely on the honesty of the seller to ship the merchandise on which the two parties originally agreed. No payment method can completely substitute for business trust.

Payment of the L/C may be made on a sight or time basis. The advising bank will pay the exporter under a sight draft L/C on receipt of the documents required by the L/C. Under a time draft, the beneficiary receives payment on maturity of the draft. In effect, an exporter who accepts a time draft is financing the importer's transaction.

There is a fee for opening an L/C as well as a fee calculated as a percentage of the value of the draft. All of these charges are made to the account of the importer, who is the applicant.

Contents of the L/C

Banks issue Letters of Credit on forms that clearly indicate the bank's name and the extent of the bank's obligations under the credit. Letters of Credit contain the following information:

Name of the Seller—beneficiary

Name of the Buyer—applicant

Amount of Credit—the value of the merchandise plus any shipping charges intended to be paid under the credit terms

Trade Terms—revised American Foreign Trade Definitions or INCOTERMS (Chapter Eight)

Tenor of the Draft—normally dependent on the requirements of the applicant

Expiration Date—specifies the latest date documents may be presented. In this way, the applicant can exercise control over the time of shipment.

Documents Required—includes commercial invoices, consular or customs invoices, insurance policies or certificates if the insurance is to be effected by the beneficiary, and original order bills of lading stamped "on board"

General Description of the Merchandise—which briefly and in a general manner only, describes the merchandise covered by the L/C

The L/C cycle involves the exchanges of documents and funds. Let's go over the steps involved in the L/C transaction:

Step 1: The buyer and seller agree on the terms of sale.

Step 2: The importer completes an application for an L/C and forwards it to his bank, which will issue the L/C.

Step 3: The issuing (importer's) bank then forwards the L/C to a correspondent bank in the United States.

Step 4: The advising (U.S.) bank relays the L/C to the exporter.

Step 5: The exporter makes the shipping arrangements when he or she receives the assurance of payment.

Step 6: The exporter prepares the documents required under the L/C and delivers them to the advising (U.S.) bank.

Step 7: The advising (U.S.) bank negotiates the documents. If it finds them in order, it sends them to the issuing (importer's) bank. The advising bank (or other named payment bank) pays the seller in accordance with the terms of the L/C.

Step 8: The issuing (importer's) bank examines the documents. If they are in order, the issuing bank will charge the importer's account and send the documents on to the buyer. The issuing bank will reimburse the advising (U.S.) bank.

Step 9: The buyer receives the documents, including the Order Bill of Lading and picks up the merchandise from the carrier.

The primary advantage to the exporter is that an L/C reduces commercial risk. The buyer under the L/C also receives some protection. Because the banks examine shipping documents, errors are more likely to be detected.

An L/C should be used when the importer's country experiences political and economic instability. Under such conditions, the L/C should be applied to all customers regardless of their credit rating.

Documentary Collection

The most prevalent method of obtaining payment in international trade is the collection of drafts drawn on the importer. Documentary collection falls between open account, which favors the buyer, and L/C, which favors the seller (especially with a sight draft). The only control the exporter has in documentary collection is that he or she retains ownership until payment or certain payment is forthcoming. Bank fees are usually specific, rather than a percentage on the transaction amount, for each separate service offered at each stage of the collection process.

Under a *sight* draft (sight draft with documents against payment, D/P), the exporter delivers all the necessary shipping documents together with his or her draft drawn at "sight" on the importer to the advising bank. Drafts "drawn at sight" are payable on presentation of the draft to the bank, that is, the exporter is entitled to payment when he or she endorses the check and turns it over to the bank. The advising bank forwards the draft and documents to its overseas correspondent bank with instructions that state the documents may be delivered to the importer only on his or her payment of the draft (documents against payment, D/P). In this way, the exporter is able to exert control over the goods because he or she retains title to the goods. The major risk is that an irresponsible buyer may refuse to accept the shipment. In that case the exporter must find another buyer for the merchandise or provide for the costly return of the merchandise.

Under a *time* draft (time draft with documents against acceptance, D/A), the exporter draws a draft on the importer that is payable a specified number of days (30, 60, 90) after date of the draft, commercial invoice, or bill of lading. The draft and documents are sent to the overseas bank with instructions to "deliver documents against acceptance only." The importer must accept the obligation to pay before the title is released. This method favors the importer because he is not required to pay until a certain number of days after the shipment is released. The exporter has given up title and control of the merchandise. He or she must rely entirely on the importer's ability and willingness to pay as expressed in the importer's acceptance of the draft. If the importer doesn't pay the draft on maturity, the exporter may have to resort to legal action to collect, especially if the buyer has already disposed of the goods.

The exporter uses sight and time drafts when the importer is considered reliable and credit worthy. The bank doesn't add its guarantee of collection. Such assurance is only provided by the L/C. The exporter should not use this method if he or she has no prior experience with the importer. Yet sometimes an L/C is so expensive, particularly in South America and the Middle East, that the importer may not be able to afford one. In such cases, a sight draft may be more appropriate. Thorough investigation into the importer's credit history is advised.

Open Account

There is little difference between this method and domestic open account. Open account is generally used when the importer is well known to the exporter and is located in nearby or established markets. This method offers the virtue of simplicity. Paperwork is minimal. The time and costs involved with using the banking system are eliminated as well. Yet no negotiable instrument is produced that proves the importer's obligations to pay. Collection could become a problem, particularly during a time of political or financial turmoil in the importer's country. Hence, open account is most commonly used in transactions between parent companies and subsidiaries.

Consignment

Goods shipped "on consignment" are paid for by the foreign wholesaler or retailer only after they have been sold. In this payment method the risk rests with the exporter. Negotiations on consignment shipments must clearly define payment responsibilities on import duties, surcharges, freight, and the like. Sometimes this method is used on merchandise shipped to foreign representatives, branches, subsidiaries, and import houses, but even in those cases commercial risk insurance should be obtained.

Obtaining Credit Information

The World Traders Data Reports (WTDRs) is a business report prepared by the Commerce Department's Foreign Commercial Service. Each report can be obtained for approximately $75. WTDRs are business reports that provide background information on potential foreign trade contacts. They include data on the foreign firm's principal owners, financial and trade references, general reputation, product lines handled, number of employees, language preferred, year established, and territory covered. Each report also contains a general narrative prepared by the U.S. commercial officer conducting the investigation as to the reliability of the foreign firm.

Another important source is your bank. It can obtain credit information through its correspondents. Private institutions, such as Dun and Bradstreet, also offer international credit reporting services.

Collection Problems

If the exporter has problems collecting payment from the importer, the first and cheapest step is to contact the buyer and try to negotiate a settlement. Sometimes the problem is merely technical. Only when negotiations fail and the merchandise sum is large enough, should the exporter seek the assistance and advice of his or her bank and legal counsel. The exporter should also contact the nearest Commerce Department District Office. A district Commerce Department officer will call, send a telegram, or write, depending on the circumstances. Being contacted by a government official often frightens importers into paying.

This chapter has concentrated on the technical problems of foreign exchange and receiving payment. But often, especially in medium- and long-term projects and for new exporters, financing must be obtained before the exporter can produce the merchandise for sale or attempt to meet the international competition by offering attractive terms to the importer. Chapter Ten discusses the financing alternatives available to the American exporter.

SUGGESTED READINGS

Kingman-Brundage, Jane and Susan A. Schultz. *The Fundamentals of Trade Finance.* New York: John Wiley & Sons, 1986.

Polk, R. L. Co. *Polk's World Bank Directory.* Information about American banks—addresses, services, branches, correspondents. P.O. Box 1340, Nashville, Tenn 37202 (615) 889-3350.

10
FINANCING

As we learned in the previous chapter, you, as the exporter, prefer to be paid cash in advance or under a letter of credit. The buyer may decide that cash in advance is too risky for his or her company, while obtaining a letter of credit is extremely expensive in his or her country. Sometimes the importer's government places restrictions on L/C transactions. Just as manufacturers often extend credit to domestic customers, international customers have come to expect credit. If the buyer asks for credit and an exporter refuses, the sale may go to a competitor who is willing to offer more generous terms. A customer's credit, as we discussed in Chapter Nine, can be checked two major ways: through the Commerce Department's World Traders Data Reports (WTDRs) and private credit institutions.

We will detail the various available financing methods in this chapter. The decision to select a particular option should be weighed against its availability and its cost compared to other options.

OBTAINING CREDIT

Banks

Banks allow exporters to use credit lines to finance international sales, but most banks require full recourse—that is, the exporter must offer security. "Bankers' Acceptance" represents another financing option offered by banks.

When the exporter receives a time draft for payment he or she has the option of holding the draft until maturity or discounting the draft immediately. Three types of international transactions can be financed through BAs: international shipments, storage of readily marketable staples, and dollar exchange. (Dollar exchange acceptances are somewhat different than the other two BAs. They are designed for the one crop Latin American countries that have seasonal shortages of dollars between harvests.)

A BA is a time draft or bill of exchange drawn on and accepted by a U.S. bank. The BA is created when the bank stamps "accepted" on the face of the draft presented by the exporter (drawer). By creating an acceptance, the bank assumes an unconditional obligation to pay the face amount of the draft at maturity to the holder. This obligation enables the exporter to sell the draft at a discount to a willing buyer who will present the draft for full payment to the accepting bank at maturity. Most BAs are discounted by the accepting bank.

The draft is a "negotiable" instrument, which means that it can be sold and ownership transferred by endorsement to another party. The BA can be traded in secondary markets because there's no limit on the number of times ownership is transferred. The bank may hold the discounted draft in its own portfolio or sell it in the secondary market through an acceptance dealer. The BA market is an over-the-counter market. The Federal Reserve's Open Market Committee is the largest investor in the United States BA market. U.S. commercial and savings banks, foreign banks, mutual funds, corporations, and individuals also participate in the BA secondary market.

If a BA conforms to the Federal Reserve Act of 1913 it is said to be "eligible." Because eligible BAs are more easily traded and at a higher discount, the secondary BA market is composed primarily of eligible BAs.

The eligible BA must conform to the Federal Reserve's requirements, which include the following:

1. Must show a bank as drawee on the draft. That bank must be a member of the Federal Reserve System.
2. Must be a two-party paper. The exporter, as the drawer, remains liable even after the bank has accepted the draft. If the accepting bank is unable to satisfy its obligation to repay the holder of the BA at maturity, the drawer is liable. (Actually the two-party feature is an important safety mechanism which makes the BA an extremely sound financial instrument for investment.)
3. The maturity of the draft can't exceed six months. The draft must conform to the "channels of trade" sequence, that is, if a shipment process and normal credit term is 60 days, the draft must mature somewhere in that time range. (BA financing for dollar exchange is limited to 90 days.)
4. No other means of financing the transaction can be used. The inves-

tor of the draft needs to be sure that there isn't a third party who can legally claim the goods as collateral if the importer defaults on payment.

5. The bank can't create a BA without specific information about the transaction—price, description of the goods, and point of shipment.

The cost of credit associated with BA financing usually compares favorably with other types of bank credit because banks usually require compensating balances under lines of credit.

Let's say the exporter receives a sight draft of $50,000 for payment of an export shipped to Italy. Its "tenor" or days until maturity, is sixty days. The exporter decides to present it to his or her bank for both acceptance and discounting. The bank quotes a 10 percent "all-in" rate, which figures in the discount and acceptance commission.

FIGURING PROCEEDS

1. Calculate the bank discount and commission for acceptance.

$$\text{Bank discount} = \text{Face value of Draft} \times \text{All-in Rate} \times \text{Tenor}/360$$
$$B = \$50,000 \times .10 \times 60/360$$
$$B = \$833.33$$

2. Calculate your proceeds.

$$\text{Proceeds} = \text{Face Value} - \text{Bank Discount}$$
$$P = \$50,000 - \$833.33$$
$$P = \$49,166.67$$

3. Calculate effective rate of interest.

The all-in rate of ten percent isn't the real rate of interest because the exporter doesn't receive the full $50,000. The actual rate of interest is called the "effective" rate. (Compare 10.17 percent, rather than the 10 percent all-in rate, with other available financing methods.)

$$\text{Effective rate} = \frac{\text{Bank Discount}}{\text{Proceeds} \times \text{Tenor}/360}$$

$$R = \frac{\$833.33}{\$49166.67 \times 60/360}$$

$$R = 10.17\%$$

"Documentary" BAs originate under Letters of Credit that use time (usance) drafts to cover export shipments. The terms of the L/C must state which party, the exporter or importer, will pay for the acceptance and discount charges. Normally the importer is responsible for these fees. If the charges are for the importer, the exporter should receive the full amount of the face value of the draft. In this case the U.S. exporter's bank will be the primary obligor of the acceptance and the exporter will be the secondary obligor. All of the documents needed under BA with L/C time drafts are handled through the L/C transaction.

"Clean" BAs are available for shipments not involving Letters of Credit. The customer must have an acceptance agreement with his or her bank. Clean acceptances don't require the presentation of shipping documents to the accepting bank. Drafts are drawn by a foreign bank or company on the U.S. bank. A statement must be included which contains the value of the merchandise, description of merchandise, countries of import and export, date of shipment, and certification attesting that the BA is the only financing obtained.

Export Management Companies

Some Export Management Companies also carry financing. Chapter Eight contains information about EMCs.

Factoring Houses

Companies purchasing the accounts receivable of manufacturers are called "Factoring Houses." The factor buys the accounts receivable at a discount, but assumes the risk of collecting from the importer when he or she buys "without recourse." Because it is assumed the manufacturer wouldn't have obtained the sale without financing, the manufacturer is willing to pay the discount, incorporating the added cost into price quotations. By freeing up his or her accounts receivable, the manufacturer is able to use the capital received from factoring for other purposes. Factors normally charge a higher discount rate than would be obtained through a bank line of credit, but the factor assumes the risk, while with a line of credit, the risk remains with the exporter. The discount paid depends on the export, the country, and the factor. If the exporter can obtain factoring agreements, it is safe to ship under open account, a method of payment that should greatly expand sales compared to cash in advance or letter of credit. It's imperative that the exporter understand the terms of the agreement with the factor. Transactions "with recourse" do not free the exporter from ultimate responsibility. The factor acts as a collection agency, but if it can't collect, the exporter is responsible for paying the draft. The discount (interest rate charged by the factor) will be lower for "with recourse" purchases.

Eximbank

The major export financing institution is an independent U.S. government agency called THE EXPORT-IMPORT BANK or Eximbank. It receives no appropriations from the U.S. Congress and must operate at a profit in order to continue its services. Eximbank finances and facilitates exports, but it is by no means a granting agency. In addition to its lending, a group of insurance companies working through the FOREIGN CREDIT INSURANCE ASSOCIATION (FCIA) cooperates with Eximbank to cover repayment risks on short- and medium-term export credit sales. Eximbank programs are divided into short-term sales (up to 180 days), medium-term (181 days to five years) and long-term (five years and longer).

Short-term Programs

Eximbank's short-term programs are designed to provide credit insurance, and as such, are coordinated through the FCIA. (Short-term sales are not eligible for loans.) Export credit insurance protects the exporter from political and commercial risks. Typical products covered are consumables, small manufactured items, spare parts, raw materials, and farm products. Examples of political risks covered are war, revolution, insurrection, expropriation, and currency inconvertibility. An insolvent importer or one who defaults on payment after the exporter has tried every available course to collect the payment, are covered under commercial risks.

Table 10.1 contains a summary of Eximbank and FCIA insurance

TABLE 10.1   Eximbank/FCIA Insurance Coverage

Policy	Commercial	Political
Short-term comprehensive	90%	100%
Short-term political risk	—	100%
Short-term/medium-term Master comprehensive	90%	100%
Short-term/medium-term Master political risk	—	100%
Agricultural commodities	98%	100%

coverage. Short-term policies cover risks on sales up to 180 days. There's an annual deductible provision similar to medical and automative collision policies.

The master policy covers both short-term and medium-term sales. This policy is most suitable for the large-volume exporter with multiple product lines. Comprehensive policies cover both commercial and political risks. If the exporter is certain that there will be no commercial risks, then he or she can obtain a reduction in the policy by only opting for political risk insurance.

A "new-to-export policy" is available for companies just entering the export business. It's similar to the master policy except that it gives 95 percent (rather than 90 percent) commercial risk protection, with no deductible for two years. Eligible companies have exported less than $750,000 per year over the last two years and have never used FCIA or Eximbank programs in the past.

"Working Capital Guarantees" is one of the newer Eximbank programs which is designed to provide small-sized, medium-sized, minority, and agricultural exporters with working capital loans from lending institutions with the Eximbank guarantee. The loan is for a specific export-related activity, for example, inventory purchases or the development of export-marketing programs. Loan terms are from one month to a year and security for the loan must have a value of at least 110 percent of the outstanding balance.

In addition to the short-term policies and master policies, the FCIA offers a policy for exporters of services as long as those services are performed by United States-based personnel. For service policies similar procedures are followed as outlined for short- and medium-term policies. Examples of previously covered service activities are telecommunications design and technical consulting.

Medium-term Programs

Medium-term policies cover exports sold on terms of 181 days to five years. Eximbank sponsors many different programs in the medium-term range. First, there are the FCIA medium-term policies. To obtain FCIA coverage, the importer must pay at least 15 percent of the contract price on or before delivery. The exporter must risk at least ten percent of the financed portion of the sale. Repayment terms must not be more liberal than is standard in international trade. Capital goods for medium-term transactions are supported on the following schedule:

Financing

Contract Value	Term
Up to $50,000	Up to 2 years
$50,001–$100,000	Up to 3 years
$100,001–$200,000	Up to 4 years
Over $200,000	Up to 5 years

There is a "single buyer" policy for single sales. A repetitive sales policy is available for sales to a specific importer. A promissory note is necessary to provide evidence that there is an arrangement for payment on a monthly, quarterly, or semiannual basis. The "short- and medium-term combination policy" protects exports that are financed to overseas dealers and distributors. The policy provides for inventory and receivables financing. Another policy covers products exported on consignment.

The "Commercial Bank Guarantee Program" works with the same 300 commercial banks that finance medium-term exports. Eximbank offers protection against commercial and political risks on loans made by commercial banks to exporters who finance exports. Repayment guidelines are the same as the above schedule for obtaining insurance. The importer must pay at least 15 percent of the contract price.

Since the debt crisis, many more U.S. banks are less willing to take on the additional risk associated with export sales. As such, a bank may demand full recourse. Many banks will take the ten percent risk Eximbank requires in the commercial bank guarantee. The exporter is required to assume five percent of the commercial risk.

Special coverages are available for switch, bank-to-bank lines, and preshipment coverage. The "Switch-Cover" option for foreign distributors allows coverage under any of the Eximbank medium-term programs (insurance or commercial bank guarantee) for exporters to be extended to the distributors in their sales to end users. "Bank-to-Bank Lines" are used in transactions with developing countries. Eximbank offers its guarantee to cover revolving lines of credit established by an American bank with foreign banks. The foreign bank assumes the risk when it makes loans to importers of American products. "Preshipment" covers the fabrication of certain products when sales contracts have already been signed.

Eximbank extends fixed-rate, medium-term export credits to commercial banks through its "Discount Loan Program." These credits are available only to banks that will not extend financing without a discount. There is also a special discount program for small businesses.

Another Eximbank program designed to cover medium-term exports is the "Cooperative Financing Facility." This program operates in developing countries. Eximbank lends capital to foreign banks which in turn extend credit to importers of American products.

The "Small Business Credit Program" enables U.S. banks to extend fixed rather than floating rates on loans to finance sales of products manufactured by small U.S. companies. The company gets the lowest possible rate allowed by credit guidelines adopted by members of the Organization for Economic Cooperation and Development. The U.S. bank borrows from Eximbank at one percent below the rate of the export loan. Finally, as in short-term financing, there is a working capital guarantee program for medium-term transactions.

Long-term Programs

Eximbank also provides financing for the export of heavy capital equipment and large-scale installations with repayment terms of from five to ten years, but sometimes longer depending on the particular nature of the export. One program is a "direct credit" to the importer. Another, often used in conjunction with direct credit, is that of a "financial guarantee" which assures repayment of a private credit. Eximbank will extend credit of up to 65 percent of the transaction. The balance must be obtained from other lenders.

Table 10.2 provides a summary of Eximbank/FCIA short-, medium-, and long-term programs.

TABLE 10.2 Summary of Eximbank Programs

Short-Term (Up to 180 days)
Export credit insurance (FCIA)
Working capital guarantee

Medium-Term (181 days to 5 years)
Export credit insurance
Commercial bank guarantee
Discount loans
Working capital guarantee
Small business credit program

Long-Term (5 years and longer)
Direct loans
Financial guarantees

Financing

Private Export Funding Corporation

The Private Export Funding Corporation (PEFCO) is a private organization owned by commercial banks and some large manufacturers. PEFCO often works with Eximbank to extend medium- and long-term loans for American exports. Eximbank guarantees the principal and interest.

The Small Business Administration

The Small Business Administration (SBA) has a regular business loan guarantee program that provides financing for the establishment, operation, or expansion of small business, including businesses engaged in exporting. Interest rates are set by the participating bank and are limited to 2.25 percent over the prime rate on loans with a maturity of less than seven years and 2.75 percent on loans with a maturity of seven years or more. Another SBA program, "Export Revolving Line of Credit Guarantee Program," provides pre-export financing for the manufacture or purchase of goods for sale to foreign markets and to help small business penetrate and/or develop a foreign market. The applicant must have been in business for 12 months before filing an application and all loans must have bank participation. The interest rate schedule is the same as that listed above for SBA's regular business loan guarantee program.

Overseas Private Investment Corporation

The Overseas Private Investment Corporation (OPIC) encourages and assists U.S. private capital and skills in the economic and social progress of developing countries through programs of political risk insurance. OPIC also has a guarantee loan program as well.

International Development Cooperation Agency

The International Development Cooperation Agency (IDCA) has two programs: the Agency for International Development (AID) and the Trade and Development Program (TDP). AID administers the U.S. bilateral foreign economic program, including the extension of loans, to less developed countries. AID invites bids from U.S. exporters on projects in LDCs. TDP promotes economic development in Third World countries, particularly in the newly industrializing countries, by financing planning services for development projects leading to the export of U.S. goods and services.

Department of Agriculture

The Department of Agriculture has two major programs: PL-480 Food for Peace and Commodity Credit Corporation (CCC). Food for Peace provides food relief for disaster and emergency-stricken countries. The CCC program provides short-term financing for U.S. agricultural commodities, enabling U.S. exporters to sell on a deferred payment basis.

World Banks

There are three major programs under the umbrella of the World Bank: the International Bank for Reconstruction and Development (IBRD), referred to as the World Bank; the International Development Association (IDA); and the International Finance Corporation (IFC). The IBRD extends loans to member governments for specific high-priority projects. The IDA promotes the economic development of lesser developed member countries by making credits on concessionary terms, thereby reducing the burden on the recipient country's balance of payments position. The IFC encourages growth of productive private enterprise in developing countries by extending loans to private firms in developing member countries.

Regional Banks

There are three development banks: Inter-American, Asian, and African. These banks make loans to governments and private corporations that are members of the regional bank.

For addresses and telephone numbers of the financing institutions listed in this chapter, consult the appendix.

SUGGESTED READING

U.S. Department of Commerce. "A Guide to Financing Exports," Brochure, June 1985.

11

DOCUMENTATION

The complex documentation required in foreign trade is necessary to protect all parties to the transaction. UNZ & Company offers a complete line of international trade documents. Call (800) 631–3098 or write to UNZ & Co., 190 Baldwin Avenue, Jersey City, N.J. 07306 for the "UNZ & Company Sourcebook: A How-to Guide for Exporters and Importers." (Check with your Chamber of Commerce or U.S. Department of Commerce District Office. They may have copies of the UNZ guide available.) Figures containing many of the documents we will discuss are included in this chapter. Table 11.1 contains a listing of the major documents used in the export trade.

TABLE 11.1   Export Documents

Pro forma invoice
Commercial invoice
Export license (covered in Chapter 12)
Shipper's export declaration
Certificate of origin
Consular invoice
Delivery instructions
Packing list
Inspection certificate
Insurance certificate
Shipper's Letter of Instructions
Dock receipt
(Ocean) bill of lading
Air waybill

COMMERCIAL INVOICE

After receiving an order, the exporter must prepare a commercial invoice. This document, like the domestic invoice, is a bill for the goods. Foreign governments often require this invoice to determine the value of goods for the assessment of customs duties. The preparation of consular documentation (if required) is often based on the commercial invoice. The importer's country may require the commercial invoice, as well as other documents, to be prepared in its language. Table 11.2 contains a checklist of the items that should be included in a commercial invoice.

When shipping under a letter of credit the commercial invoice must satisfy these requirements:

1. Invoice is made by the exporter.
2. Invoice is addressed to the importer.
3. Description of the merchandise is *exactly* as stated in the L/C.
4. Quantity agrees with the L/C.
5. Invoice is signed.
6. Marks and weights agree with all other documents.
7. Unexpected expenses (such as extra labor required, commission or storage while awaiting loading on the ship) are not included in the invoice *unless* the terms of the L/C allow for such charges.

Attention to detail is crucial. The importer can refuse to accept the shipment and his or her bank will not release funds to the exporter's bank if the exporter doesn't comply with the exact terms of the L/C.

Some countries require a specific format for the commercial invoice.

TABLE 11.2   Commercial Invoice Checklist

Addresses of exporter, importer
Date
Order number
Shipment details
Quantity
Unit price, total price
Weight of goods
Number of packages
Shipping marks
Delivery date
Terms of delivery and payment

Documentation

UNZ & Company prints special invoices for many countries. *Exporter's Encyclopedia* lists country regulations. (See "Suggested Readings" at the end of this chapter.)

Packing List

Shown in Figure 11.1, the packing list itemizes the material in each package, describes the type of package, gives net, legal, tare, gross weights, and measurements. Package markings are supplied as well as the exporter's and importer's names. Freight forwarders require the packing list to figure the total shipping weight or volume in order to reserve adequate shipping space. Customs officials check the packing list at the port of export and import. And the importer will use the list to inventory the cargo. The packing list is attached to the shipment in a waterproof envelope or placed inside the box.

Shipper's Export Declaration

The SED or "export dec" is used by the U.S. Bureau of the Census to collect export statistics and by the Commerce Department to enforce export control laws. Forms may be obtained from the U.S. Government Printing Office, U.S. Customs Offices, freight forwarders or commercial printers. The exporter prepares the SED and signs it. The publication entitled *Schedule B Statistical Classification of Domestic and Foreign Commodities Exported from the United States* lists Schedule B numbers. This publication is available in some libraries or for sale through the U.S. Government Printing Office. Figure 11.2 includes an SED as well as an instructional pamphlet issued by the U.S. Department of Commerce/Bureau of the Census.

A "Shipper's Summary Export Declaration" (Form 7525-M) allows exporters to report on a monthly basis (rather than per shipment) if they meet certain criteria. Section 30.39 of the *Foreign Trade Statistics Regulations*, a Bureau of Census publication, provides guidelines. The summary form 7525-M can only be used on shipments to Country Groups Q, T, V, W, Y, and Canada. (Group Q—Poland and Romania; Group T—all countries in the Western Hemisphere, except Cuba; Group V—all other countries not in any group; Group W—Hungary and Poland; Group Y—Albania, Bulgaria, Czechoslovakia, Estonia, East Germany, Laos, Latvia, Lithuania, People's Republic of Mongolia.)

Form 30-035   Printed and Sold by Unz & Co., 190 Baldwin Ave., Jersey City, New Jersey 07306
(201) 795-5400   (800) 631-3098

PACKING LIST

_____ 19 _____
Place and Date of Shipment

To

Gentlemen:

Under your Order No. _____ the material listed below

was shipped   via

To
_____

Shipment consists of:		Marks
_____ Cases	_____ Packages	
_____ Crates	_____ Cartons	
_____ Bbls.	_____ Drums	
_____ Reels	_____	

*LEGAL WEIGHT IS WEIGHT OF ARTICLE PLUS PAPER, BOX, BOTTLE, ETC., CONTAINING THE ARTICLE AS USUALLY CARRIED IN STOCK.

PACKAGE NUMBER	WEIGHTS IN LBS. or KILOS			DIMENSIONS			QUANTITY	CLEARLY STATE CONTENTS OF EACH PACKAGE
	GROSS WEIGHT EACH	*LEGAL WEIGHT EACH	NET WEIGHT EACH	HEIGHT	WIDTH	LENGTH		

Figure 11.1
(*Source:* UNZ & Company, Jersey City, New Jersey.)

Documentation

CORRECT WAY TO FILL OUT THE SHIPPER'S EXPORT DECLARATIONS
(Follow Carefully to Avoid Delay at Shipping Point)

1. Purpose

The Shipper's Export Declarations (SEDs), Forms 7525-V and 7525-V-Alternate (Intermodal) and the Shipper's Export Declaration for In-Transit Goods, Form 7513, are joint Bureau of the Census — International Trade Administration documents used for compiling the official U.S. export statistics and administering the requirements of the Export Administration Act, as provided for in the Foreign Trade Statistics Regulations (FTSR) (15 CFR, Part 30) and the Export Administration Regulations (15 CFR, Parts 368—399).

2. Forms

The SED, Form 7525-V, its continuation sheet, and the in-transit SED, Form 7513, may be purchased from the Superintendent of Documents, Government Printing Office, Washington, D.C. 20402, local Customs District Directors, or privately printed. Form 7525-V-Alternate (Intermodal) and its continuation sheet must be privately printed. Sample copies may be obtained from the Bureau of the Census, Washington, D.C. 20233. When privately printing SEDs, the forms must conform in every respect to the official forms in size, wording, color **(black ink on buff paper — Form 7513 on pink paper)**, weight of paper stock (not less than 16 nor more than 20 pounds commercial substance), and arrangement including the Office of Management and Budget Approval Number printed in the upper right-hand corner of the face of the form. Form 7525-V-Alternate (Intermodal) may be used in lieu of the basic SED, Form 7525-V, without limitation.

The Bureau of the Census has a program whereby exporters, carriers, or freight forwarders may submit monthly reports via the Shipper's Summary Export Declaration, computer tape, or direct computer-to-computer transmission in lieu of filing an individual Shipper's Export Declaration for each shipment.

3. When Required

SEDs are required to be filed for virtually all shipments, including hand-carried merchandise, **(see Section 9 for exemptions, particularly if the shipment is valued $1,000 or less)** from the United States (50 states and the District of Columbia); Puerto Rico; U.S. or Puerto Rican Foreign Trade Zones (FTZs); and the U.S. Virgin Islands to all foreign countries (including FTZs located therein) and to the U.S. Trust Territories, excluding the Northern Mariana Islands.

SEDs are also required to be filed for shipments between the United States and Puerto Rico and from the United States or Puerto Rico to the U.S. Virgin Islands.

SEDs are not required for shipments from the United States or Puerto Rico to U.S. Possessions (except the U.S. Virgin Islands) or from a U.S. Possession to the United States, Puerto Rico, or another U.S. Possession.

The SED for in-transit merchandise (Form 7513) is required to be filed for:

(a) merchandise destined from one foreign country to another which transits the United States, Puerto Rico or the U.S. Virgin Islands and is **exported by vessel** regardless of the method of transportation by which the merchandise entered. If a validated export license is required this form must be filed regardless of the method of transportation for the export;

(b) foreign merchandise exported from General Order Warehouses; and

(c) imported merchandise which has been rejected by government inspection and is being exported. (Form 7513 is **not** to be used for the reexport of imported merchandise (except rejected merchandise) documented on Customs Entry Forms other than Form 7512.)

4. Number of Copies Required

(a) One copy for shipments to Canada, Puerto Rico, and the U.S. Virgin Islands

(b) One copy for exports through the U.S. Postal Service

(c) Two copies for all other shipments

Additional copies may be required for export control purposes by the Office of Export Administration, other Government agencies (when authorized), Customs Directors, or the Postmaster.

5. Preparation and Signature

The SED shall be prepared in English in a permanent medium with the original signed (signature stamp acceptable) by the exporter or his duly authorized agent. The agent's authority to sign the SED must be executed by a power-of-attorney or as authorized on the SED.

6. Requirement for Separate SEDs

Separate SEDs are required for each shipment from one consignor to one consignee on a single carrier (including **each** rail car, truck, or other vehicle). However, Customs Directors may waive this requirement if multiple car shipments are made under a single loading document and cleared simultaneously. Also, merchandise requiring a validated export license shall not be reported on the same SED with merchandise moving under general license.

7. Presentation

(a) Postal Shipments — the SEDs shall be delivered to the Postmaster with the packages at the time of mailing.

(b) Pipeline shipments — the SEDs shall be submitted to the Customs Director within 4 working days after the end of the calendar month.

(c) All other shipments — the SEDs shall be delivered to the exporting carrier **prior** to exportation.

(d) Exporting carriers are required to file SEDs and manifests with Customs — See Sections 30.20 through 30.24 of the FTSR.

Shipments from an interior point — SED may accompany the merchandise being transported to the exporting carrier or the port of exportation, or it may be delivered directly to the exporting carrier.

Shipments exempt from SED filing requirements — a reference to the exemption must be noted on the bill of lading, air waybill, or other loading document for verification that no SED is required.

Page 3

Figure 11.2
(*Source:* U.S. Department of Commerce.)

Documentation

8. Corrections

Corrections, amendments, or cancellations of data may be made directly on the originally filed SED, if it has not been forwarded to the Bureau of the Census. If the SED has been forwarded to the Bureau, corrections, amendments, or cancellations should be made on a copy of the originally filed SED (marked "Correction Copy") and filed with the Customs Director or the Postmaster where the declaration was originally presented.

9. Exemptions

A. Shipments (excluding postal shipments) where the value of commodities classified under each individual Schedule B number is **$1000 or less** and for which a validated export license is not required and when shipped to countries not prohibited by the Export Administration Regulations (15 CFR, Parts 368 — 399).

B. Shipments through the U.S. Postal Service that do not require a validated license when the shipment is: (1) valued **$500** or under, (2) either the consignee or the consignor is not a business concern, or (3) the shipment is not for commercial consideration.

C. In-transit shipments not requiring a validated export license and leaving for a foreign destination by means other than vessel.

D. Shipments from one point in the United States to another point thereof by routes passing through Canada or Mexico, and shipments from one point in Canada or Mexico to another point thereof by routes passing through the United States.

E. Shipments to the U.S. Armed Services

(1) All commodities consigned to the U.S. Armed Services, including exchange systems.

(2) Department of Defense Military Assistance Program Grant-Aid shipments being transported as Department of Defense cargo.

F. Shipments to U.S. Government Agencies and Employees

(1) Office furniture and supplies for use in Government offices.

(2) Household goods and personal property for the use of U.S. Government employees.

(3) Food, medicines, and related items and other commissary items for use by U.S. Government employees and offices.

(4) Government shipments of books, charts, maps, and so forth, for use by libraries or similar institutions.

G. Miscellaneous Exemptions

(1) Diplomatic pouches and their contents.

(2) Human remains and accompanying appropriate receptacles and flowers.

(3) Shipments of gift parcels moving under Office of Export Administration General License GIFT.

(4) Shipments of interplant correspondence and other business records from a U.S. firm to its subsidiary or affiliate.

(5) Shipments of pets as baggage, accompanying or unaccompanying persons leaving the United States.

(6) Shipments under Office of Export Administration Project License DL-5355-S, General License G-NOAA, and General License RCS.

H. Conditional Exemptions

SEDs are not required for the following if they are not shipped as cargo under a bill of lading or air waybill and do not require a validated export license.

(1) Baggage and household effects and tools of trade of persons leaving the United States when such are owned by the person, in his possession at the time of departure and intended for his use only.

(2) Carriers' stores, supplies, equipment, bunker fuel, and so forth, when not intended for unlading in a foreign country.

(3) Usual and reasonable kinds and quantities of dunnage necessary to secure and stow cargo. (For sole use on board the carrier.)

If the shipments indicated above are shipped under a bill of lading or air waybill, the SED should show in the description column in lieu of a description, a statement that the shipment consists of baggage, personal effects, and so forth, and Schedule B Commodity Numbers should not be shown.

If these shipments require a validated export license, the SED must identify the shipment as baggage, personal effects, and so forth, and must contain all of the information required on the SED.

10. Retention of Shipping Documents

The Bureau of the Census and the U.S. Customs Service may require the exporters or their agents to produce copies of shipping documents within 3 years of exportation.

11. Administrative Provisions

SEDs and the information contained thereon are confidential and used solely for official purposes authorized by the Secretary of Commerce in accordance with 13 U.S.C. Section 301(g). Neither may be disclosed to anyone except the exporter or his agent by those having possession of or access to any official copy.

Information from SEDs (except common information) may not be copied to manifests or other shipping documents. Exporters may not furnish SEDs or their information to anyone for unofficial purposes.

Copies of the SEDs may be supplied to exporters or their agents when such copies are needed to comply with official requirements as authorization for export, export control requirements, or U.S. Department of Agriculture requirements for proof of export in connection with subsidy payments. Such copies will be stamped certified, and not for any other use and may not be reproduced in any form.

When the Secretary of Commerce or delegate determines that the withholding of information provided on an individual SED is contrary to the "National Interest," the Secretary or delegate may make such information available taking safeguards and precautions as deemed appropriate.

A SED presented for export constitutes a representation by the exporter that all statements and information are in accordance with the export control regulations. The commodity described on the declaration is authorized under the particular license as identified on the declaration, all statements conform to the applicable licenses, and all conditions of the export control regulations have been met.

Page 4

Figure 11.2 *(cont.)*

Documentation

11. Administrative Provisions — Continued

It is unlawful to knowingly make false or misleading representation for exportation. This constitutes a violation of the Export Administration Act, 50. U.S.C. App. 2410. It is also a violation of export control laws and regulations to be connected in any way with an altered SED to effect export.

Commodities that have been, are being, or for which there is probable cause to believe they are intended to be exported in violation of the Export Administration Act are subject to seizure, detention, condemnation, or sale under 22 U.S.C. Section 401.

To knowingly make false or misleading statements relating to information on the SED is a criminal offense subject to penalties as provided for in 18 U.S.C. Section 1001.

Violations of the Foreign Trade Statistics Regulations are subject to civil penalties as authorized by 13 U.S.C. Section 305.

12. Regulations

Detailed information regarding the SED and its preparation is contained in the Foreign Trade Statistics Regulations (FTSR) (15 CFR, Part 30). Also, the FTSR should be consulted for special provisions applicable under particular circumstances. Copies may be purchased from the Bureau of the Census, Washington, D.C. 20233. Information concerning export control laws and regulations of the Office of Export Administration is contained in the Export Administration Regulations, which may be purchased from the Superintendent of Documents, Government Printing Office, Washington, D.C. 20402.

Reference Schedules

Schedule B — Statistical Classification of Domestic and Foreign Commodities Exported from the United States. For sale by the Superintendent of Documents, U.S. Government Printing Office, Washington, D.C. 20402 and local U.S. Customs District Directors.

Schedule C-E — Classification of Country and Territory Designations for U.S. Export Statistics. Free from the Bureau of the Census, Washington, D.C. 20233.

Schedule C-I — Classification of Country and Territory Designations for U.S. Import Statistics. Free from the Bureau of the Census, Washington, D.C. 20233.

Schedule D — Classification of Customs Districts and Ports. Free from the Bureau of the Census, Washington, D.C. 20233.

Schedule K — Classification of Foreign Ports by Geographic Trade Area and Country. Free from the Bureau of the Census, Washington, D.C. 20233.

Foreign Trade Statistics Regulations. For sale by the Bureau of the Census, Washington, D.C. 20233.

Export Administration Regulations. For sale by the Superintendent of Documents, U.S. Government Printing Office, Washington, D.C. 20402 and U.S. Department of Commerce District Offices.

NOTE: This is an instructional pamphlet summarizing the preparation of the SED. It is in no way intended as a substitute for either the *Foreign Trade Statistics Regulations* or the *Export Administration Regulations*.

Page 5

Figure 11.2 *(cont.)*

Documentation

		SED Item Number		
Data	FTSR Reference	7525-V	7525-V Alternate (Intermodal)	7513
INFORMATION TO BE REPORTED ON SEDS				
Exporter — The name and address of the principal party responsible for effecting export from the United States. The exporter as named on the validated export license. Report only the first five digits of the ZIP code.	30.7(d)	1(a)	2	5
Exporter Identification Number — The exporter's Internal Revenue Service Employer Identification Number (EIN) or Social Security Number (SSN) if no EIN has been assigned.	30.7(d)	1(b)	34	N A
Related Party Transaction — One between the U.S. exporter and the foreign consignee, that is an export from a U.S. person to a foreign business enterprise or from a U.S. business enterprise to a foreign person, when the person owns (directly or indirectly) at any time during the fiscal year, **10 percent** or more of the voting securities of the incorporated business enterprise, or an equivalent interest if an unincorporated business enterprise, including a branch.	30.7(v)	1(c)	35	N A
Agent of Exporter — The name and address of the duly authorized forwarding agent.	30.7(e)	5	7	4
Ultimate Consignee — The name and address of the party actually receiving the merchandise for the designated end-use or the party so designated on the validated export license.	30.7(f)	4(a)	3 31	6
Intermediate Consignee — The name and address of the party in a foreign country who effects delivery of the merchandise to the ultimate consignee or the party so named on the export license.	30.7(g)	4(b)	4	N A
Exporting Carrier — The carrier transporting the merchandise out of the United States. For vessel shipments, give the vessel's name and flag.	30.7(c)	10	14	1
U.S. Port of Export (a) Overland — the U.S. Customs port at which the surface carrier crosses the border. (b) Vessel and Air — the U.S. Customs port where the merchandise is loaded on the carrier which is taking the merchandise out of the United States. (c) Postal — the U.S. Post Office where the merchandise is mailed.	30.7(a) 30.20	11	15	2
Method of Transportation — The mode of transport by which the merchandise is exported. Specify by name, i.e., vessel, air, rail, truck, etc.	30.7(b)	9	30	N A
Loading Pier/Terminal — (For vessel shipments only) The number or name of the pier at which the exporting vessel.	30.7(c)	8	10	N A
Containerized — (For vessel shipments only) Cargo originally booked as containerized cargo and that placed in containers at the vessel operator's option.	30.7(u)	13	11(a)	N A
Point (State) of Origin or Foreign Trade Zone (FTZ) Number (a) The two-digit U.S. Postal Service abbreviation of the state in which the merchandise actually starts its journey to the port of export, or (b) The state of the commodity of the greatest value, or (c) The state of consolidation, or (d) The Foreign Trade Zone Number for exports leaving a FTZ.	30.7(t)	6	8	N A
Foreign Port of Unloading — (For vessel and air shipments only) The foreign port and country at which the merchandise will be unladen from the exporting carrier.	30.7(h)	12	16	7
Country of Ultimate Destination — The country in which the merchandise is to be consumed, further processed, or manufactured; the final country of destination as known to the exporter at the time of shipment; or the country of ultimate destination as shown on the validated export license.	30.7(i)	7	33	8
Marks and Numbers — Marks, numbers, or other identification shown on the packages.	30.7(j)	15	18	12

Figure 11.2   (cont.)

Documentation

INFORMATION TO BE REPORTED ON SEDS				
			SED Item Number	
Data	FTSR Reference	7525-V	7525-V Alternate (Intermodal)	7513
Numbers and Kinds of Packages — The numbers and kinds of packages (boxes, barrels, baskets, etc.).	30.7(k)	15	19	14
Commodity Description — A sufficient description of the commodity to permit verification of the Schedule B Commodity Number or the description shown on the validated export license.	30.7(l)	14	20	14
Schedule B Commodity Number — The commodity number as provided in Schedule B — Statistical Classification of Domestic and Foreign Commodities Exported from the United States.	30.7(l)	17	24	15
Gross Shipping Weight — **(For vessel and air shipments only)** The gross shipping weight in pounds, including the weight of containers but excluding carrier equipment.	30.7(o)	19	21	13
"D" (Domestic) or "F" (Foreign) **(a)** Domestic exports — merchandise grown, produced, or manufactured (including imported merchandise which has been enhanced in value) in the United States. **(b)** Foreign exports — merchandise that has entered the United States and is being reexported in the same condition as when imported.	30.7(p)	16	23	NA
Net Quantity — The amount in terms of the unit(s) specified in Schedule B with the unit indicated or the unit as specified on the validated export license.	30.7(n)	18	25	16
Value — Selling price or cost if not sold, including inland freight, insurance, and other charges to U.S. port of export and conditional discounts, but **excluding** unconditional discounts and commissions (nearest whole dollar, omit cents).	30.7(q)	20	26	17
Export License Number or Symbol — Validated export license number and expiration date or general license symbol.	30.7(m)	21	27	14
Export Control Commodity Number (ECCN) — **(When required)** ECCN number of commodities listed on the Commodity Control List (commodities subject to U.S. Department of Commerce export controls) in the Export Administration Regulations.	NA	22	28	15
Bill of Lading or Air Waybill Number — The exporting carrier's bill of lading or air waybill number.	30.22(b)	3	5(a)	NA
Date of Exportation — **(Not required for vessel and postal shipments)** The date of departure or date of clearance, if date of departure is not known.	30.7(r)	2	32	NA
Designation of Agent — Signature of exporter authorizing the named agent to effect the export when such agent does not have formal power of attorney.	30.7(s) 30.4	23	29	NA
Signature — Signature of exporter or authorized agent certifying the truth and accuracy of the information on the SED.	30.7(s) 30.4	24	36	18
Additional Information Required Only on Form 7513				
U.S. Port of Arrival — The U.S. port at which the merchandise arrived from a foreign country.	30.8(a)	NA	NA	9
Country from Which Shipped — The foreign country where the merchandise was loaded on the carrier that brought it to the United States.	30.8(b)	NA	NA	10
Date of Arrival — The date on which the merchandise arrived in the United States.	30.8(c)	NA	NA	11
Country of Origin — The country in which the merchandise was mined, grown, manufactured or substantially transformed. If the country of origin is not known, show the country of shipment designated as "Country of Shipment."	30.8(d)	NA	NA	12

Page 7

Figure 11.2 *(cont.)*

Documentation

U.S. DEPARTMENT OF COMMERCE — BUREAU OF THE CENSUS — INTERNATIONAL TRADE ADMINISTRATION

FORM **7525-V** (3-19-85)   **SHIPPER'S EXPORT DECLARATION**   OMB No. 0607-0018

1a. EXPORTER *(Name and address including ZIP code)*

| ZIP CODE | **2.** DATE OF EXPORTATION | **3.** BILL OF LADING/AIR WAYBILL NO. |

b. EXPORTER EIN NO.

c. PARTIES TO TRANSACTION
☐ Related ☐ Non-related

4a. ULTIMATE CONSIGNEE

b. INTERMEDIATE CONSIGNEE

5. FORWARDING AGENT

6. POINT (STATE) OF ORIGIN OR FTZ NO. **7.** COUNTRY OF ULTIMATE DESTINATION

8. LOADING PIER/TERMINAL

9. MODE OF TRANSPORT *(Specify)*

10. EXPORTING CARRIER

11. PORT OF EXPORT

12. FOREIGN PORT OF UNLOADING

13. CONTAINERIZED *(Vessel only)*
☐ Yes ☐ No

14. SCHEDULE B DESCRIPTION OF COMMODITIES, *(Use columns 15—19)*

MARKS, NOS., AND KINDS OF PKGS. (15)	D/F (16)	SCHEDULE B NUMBER (17)	QUANTITY — SCHEDULE B UNIT(S) (18)	SHIPPING WEIGHT *(Pounds)* (19)		VALUE (U.S. dollars, omit cents) *(Selling price or cost if not sold)* (20)

21. VALIDATED LICENSE NO./GENERAL LICENSE SYMBOL   **22.** ECCN *(When required)*

23. Duly authorized officer or employee | The exporter authorizes the forwarder named above to act as forwarding agent for export control and customs purposes.

24. I certify that all statements made and all information contained herein are true and correct and that I have read and understand the instructions for preparation of this document, set forth in the **"Correct Way to Fill Out the Shipper's Export Declaration."** I understand that civil and criminal penalties, including forfeiture and sale, may be imposed for making false or fraudulent statements herein, failing to provide the requested information or for violation of U.S. laws on exportation (13 U.S.C. Sec. 305; 22 U.S.C. Sec. 401; 18 U.S.C. Sec. 1001; 50 U.S.C. App. 2410).

Signature

Title

Date

Confidential – For use solely for official purposes authorized by the Secretary of Commerce (13 U.S.C. 301 (g)).

Export shipments are subject to inspection by U.S. Customs Service and/or Office of Export Enforcement.

25. AUTHENTICATION *(When required)*

Figure 11.2   *(cont.)*

Certificate of Origin

Shown in Figure 11.3, this document certifies that the goods were manufactured in the United States. Sometimes the importer's country requires that this certificate be endorsed by one's local (accredited) Chamber of Commerce or Commerce Department district office and/or its consulate.

Consular Invoice

Some countries require this form, which is prepared in the language of the importer's country. The form is available at the country's consulate. It covers the same details as the commercial invoice and packing list. Latin American countries, in particular, require a consular invoice (in addition to the commercial invoice). The consulate uses the invoice (which a freight forwarder will prepare) to determine if the shipment complies with its country's import regulations. The consulate charges a fee for checking and certifying the consular invoice.

Certificate of Insurance

If insurance is provided by the shipper (C.I.F. terms), this certificate must be included. The certificate of insurance is issued by the exporter's insurance broker on behalf of the exporter. If the exporter ships under his or her freight forwarder's policy, the forwarder will issue the certificate.

Shipping Instructions

The exporter should provide his or her forwarder with all the details and requirements of the shipment. It shouldn't be assumed that the forwarder provides all the necessary services. The forwarder and the exporter must understand who pays for insurance and the coverage desired, which documents the forwarder is expected to prepare, how documents are distributed, and how ocean or air freight is to be paid (collect or prepaid). See Figure 11.4.

Delivery Instructions

This letter, prepared by the forwarder, directs the inland carrier where to deliver the goods (which ocean pier, air cargo line). Delivery instructions shouldn't be confused with "delivery order," which is used for the import trade.

CERTIFICATE OF ORIGIN

The undersigned _____
(Owner or Agent, or &c)

for _____ declares
(Name and Address of Shipper)

that the following mentioned goods shipped on S/S _____
(Name of Ship)

on the date of _____ consigned to _____

_____ are the product of the United States of America.

| MARKS AND NUMBERS | NO. OF PKGS., BOXES OR CASES | WEIGHT IN KILOS | | DESCRIPTION |
		GROSS	NET	

Sworn to before me .

Dated at _____ on the _____ day of _____ 19 _____

this _____ day of _____ 19 _____

_____   _____
                                                                      (Signature of Owner or Agent)

The _____ , a recognized Chamber of Commerce under the laws of the State of

_____ , has examined the manufacturer's invoice or shipper's affidavit concerning the
origin of the merchandise and, according to the best of its knowledge and belief, finds that the products named originated in the
United States of North America.

Secretary _____

Form 10-900 ©, 1986 *UNZCO* 190 Baldwin Ave., Jersey City, NJ 07306 • (800) 631-3098 • (201) 795-5400

Figure 11.3
(*Source:* UNZ & Company, Jersey City, New Jersey.)

SHIPPER (Name and address including ZIP code)

ZIP CODE

EXPORTER EIN NO.

PARTIES TO TRANSACTION
☐ Related   ☐ Non-related

ULTIMATE CONSIGNEE

INTERMEDIATE CONSIGNEE

FORWARDING AGENT

POINT (STATE) OF ORIGIN OR FTZ NO.   COUNTRY OF ULTIMATE DESTINATION

SHIPPER'S LETTER OF INSTRUCTIONS

NOTE: ① IF YOU ARE UNCERTAIN OF THE SCHEDULE B COMMODITY NO.—DO NOT TYPE IT IN—WE WILL COMPLETE WHEN PROCESSING 7525-V.
② IF YOU HAVE SHIPPED THIS MATERIAL TO US VIA AN INLAND CARRIER—PLEASE GIVE US THE INLAND CARRIER'S NAME, SHIPPING DATE, AND RECEIPT OR PRO. NO. (IF AVAILABLE). THIS WILL HELP US EXPEDITE YOUR SHIPMENT WITH THE INLAND CARRIER.
③ BE SURE TO PICK UP TOP SHEET AND SIGN THE FIRST BUFF EXPORT DECLARATION WITH PEN AND INK.

SHIPPER'S REF. NO.   DATE   SHIP VIA
☐ AIR   ☐ OCEAN   ☐ CONSOLIDATE   ☐ DIRECT

MARKS. NOS., AND KINDS OF PKGS.	D/F	SCHEDULE B NUMBER	QUANTITY— SCHEDULE B UNIT(S)	SHIPPING WEIGHT (Pounds)	PRICE PER UNIT (U.S. Dollars)	VALUE (U.S. dollars, omit cents) (Selling price or cost if not sold)

VALIDATED LICENSE NO./GENERAL LICENSE SYMBOL   ECCN (When required)   SHIPPER MUST CHECK ♦ ☐ PREPAID OR ☐ COLLECT

Duly authorized officer or employee   The exporter authorizes the forwarder named above to act as forwarding agent for export control and customs purposes.   C.O.D. AMOUNT $

SPECIAL INSTRUCTIONS

BE SURE TO PICK UP TOP SHEET AND SIGN THE FIRST BUFF EXPORT DECLARATION WITH PEN & INK.

SHIPPER'S INSTRUCTIONS IN CASE OF INABILITY TO DELIVER CONSIGNMENT AS CONSIGNED: ☐ ABANDON ☐ RETURN TO SHIPPER
☐ DELIVER TO

SHIPPER REQUESTS INSURANCE   ☐ NO   If Shipper has requested insurance as provided for at the left hereof, shipment is insured in the amount indicated (recovery is limited to actual loss) in accordance with the provisions as specified in the Carrier's Tariffs. Insurance is payable to Shipper unless payee is designated in writing by the shipper.
☐ YES $

NOTE: The Shipper or his Authorized Agent hereby authorizes the above named Company, in his name and on his behalf, to prepare any export documents, to sign and accept any documents relating to said shipment and forward this shipment in accordance with the conditions of carriage and the tariffs of the carriers employed. The shipper guarantees payment of all collect charges in the event the consignee refuses payment. Hereunder the sole responsibility of the Company is to use reasonable care in the selection of carriers, forwarders, agents and others to whom it may entrust the shipment.

Form 15-305 Printed and Sold by UNZ&Co. 190 Baldwin Ave., Jersey City, NJ 07306 • (800) 631-3098 • (201) 795-5400

Figure 11.4
(*Source:* UNZ & Company, Jersey City, New Jersey.)

Documentation

Dock Receipt

When the inland carrier delivers the cargo to the pier, the pier operator issues a "dock receipt." The pier operator retains the original dock receipt, forwarding it to the steamship company while issuing a signed copy to the inland carrier. The dock receipt transfers accountability for the cargo from the inland carrier to the ocean carrier. The exporter or forwarder prepares the dock receipt, which the inland carrier presents. See Figure 11.5.

Ocean Bill of Lading

The ocean bill of lading, shown in Figure 11.6, serves three important functions in international trade. It is evidence of a contract of carriage or the final receipt from the ocean carrier for the goods shipped; second, it is a receipt for the cargo and third, it is a document of title with which the consignee claims the goods. The bill of lading contains information such as the party to notify, port of loading and discharge, destination, number of packages, marks, description of cargo, gross weight, and condition of the goods. There are two types of bills of lading used for transferring ownership: straight and shipper's order.

Straight: This is a nonnegotiable bill of lading that provides for the delivery of the goods to the person named in the bill of lading and to no one else. Because only the named person can pick up the goods, the cargo can be released to that person if he or she presents proper identification and a copy (rather than the original) of the bill of lading. If the importer doesn't have a copy of the bill, the cargo can still be released but the steamship will ask to be released from responsibility. The bill must be clearly marked "nonnegotiable" or "not negotiable."

A straight bill of lading is used with open account (the exporter trusts the importer to pay and doesn't need to use the title for financial security), cash in advance (no need to hold the title because the exporter already has been paid), or with shipment to subsidiaries (the shipper is the consignee).

Shipper's order: This bill of lading is negotiable because it provides for the delivery of goods to a named person *or* anyone he or she designates, but only on proper endorsement and surrender of the bill of lading to the carrier or carrier's agents. It is used with a sight draft (documentary) and letter of credit shipments because both the exporter's bank and the importer's bank want to be able to hold the title in the event that the importer defaults on the payment. The exporter endorses the original copy of the bill of lading before presenting it to the bank for collection.

One original bill of lading is required to pick up the cargo, but the

Documentation

Form 35-585 ©, 1986 UNZCO 190 Baldwin Ave., Jersey City, NJ 07306 • (800) 631-3098 • (201) 795-5400

(SPACES IMMEDIATELY BELOW ARE FOR SHIPPERS MEMORANDA—NOT PART OF DOCK RECEIPT)

DELIVERING CARRIER TO STEAMER:	CAR NUMBER—REFERENCE
FORWARDING AGENT—REFERENCES	EXPORT DEC. No.

DOCK RECEIPT
NON-NEGOTIABLE

SHIPPER --

SHIP	VOYAGE NO.	FLAG	PIER	PORT OF LOADING
FOR. PORT OF DISCHARGE *(Where goods are to be delivered to consignee or on-carrier)*			For TRANSSHIPMENT TO *(If goods are to be transhipped or forwarded at port of discharge)*	

PARTICULARS FURNISHED BY SHIPPER OF GOODS

MARKS AND NUMBERS	No. of PKGS.	DESCRIPTION OF PACKAGES AND GOODS	MEASURE-MENT	GROSS WEIGHT

DIMENSIONS AND WEIGHTS OF PACKAGES TO BE SHOWN ON REVERSE SIDE

DELIVERED BY:

RECEIVED THE ABOVE DESCRIBED MERCHANDISE FOR SHIPMENT AS INDICATED HEREON, SUBJECT TO ALL CONDITIONS OF THE UNDERSIGNED'S USUAL FORM OF DOCK RECEIPT AND BILL OF LADING. COPIES OF THE UNDERSIGNED'S USUAL FORM OF DOCK RECEIPT AND BILL OF LADING MAY BE OBTAINED FROM THE MASTER OF THE VESSEL, OR THE VESSEL'S AGENT

LIGHTER ⎱
TRUCK ⎰ ....

ARRIVED— DATE .... TIME ....

UNLOADED— DATE .... TIME ....

AGENT FOR MASTER

CHECKED BY ....

BY ....
RECEIVING CLERK

PLACED IN SHIP / ON DOCK LOCATION ....

DATE ....

Figure 11.5
(*Source:* UNZ & Company, Jersey City, New Jersey.)

Documentation

MARKS	No. of Pkge.	MEASUREMENTS						TOTAL Cubic Ft.		Gross Weight
		Length		Breadth		Depth				
		Ft.	In.	Ft.	In.	Ft.	In.	Ft.	In.	
							Totals			

Printed in U.S.A.
UNZ & CO., Inc.
New York

Figure 11.5 *(cont.)*

Documentation

DELIVERING CARRIER TO STEAMER:	CAR NUMBER—REFERENCE
FORWARDING AGENT—REFERENCES	EXPORT DEC. No.

BILL OF LADING
(Conditions Continued from Reverse Side Hereof)

SHIPPER.....................

CONSIGNEE: ORDER OF.....................

ADDRESS ARRIVAL NOTICE TO	ALSO NOTIFY

SHIP	VOYAGE NO.	FLAG	PIER	PORT OF LOADING

FOR. PORT OF DISCHARGE (Where goods are to be delivered to consignee or on-carrier) | For TRANSSHIPMENT to (If goods are to be transshipped or forwarded at port of discharge)

PARTICULARS FURNISHED BY SHIPPER OF GOODS

MARKS AND NUMBERS	No. of PKGS.	DESCRIPTION OF PACKAGES AND GOODS	MEASURE-MENT	GROSS WEIGHT

FREIGHT PAYABLE IN

..............@............PER 2240 LBS...... $..............		
..............@............PER 100 LB......... $..............		
.......FT..........IN. @..............PER 40 CU. FT...... $..............		
.......FT..........IN. @.... ....PER CU. FT........ $..............		
.... $..............		
.... $..............		
.... $..............		
TOTAL........... $..............		

(CONDITIONS CONTINUED FROM REVERSE SIDE HEREOF)

IN WITNESS WHEREOF, THERE HAVE BEEN EXECUTED........
BILLS OF LADING, ALL OF THE SAME TENOR AND DATE, ONE OF WHICH BEING ACCOMPLISHED, THE OTHERS TO STAND VOID.

BY..
FOR THE MASTER

ISSUED AT..
(DATE)

B/L No..

Form 35-084 ©, 1986 *UNZCO* 190 Baldwin Ave., Jersey City, NJ 07306 • (800) 631-3098 • (201) 795-5400

Figure 11.6
(*Source:* UNZ & Company, Jersey City, New Jersey.)

Documentation

BILL OF LADING
(SHORT FORM)

RECEIVED from the shipper named on the reverse side hereof the goods, or packages said to contain goods hereinafter mentioned in apparent good order and condition unless otherwise indicated in this bill of lading, to be transported to the port of discharge and there to be delivered or transshipped and forwarded on the terms hereinafter stated. In every contingency whatsoever and even in case of deviation or of unseaworthiness of the ship at time of loading or at any subsequent time, the rights and obligations, whatsoever they may be, of each and every person having any interest of duty whatsoever in respect of the receipt, care, custody, carriage, delivery or transshipment of the goods whether as shipper, consignee, holder or endorsee of the bill of lading, receiver or owner of the goods, master of the ship, carrier, ship-owner, demise charterer, time charterer, operator, agent, bailee, warehouseman, forwarder or otherwise howsoever, shall be subject to and governed by the terms of the carrier's regular bill of lading, which shall be deemed to be incorporated herein, including any amendments thereto or special provisions thereof which may be in effect at the time the goods are received for shipment and applicable to the intended voyage. Copies of such regular bill of lading and amendments may be obtained on application to the office of the Company or its Agent at the port of loading or port of discharge. This shipment shall have effect subject to the provisions of the Carriage of Goods by Sea Act of the United States, approved April 16, 1936, which shall be deemed to be incorporated herein and nothing herein contained shall be deemed a surrender by the carrier of any of its rights or immunities or an increase of any of its responsibilities or liabilities under said Act. The provisions stated in said Act shall (except as may be otherwise specifically provided in the bill of lading referred to above) govern before the goods are loaded on and after they are discharged from the ship and throughout the entire time the goods are in the custody of the carrier. Nothing herein contained, whether by express statement, reference, implication or otherwise, shall be deemed a surrender of any rights or immunities or an increase of any responsibilities or liabilities which the ship, her owner, charterer, operator, agent or master or any carrier, bailee, warehouseman, or forwarder of the goods or the agent of any of them would have in the absence of this bill of lading. None of the terms of this bill of lading shall be deemed to have been waived by any person unless by express waiver signed by such person, or his duly authorized agent.

IN ACCEPTING THIS BILL OF LADING, the shipper, consignee, pledgee, holder or endorsee of this bill of lading, receiver, owner of the goods and each of them agree that all freight engagements, dock receipts or other agreements whatsoever in respect of the shipment of the goods are superseded by this bill of lading, and agree to be bound by all its terms whether written, printed or stamped on the front or back thereof or incorporated by reference therein, any local customs or privileges to the contrary notwithstanding.

If requested, one signed bill of lading duly endorsed must be surrendered to the agent of the ship at the port of discharge in exchange for delivery order.

(CONDITIONS CONTINUED ON REVERSE SIDE HEREOF)

DO NOT USE THIS SPACE FOR DESCRIPTION OF SHIPMENT

Figure 11.6   (cont.)

importer needs the full set of bills to claim title. The exporter or bank won't release the full set until the importer pays or acknowledges the obligation to pay. Hence, the order bill of lading can be used as collateral.

Either of these bills (straight or order) can be further identified in the following ways:

Clean: Such a bill of lading is issued when the shipment is received by the ocean carrier in good order. Actually "clean" is the only acceptable bill of lading, especially for documentary and letter of credit shipments.

Foul (or not clean): Goods arrive at the pier inadequately packed, damaged, or broken.

On board: When the bill of lading is stamped "on board," the ocean carrier is certifying that the cargo has been placed aboard the named vessel. In documentary or letter of credit transactions an on board bill of lading is required by the bank to release funds to the exporter.

Stale: A bill of lading is termed "stale" when the exporter (or his or her agent) fails to present the bill of lading to the issuing bank under a letter of credit transaction within a reasonable time after its date. The requirement is such that the bill of lading arrives at the port of importation before the steamer arrives. If the bill of lading is late, fines and storage charges may be assessed against the cargo until the bill arrives and the party can obtain its release. Banks withhold funds to the exporter on a stale bill of lading unless the importer gives his or her bank permission.

Through: Also termed a "combined transport document" when more than one carrier is handling the shipment (such as railroad, carload, and steamship), the same bill of lading can be used by all the carriers involved. One set of bills prevents confusion, and errors may result if each carrier makes out a new set of bills at each transfer. This document shows, in addition to the information already contained in the ocean bill of lading, the place of delivery and evidence that the shipment is "taken in charge." The through bill can be issued by an operator other than the steamship line.

The ocean bill of lading must contain the following information:

1. Name of the vessel
2. Exporter's and importer's names
3. "Notify" party
4. To whom arrival notice is to be sent
5. Port of loading and discharge
6. Destination of goods

7. Description of goods
8. Forwarders' Federal Maritime Board registration numbers

Blank bills of lading are supplied by the ocean carrier or his or her agents, but are prepared by the exporter or the freight forwarder. The required number of bills varies. There can be many "original" bills of lading, but only one is needed to secure the cargo at the port of destination. Each of the endorsed, original set of bills is submitted to the bank.

Air Waybill

The air waybill provides evidence of contract of carriage, receipt of goods, and transfer of ownership to the importer. The air waybill is analogous to the straight or nonnegotiable ocean bill of lading. The air waybill is always nonnegotiable because there isn't time for a negotiable bill to travel through the mail. The shipment arrives before the bill. The air carrier must be able to deliver the cargo to the named party on the presentation of identification. In that a negotiable bill is not used in air shipments, the exporter and bank lose control of the title to the shipment. The air waybill also serves as a document for customs declaration.

SUGGESTED READINGS

Dun's Marketing Services. *Exporter's Encyclopedia*. Country profiles: communications, key contacts, trade regulations, documentation, marketing data, transportation, business travel. Annual. (800) 526–0651. $365.

Murr, Alfred. *Export/Import Traffic Management and Forwarding*. Cornell Maritime Press, 1979. Box 456 Centerville, MD 21617. $22.50.

"UNZ & Company Sourcebook: A How-to Guide for Exporters and Importers," 190 Baldwin Ave., Jersey City, N.J. 07306.

12

EXPORT LICENSING

Export controls have been in effect since July 1940. Originally formulated to conserve scarce supplies of commodities during wartime shortages, in 1949 the Cold War precipitated passage of the Export Control Act. On January 1, 1970, the Export Control Act was replaced by the Export Administration Act (EAA) of 1969, which is amended and extended periodically. The most recent amendment was signed into law by President Ronald Reagan in July of 1985 and will expire on September 30, 1989.

The EAA of 1969 mirrored the spirit of détente by encouraging peaceful trade with the U.S.S.R. and Eastern Europe. In 1972 the People's Republic of China was placed in the same category as the Soviet Union. (Prior to June 1971, China was on a total embargo list with North Korea, Vietnam, Cambodia, and Cuba.) Strategic controls continued on trade with the Soviet Bloc and China.

The EAA controls exports for three purposes. First, to restrict the export of goods and technology which would make a contribution to the military potential of any other country or combination of countries that might threaten the national security of the United States; second, to restrict the export of goods and technology where necessary to further the foreign policy of the United States or to fulfill its declared international obligations; third, to restrict the export of goods where necessary to protect the domestic economy from the excessive drain of scarce materials and to reduce the serious inflationary impact of foreign demand.

Coordination of export controls with allied countries takes place through the Coordinating Committee (COCOM) composed of all the NATO nations except Iceland but including Japan. The fifteen member committee is based in Paris. COCOM develops a common embargo list. Exceptions are granted only if all member government representatives agree. Export control authority was delegated by the President to the Secretary of Commerce and is administered by the Office of Export Administration (OEA) of the Bureau of Trade Regulations within the International Trade Administration of the U.S. Department of Commerce.

All exports leaving the United States require licensing. Most American exports are shipped out under a general license that doesn't require specific application. To export commodities on the Commodity Control List (CCL) maintained by the Commerce Department a firm must apply and receive a validated license. Until the 1985 amendment to the Export Administration Act, Commerce had sole jurisdiction in the review of license applications for free world shipments while Defense was permitted to review applications to communist countries. Under the current act, the Pentagon is authorized to review the licensing of goods and technology to 15 non-Communist nations with a time limit of 15 days to make a denial. To reduce document handling time, the Commerce Department was instructed to transmit application by computer to the Pentagon's Office of Strategic Trade.

The Customs Service assists in search and seizure at ports of entry and exit through its "Operation Exodus" program. The State Department serves principally in an advisory capacity, but has also assisted Commerce in performing overseas compliance activities. With the growth of the foreign commercial officer service, staffed by Commerce at American embassies, the State Department has taken a less active role in investigating suspected overseas violations of the Export Administration Act. Commerce conducts, outside the United States, prelicense investigations and post-shipment verifications. Commerce also has search and seizure authority, subject to guidelines set by the Attorney General.

The 1985 Act prohibits exports to foreign companies that sell to the Soviets in violation of agreed multilateral export controls. Stricter penalties were added for persons discovered selling controlled U.S. goods and technology to the Soviet Bloc.

In the area of licensing, the 1985 Act required Commerce to improve its turnaround time on license applications. Export licenses for COCOM countries are processed in about seven days: below the statutory limit of 15 days. Table 12.1 lists processing deadlines. The Commerce Department utilizes an audio response system termed "STELA" (Status Tracking Export License Applications) that automatically handles requests for status checks on export license applications using voice-generated technology.

An exporter can determine if he or she should apply for a license by following these steps:

1. Purchase a copy of *Export Administration Regulations*, U.S. Department of Commerce, International Trade Administration, annual and

TABLE 12.1 Export License Application Processing Deadlines

	Licensing—Non-COCOM Countries Issue or deny a license if it does not require outside referral.	90 days	60 days
	Licensing—Non-COCOM Countries and Outside Referral		
The new	Refer a license to another agency or department if outside position required.	30 days	20 days
legislation	Outside agency must return its rec-	30 days	20 days
contains	ommendation to Commerce.		
some 55	(If recommendation not received,		
revisions	Commerce assumes approval.)		
or additions	Maximum extension an outside agency	30 days	20 days
to the 1979	may request to provide its recom-		
law.	mendation.		
	After receipt of outside agency rec- ommendations, Commerce must issue or deny a license.	90 days	60 days
	TOTAL	180 days	120 days
	Licensing—COCOM Countries Issue or deny license for COCOM country.	N/A	15 working days*

*Commerce can request an additional 15 working days for review.

supplements, $86 for October 1, 1986 edition, or ask the librarian in government documents. To purchase, write to: Superintendent of Documents, U.S. Government Printing Office, Washington, D.C. 20402.

2. Other helpful publications available:

Export Licensing Checklist (U.S. Government Printing Office) assists exporters in obtaining export licenses for demonstration purposes in overseas trade fairs, exhibitions, and other promotional events.

Quick Reference Guide to the Export Administration Regulations (Office of Export Administration, Room 1622, ITA, U.S. Department of Commerce, Washington, D.C. 20230).

How to Fill Out the Export License Application (available from Commerce Department district offices).

Export Licensing Information and Assistance (Office of Export Administration).

3. Parts 371, 379, and 399 of the *EAR* explains whether an export can be shipped under a general license or needs a validated export license

for which the exporter must apply through EAA. Individual validated licenses are valid for 24 months.

4. Commodity groups under the Office of Export Administration's jurisdiction are grouped on the Commodity Control List (CCL) under ten general categories. See Table 12.2.

5. If a commodity doesn't fall into any of the CCL categories, it can be shipped under a general license—that is, the exporter doesn't need to apply for a license. Under the "Table of General Licenses," provided in the *EAR*, you can find the appropriate General License Symbol (usually "G-DEST"), which must be entered in Box #21 of the Shipper's Export Declaration.

6. If your product falls into one of the ten general categories of the CCL, find the CCL and explanations of how to use it—see Section 399.1 of the *Export Administration Regulations*. See Table 12.3 for a sample entry of the CCL from the *EAR*.

7. After locating the CCL entry, look for its Export Control Commodity Number (ECCN). This four-digit number must appear on the export license application. The code letter that follows the ECCN is a "country group." See Table 12.4 for "Country Groups Code Letters."

8. The "Country Groups" table in the *EAR*, (Table 12.5) places countries into categories. The President has the authority to move countries into different groupings. Consult the most recent *EAR* country group table.

9. Figure 12.1 shows an Export License. If an application is approved, a license will be sent to the exporter. There are five types of validated licenses:

1. Individual
2. Project
3. Distribution
4. Qualified general
5. Service supply

10. Figure 12.2 displays the back portion of the license on which shipments are recorded. When the license expires or shipment for which the license covers is expired, the license, with shipments recorded, is returned to the DEA.

11. Figure 12.3 shows Form ITA-6019P which is a "Request for, and Advice on, Status of Pending Application, Amendment, or Reexport Re-

Export Licensing

TABLE 12.2 Commodity Categories
(Appear as second digit for ECCN)

Group	Type of Commodities
0	Metal-working machinery
1	Chemical and petroleum equipment
2	Electrical and power-generating equipment
3	General industrial equipment
4	Transportation equipment
5	Electronics and precision instruments
6	Metals, minerals, and their manufactures
7	Chemical, metalloids, petroleum products and related materials
8	Rubber and rubber materials
9	Miscellaneous

TABLE 12.3 Sample CCL Entry

4592B	Equipment for measuring pressures to 100 Torr or less having corrosion-resistant sensing elements of nickel, nickel alloys, phosphor bronze, stainless steel, or aluminum.
	Controls for ECCN 4592B
	Unit: Report in "$ value."
	Validated License Required: Country Groups PQSTVWYZ
	GLV $ value limit: $0 for all destinations
	Processing Code: TE
	Reason for Control: National security; nuclear nonproliferation. Nuclear nonproliferation controls do not apply to those countries listed in Supp. Nos. 2 or 3 to Part 373.
	Special Licenses Available: Distribution License is available for shipments to countries listed in Supp. Nos. 2 or 3 to Part 373. No other special licenses are available.

TABLE 12.4 Country Groups for Which Validated License Is Required

Code Letters	
A	PQSTVWYZ (multilaterally controlled to all destinations)
B	PWSTVWYZ (unilaterally controlled to all destinations)
C	PQSWYZ and certain other countries
D	PQSWYZ only
E	PSWYZ
F	SZ and certain other countries
G	SZ only
I	None
M	Various (country group control level is governed by another entry on the CCL)

TABLE 12.5 Country Groups

For export control purposes, foreign countries are separated into seven country groups designated by the symbols "Q", "S", "T", "V", "W", "Y", and "Z". Listed below are the countries included in each country group. Canada is not included in any country group and is referred to by name throughout the Export Administration Regulations.

Country Group Q
Romania

Country Group S
Libya

Country Group T
North America
Northern Area:
  Greenland
  Miquelon and St. Pierre Islands
Southern Area:
  Mexico (including Cozumel and Revilla Gigedo Islands)

Central America
  Belize
  Costa Rica
  El Salvador
  Guatemala
  Honduras (including Bahia and Swan Islands)
  Nicaragua
  Panama
Bermuda and Caribbean Area:
  Bahamas
  Barbados
  Bermuda
  Dominican Republic
  French West Indies
  Haiti (including Gonave and Tortuga Islands)
  Jamaica
  Leeward and Windward Islands
  Netherlands Antilles
  Trinidad and Tobago

South America
Northern Area:
  Colombia
  French Guiana (including Inini)
  Guyana
  Surinam
  Venezuela

Western Area:
  Bolivia
  Chile
  Ecuador (including the Galapagos Islands)
  Peru

Eastern Area:
  Argentina
  Brazil
  Falkland Islands (Islas Malvinas)
  Paraguay
  Uruguay

Country Group V
All countries not included in any other country group (except Canada).

Country Group W
Hungary
Poland

Country Group Y
Albania
Bulgaria
Czechoslovakia
Estonia
German Democratic Republic (including East Berlin)
Laos
Latvia
Lithuania
Mongolian People's Republic
Union of Soviet Socialist Republics

Country Group Z
Cuba
Kampuchea
North Korea
Vietnam

Export Licensing

Form ITA-622P (REV. 4-87)	U.S. DEPARTMENT OF COMMERCE INTERNATIONAL TRADE ADMINISTRATION	Not approved unless the official validation stamp appears hereon.	LICENSE NUMBER
EXPORT **LICENSE**	Information furnished herewith is subject to the provisions of Section 12(c) of the Export Administration Act of 1979, 50 U.S.C. app. 2411(G), and its unauthorized disclosure is prohibited by law.	VALIDATION	

This License authorizes the Licensee to carry out the export transaction described on the License ("License" includes all attachments). It may not be transferred without prior written approval of the Office of Export Licensing. This License has been granted in reliance on representations made by the Licensee and others in connection with the application for export and is expressly subject to any conditions stated on the License, as well as all applicable export control laws, regulations, rules and orders. This License is subject to revision, suspension, or revocation without prior notice.

APPLICANT'S REFERENCE NO.

LICENSEE   EXPORTER'S I.D. NO.

PURCHASER   OEL USE ONLY

CONSIGNEE IN COUNTRY OF ULTIMATE DESTINATION   OEL USE ONLY

INTERMEDIATE CONSIGNEE   OEL USE ONLY

QUANTITY	DESCRIPTION OF COMMODITIES OR TECHNICAL DATA	EXPORT CONTROL COMMODITY NUMBER AND PROCESSING CODE	UNIT PRICE	TOTAL PRICE
			TOTAL	$

The Export Administration Regulations require you to take the following actions when exporting under the authority of this license.
A. Record the Export Control Commodity Number in parentheses directly below the corresponding Schedule B Number on each Shipper's Export Declaration (SED).
B. Record your License Number in the Commodity description column on each SED.
C. Place a *Destination Control Statement* on all bills of lading, airway bills, and commercial invoices.
D. Enter details of each shipment made against the license, on the reverse side of license.
E. Sign and return license to the Office of Export Licensing, P.O. Box 273, Washington, D.C. 20044, (a) when it is fully used, (b) when it has expired, or (c) when it has been determined that it will no longer be used.

Figure 12.1

quest" Check Section 370.11 of the *EAR* before requesting advice on the progress of an application.

    12. Sometimes a destination control statement is required. Check Section 386 of the *EAR*. Figure 12.4 shows Form ITA-629 which is a "Statement by Ultimate Consignee and Purchaser." This is a destination control statement that must be completed by the importer (when required). The DEA requires this form to gather information about the foreign buyer. The OEA must be certain that the shipment won't be subverted to the Soviet Union or another country where the export of that particular commodity is forbidden.

Export Licensing

RECORD OF SHIPMENTS

Each Shipment made against this Export License shall be recorded below. If more space is needed, use a continuation sheet. (See Export Administration Regulations §386.2 (d). Shipping tolerances apply only to the unshipped balance remaining on the license at the time of shipment (§386.7)

QUANTITY SHIPPED	DESCRIPTION OF COMMODITIES	DOLLAR VALUE	NAME OF EXPORTING CARRIER	POINT OF EXPORT OR POST OFFICE OF MAILING	DATE OF EXPORT	INITIALS OF PERSON MAKING ENTRY

I certify that shipments have been made under this license as indicated above. There is no material or substantive change in facts on which the license or subsequent amendments were issued.

_____   _____   _____
Signature of Licensee   Address   Date
or duly authorized agent

Figure 12.2

Export Licensing

OMB No. 0625—0050

FORM ITA-6019P
(REV. 1-84)

U.S. DEPARTMENT OF COMMERCE
INTERNATIONAL TRADE ADMINISTRATION

**REQUEST FOR, AND ADVICE ON, STATUS OF PENDING
APPLICATION, AMENDMENT, OR REEXPORT REQUEST**

This report is authorized by law (50 U.S.C. app. 2401 et seq.; 15 C.F.R. 370.11). While you are not required to respond to this form, your desire to secure status information necessitates our obtaining certain basic information from you so that we can more adequately respond to your request.

INSTRUCTIONS: This page is to be filled out by applicant or applicant's agent. Please submit, in duplicate, to Office of Export Administration, Exporters' Service Staff, P.O. Box 273, U.S. Department of Commerce, Washington, D.C. 20044. One copy will be returned with the appropriate advice noted on the reverse side.

Requesters should allow the period of time set forth in §370.11 of the Export Administration Regulations to expire before requesting advice on progress of an application, amendment, or reexport request. No action will be taken on earlier requests, unless an emergency exists and is explained. A status request should relate to only one application, amendment, or reexport request.

1. Firm Name

Name and Telephone No. of Person to Contact

Address
(Street,
City,
State,
ZIP Code)

2. Date

3. Type of Request	4. Request Date	5. Requestor's Ref. No.	6. Case No. *(If known)*
☐ Application ☐ Reexport Request ☐ Amendment ☐ Other *(Specify)*			

7. Country of Ultimate Destination	8. Name of Ultimate Consignee

9. Commodity Description

10. Export Control Commodity No.	11. Exporter's I.D. No. *(If known)*	12. Processing Code	13. Dollar Value

14. Applicant's Signature	15. Signature and Address of Authorized Agent *(If different from items 1 and 11)*

16. Remarks

(If more space is needed, please use reverse side.)

Information furnished herewith is subject to the provisions of Section 12(c) of the Export Administration Act of 1979, 50 U.S.C. app. 2411(c), and its unauthorized disclosure is prohibited by law.

USCOMM-DC 84-20580

Figure 12.3

Export Licensing

In accordance with the processing schedule prescribed in the Export Administration Act of 1979 (Section 10), your

application Case No. _____ dated _____ is currently:

☐ Undergoing review for final decision in the Office of Export Administration (OEA) and, this review should be completed within 90 days of its date of receipt by OEA.

☐ Undergoing review in OEA prior to being referred to one or more of the agencies from which we seek advice and information. Referral to such agencies must be made within 30 days after receipt of the application by OEA.

☐ Undergoing review by one or more of the government agencies from which OEA seeks advice and information. This review should be completed within a maximum of 60 days after referral by OEA. OEA referral was made on _____.

☐ Undergoing additional review and consultation with OEA and other agencies to resolve divergent recommendations on appropriate U.S. Government action on the application. Decision must be reached within 180 days of date of receipt by OEA of the application.

☐ Undergoing multilateral review for approval as an exception to the general embargo exercised over this equipment by the International Control Organization (COCOM). The U.S. Government believes this exception is merited but is obligated to obtain the concurrence of COCOM with this judgement.

☐ Undergoing review by COCOM. The subject case was submitted to COCOM on _____. COCOM review is generally completed within 60 days after a case is referred to it. You will be informed by OEA if your case is delayed beyond 60 days.

☐ In the mail. Your application was validated and mailed to you on _____.

16. Remarks (continued)

17. Exporters' Service Staff

18. Date

Figure 12.3 *(cont.)*

Export Licensing

FORM ITA-629P (REV. 6-84)	U.S. DEPARTMENT OF COMMERCE INTERNATIONAL TRADE ADMINISTRATION

STATEMENT BY ULTIMATE CONSIGNEE AND PURCHASER

GENERAL INSTRUCTIONS – This form must be submitted by the importer (ultimate consignee shown in Item 1) and the overseas buyer or purchaser, to the U.S. exporter or seller with whom the order for the commodities described in Item 3 is placed. This completed statement will be submitted in support of one or more export license applications to the U.S. Department of Commerce. **All items on this form must be completed.** Where the information required is unknown or the item does not apply, write in the appropriate words "UNKNOWN" or "NOT APPLICABLE." If more space is needed, attach an additional copy of this form or sheet of paper signed as in Item 8. Submit form within 180 days from latest date in Item 8. Information furnished herewith is subject to the provisions of Section 12(c) of the Export Administration Act of 1979, 50 USC app. 2411(c), and its unauthorized disclosure is prohibited by law.

1. Ultimate consignee name and address

Name

Street and number

City and Country

Reference *(if desired)*

2. Request *(Check one)*

a. ☐ We request that this statement be considered a part of the application for export license filed by

_____
U.S. exporter or U.S. person with whom we have placed our order (order party)

for export to us of the commodities described in item 3.

b. ☐ We request that this statement be considered a part of every application for export license filed by

_____
U.S. exporter or U.S. person with whom we have placed or may place our order (order party)

for export to us of the type of commodities described in this statement, during the period ending June 30 of the

second year after the signing of this form, or on _____

3. Commodities

We have placed or may place orders with the person or firm named in Item 2 for the commodities indicated below:

COMMODITY DESCRIPTION	*(Fill in only if 2a is checked)*	
	QUANTITY	VALUE

4. Disposition or use of commodities by ultimate consignee named in Item 1 *(Check and complete the appropriate box(es))*

We certify that the commodity(ies) listed in Item 3:

a. ☐ Will be used by us (as capital equipment) in the form in which received in a manufacturing process in the country named in Item 1 and will not be reexported or incorporated into an end product.

b. ☐ Will be processed or incorporated by us into the following product(s) _____
(Specify)

to be manufactured in the country named in Item 1 for distribution in _____
(Name

of country or countries)

c. ☐ Will be resold by us in the form in which received in the country named in Item 1 for use or consumption therein.

The specific end-use by my customer will be _____
(Specify, if known)

d. ☐ Will be reexported by us in the form in which received to _____
(Name of country(ies))

e. ☐ Other *(Describe fully)* _____

NOTE: If Item (d) is checked, acceptance of this form by the Office of Export Administration as a supporting document for license applications shall not be construed as an authorization to reexport the commodities to which the form applies unless specific approval has been obtained from the Office of Export Administration for such reexport.

(Reproduction of this form is permissible, providing that content, format, size and color of paper are the same)

Please continue form and sign certification on reverse side.

Figure 12.4

159

Export Licensing

5. Nature of business of ultimate consignee named in Item 1 and his relationship with U.S. exporter named in Item 2.

a. The nature of our usual business is _____
(Broker, distributor, fabricator, manufacturer, wholesaler, retailer, etc.)

b. Our business relationship with the U.S. exporter is _____
(Contractual, franchise, exclusive distributor, distributor,

wholesaler, continuing and regular individual transaction business, etc.)
and we have had this business relationship for _____ years.

6. Additional information _(Any other material facts which will be of value considering applications for licenses covered by this statement.)_

7. Assistance in preparing statement _(Names of persons other than employees of consignee or purchaser who assisted in the preparation of this statement.)_

8. CERTIFICATION OF ULTIMATE CONSIGNEE AND PURCHASER (This item is to be signed by the ultimate consignee shown in Item 1 and by the purchaser where the latter is not the same as the ultimate consignee. Where the ultimate consignee is unknown, this item should be signed by the purchaser.)

We certify that all of the facts contained in this statement are true and correct to the best of our knowledge and belief and we do not know of any additional facts which are inconsistent with the above statement. We shall promptly send a supplemental statement to the person named in Item 2, disclosing any change of facts or intentions set forth in this statement which occurs after the statement has been prepared and forwarded. Except as specifically authorized by the U.S. Export Administration Regulations, or by prior written approval of the U.S. Department of Commerce, we will not reexport, resell, or otherwise dispose of any commodities listed in Item 3 above: (1) to any country not approved for export as brought to our attention by means of a bill of lading, commercial invoice, or any other means; or (2) to any person if there is reason to believe that it will result directly or indirectly, in disposition of the commodities contrary to the representations made in this statement or contrary to U.S. Export Administration Regulations.

Ultimate Consignee

Signature
in ink _____
(Signature of official of ultimate consignee)

Type or
print _____
(Name and title of official of ultimate consignee)

Date _____

Purchaser

Signature
in ink _____
(Signature of official of purchaser firm)

Type or
print _____
(Name and title of official of purchaser firm)

Type or
print _____
(Name of purchaser firm)

Date _____

9. CERTIFICATION FOR USE OF U.S. EXPORTER in certifying that any correction, addition, or alteration on this form was made prior to the signing by the ultimate consignee and purchaser in Item 8.

We certify that no corrections, additions, or alterations were made on this form by us after the form was signed by the (ultimate consignee) (purchaser).

Type or
print _____
(Name of exporter firm)

_____
(Date signed)

Sign here
in ink _____
(Signature of person authorized to certify for exporter)

Type or
print _____
(Name and title of person signing this document)

The making of any false statement, the concealment of any material fact, or failure to file required information may result in denial of participation in U.S. exports. Notarial or governmental certification is not required.

FORM ITA-629P (Rev. 6-84)   USCOMM-DC 84-21766

Figure 12.4 _(cont.)_

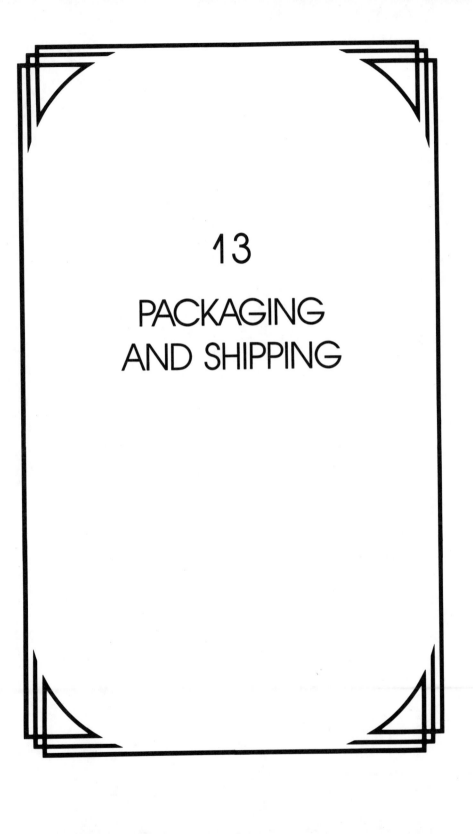

13

PACKAGING
AND SHIPPING

Shipping documents accompany cargo. To illustrate this process, let's trace a truck shipment to an ocean pier. The exporter prepares an inland bill of lading showing the movement of cargo to the pier. Copies of the bill of lading and packing list are sent to the exporter's forwarder at the port of exportation. The exporter marks the cargo to show gross and net weights, cubic measurement, foreign destination, shipping marks, and country of origin. The motor carrier advises the exporter's forwarder of the cargo's arrival at the port. The forwarder communicates the name of the vessel, sailing date, pier number and location, and any special requirements particular to the cargo or pier to the motor carrier. The motor carrier gets a dock receipt from the forwarder to verify that the shipment is delivered. After the driver unloads the truck at the pier, he or she obtains a signed copy of the dock receipt. The pier operator retains the original dock receipt, forwarding it to the steamship company. The steamship company issues a bill of lading and sends it to the exporter's forwarder.

Yet even before the cargo was picked up at the factory's loading dock, many questions about its shipment had to be resolved. Should the cargo be shipped by air or ocean? What type of export packing should be selected? What identification marks should be placed outside? Who will repackage the cargo if Customs decides to inspect it? Who bears the cost of repackaging?

By Air or Sea

Air freight is costly but successful marketing of your product may depend on speedy delivery. If an item is perishable or seasonable—for example, food or fashion—ocean shipment is not a feasible alternative. But for other products the decision is made less easily. You must calculate the direct and hidden costs of air versus ocean freight.

Direct costs can be calculated by considering differences in insurance (air insurance is cheaper), inland transportation to seaport/airport, freight forwarder's fees, wharfage/airport terminal charges, actual cost of ocean/air freight. Unloading charges, customs duties, and inland transportation from seaport/airport are costs to consider.

Hidden costs are more difficult to calculate than direct costs, yet they are equally important to consider in developing profit projections:

1. Ocean freight is slow and less reliable than air freight. You may lose sales because the shipment arrives late. An entire season may be lost. Many countries have laws that impose penalties on manufacturers, both foreign and domestic, that do not deliver the merchandise when promised.

2. Each day cargo is in transit the exporter is losing money, unless he or she was paid cash in advance. The sooner the importer receives the cargo, the sooner the exporter receives payment.

3. Distributors dislike carrying the huge inventories necessary when ocean freight is involved. It's capital tied up in the warehouse that could be profitably invested in other business activities. When a distributor maintains large inventories, he or she always runs the risk of holding obsolete products. No distributor wants to mark down products in order to get them to move. Pilferage and damage that result from shifting the merchandise around is another cost to the distributor. If the importer's currency appreciates next to the dollar and the price of the import declines, then the distributor is stuck with merchandise that cost him or her more than the current price, and the distributor won't be able to realize the profit he or she had expected.

Export Packing

The four crucial considerations for export packing are: avoid breakage, minimize weight, keep moisture out, and prevent pilferage. The characteristics of the product, whether it is being shipped by air or sea, and the destination (climate, length and conditions of inland transportation) will determine the materials chosen to protect the cargo. Ocean freight takes a beating. It might be dragged, slung, rolled, pushed, dropped, buried at the bottom of a stack of cargo, or tossed around in rough weather. Shipping to the tropics requires protection from excessive humidity, while shipping to extremely cold climates requires protection from freezing. Roads may be bumpy and the travel time long in the importer's country. Cargo that changes hands many times needs extra protection.

There are many different ways to pack a product for export sale:

1. Fiberboard box
2. Nailed wood box
3. Crates
4. Wirebound box and crate
5. Cleated plywood box
6. Steel drum
7. Fiber drum
8. Barrel/cask/keg
9. Multiwall shipping sack
10. Bale

Ways to Combine Cargo

Unitize/Palletize

The ocean terminal needs to load the ship quickly but safely. Loading boxes, crates, bales, and other cargo individually involves high labor costs. Unitized and palletized shipments are handled easily by equipment such as forklifts and crane trucks. Less handling of packages decreases the occurrence of breakage. Some products are too bulky to be stuffed into any container, lending themselves naturally to unitizing. Pallets are very suitable for bagged goods because palletization eliminates the worry of the bags breaking open or getting wet.

Unitized cargo is secured together and placed on skids so that a forklift can be slid underneath. Unitizing is often done before the shipment arrives at the terminal (at the exporter's or forwarder's facilities). Palletized loads work on the same principle but are secured to pallets. Waterproof plastic shrink wrap often encases the entire load. The unitized/palletized shipment isn't broken up until it's delivered to the importer. Each piece of the unit must be marked separately to prevent loss once the unit is broken up.

Containerization

Since the mid-1960s when steamships began to containerize, the cost of shipping has decreased substantially. Most containers are made of aluminum because it is lightweight, durable, and rustproof. Containers are watertight and weatherproof. Containers fit many needs—dry, bulk liquid, dry bulk, and refrigerated. "Door-to-door" service is offered because trains or trucks can haul the containers that the exporter stuffs directly to the port. If the exporter's shipment is too small to fill a container, a forwarder will consolidate shipments and earn a cost reduction. If you export through an export management company (EMC), the company also may have enough business to consolidate shipments in a single container. Another advantage of consolidation is that a shipment isn't spread all over the hold. The container is sealed and locked, therefore pilferage, loss, and damage are reduced drastically.

Yet containerization doesn't eliminate all shipping problems. Documents are normally prepared before the container is stuffed. But what if, upon stuffing the container, it turns out that the forwarder or shipping department has too much cargo to put into one container, but not enough to fill another? You will have to ship the excess loose or get the extra cargo stuffed at the pier with other loose cargo. Did the packing department bother to make the necessary changes in the documents? The "checker" who keeps a record of what is stuffed at the pier might have left a box out or marked it in the wrong container. A shipment may be in the container indicated, but it may have been stuffed into another in which case the importer is going to have a lot of trouble locating his or her cargo. The goods may be sitting in a warehouse and the terminal will stick the importer with storage for not picking up the cargo in a timely fashion, although the importer didn't know where the cargo was located. Any problem the importer faces will ultimately reflect on the exporter's reliability and may cost the exporter customers.

Shipping Marks

Identification: The importer needs to identify the shipment. He or she will be able to recognize the marks from the facsimile provided in the commercial invoice and other documents. Always use "blind" marks (unless prohibited by local laws). A well known product or tradename is a target for pilferage. Provide neither the exporter's nor importer's name; these may give a clue to the contents. The country of origin must appear on the package.

Figure 13.1

Cautionary: There are several internationally recognized symbols (displayed in Figure 13.1). Such symbols should be placed on three faces of the package. If you use cautionary wording such as "fragile," stencil it in with waterproof ink in both English and the importer's language. The net and gross weights of the package should also be marked on the container.

14

MAJOR PRIVATE AND GOVERNMENT ACTORS

Customhouse Broker

A U.S. customhouse broker must be licensed by U.S. Customs to act as the importer's agent. A customhouse broker provides three major services for an importer:

1. Prepares and files necessary custom entries
2. Arranges for payments of duties
3. Arranges for the release of the goods in customs custody

Getting through Customs is a complicated matter, especially if the importer isn't located near one of the Customs ports of entry listed in the appendix. A Customs officer, at his or her discretion, can open a package for inspection. It is the importer's responsibility to reseal the package for shipment. A customhouse broker will take care of these details for his or her clients.

Customs regulations and tariffs change. A customhouse broker is in a better position to stay informed. Customs also has the right to reconstruct entries after the fact, which can be a few years after the shipment. A broker can provide Customs with the proper information. Before choosing a broker, ask for references and check his or her credit rating. Ask for an itemized schedule of charges: Brokers are very competitive; shopping around is a good idea. In addition, the importer should be certain that the broker has facilities for securing expensive or fragile cargo.

U.S. Customs Service

The U.S. Customs Service is an agency of the U.S. Treasury. Its primary responsibility is to administer the Tariff Act of 1930, as amended. Customs appraises imports, collects duties, taxes, and fees on imported goods, enforces customs and related laws, and administers certain navigation laws and treaties. Customs also works as an enforcement agency. It combats smuggling of contraband goods into the United States. Through its "Operation Exodus" program, Customs is authorized to assist the Commerce Department in seizing illegal exports.

International Trade Commission

Formerly known as the "Tariff Commission," the ITC operates under some 22 federal laws. It acts as an information agency for Congress and the President. A better known function of the ITC is that of a judge on import rulings, determining whether foreign competition is unfairly competing and damaging domestic manufacturers. Domestic manufacturers file complaints with the ITC and the ITC must decide if these industries deserve protection. Over the past years complaints have been filed by companies in industries such as pasta, tuna, copper, shoes, steel, flatware, apparel, and aircraft.

An industry or manufacturer usually cites dumping, unfair subsidies, or infringement of copyrights, trademarks, or patents as the basis for filing a complaint with the ITC. Decisions made by the ITC can be appealed to the Court of International Trade in New York.

SUGGESTED READINGS

Guide to International Air Freight Shipping, $17.50.

Guide to International Ocean Freight Shipping, $34.50. International Trade Institute, 5055 N. Main St., Dayton, Ohio, 45415.

15

MARKETING
CONSIDERATIONS

In Chapter Eight we learned that product, promotion, price, and distribution are the major elements of the marketing mix. This chapter evaluates your import potential within a similar framework.

Product

Let's look at some of the alternative ways to gather information about foreign suppliers or manufacturers.

1. *Contact foreign consulates.* A vital part of a consulate's job is to increase sales of its country's exports to the United States. Consulates provide updated information about manufacturers and distributors in their countries that are looking for American buyers. In addition to consulates, many countries maintain special foreign trade promotion offices. Check with the local consulate for information on availability.

2. *Read trade directories.* These are annually updated compilations of foreign manufacturers and distributors. These directories can be found in libraries. Purchasing them is costly, running on the average of $100. The section on Suggested Readings at the end of this chapter provides names of some helpful directories.

3. *Study trade journals.* Manufacturers and suppliers advertise products.

4. *Combine an overseas vacation with a buyer search.* Search for products that will complement current product lines. It's better to make contact with the manufacturer or supplier while overseas. If not, names, addresses, and contact persons should be carefully recorded so that cor-

respondence can begin upon return to the United States. Similarly, ask friends and business associates if they saw or purchased unique products on their overseas trips.

5. *Look for special initiatives.* Updated import opportunities are made available for initiatives such as the current "Caribbean Basin Initiative," sponsored by the U.S. Department of Commerce International Trade Administration. For instance, the Caribbean Basin Business Information Center of Commerce's International Trade Administration publishes the "Caribbean Basin Initiative Business Bulletin" which contains investment and import/export business opportunities with Caribbean and Central American countries. See Figure 15.1 for a sample listing.

Another special initiative is the recent free trade area created between the United States and Israel. Further details on the CBI and U.S.-Israeli free trade agreement appear later in this chapter.

6. *Talk to freight forwarders, banks, and other service groups with international contacts.* Foreign freight forwarders and banks have contacts throughout the world. They may know of foreign manufacturers and distributors looking for American buyers.

Contacting Foreign Suppliers

Mail queries on company letterhead in the language of the supplier. If you already have an established distribution network or complementary products, provide details in this letter. C.I.F. terms are most appropriate (Chapter Eight). If the foreign supplier delivers an F.O.B. quote, contact a foreign freight forwarder for assistance in finding out the cost of getting the product to the United States. Request samples. If samples are unavailable or are inappropriate for the product, request a catalog or flyer.

Price

The product may be suitable, but the import price must be considered carefully. There are many factors to evaluate, but let's begin with the effects of tariffs and quotas. All goods imported into the United States are subject to duty or duty-free entry. Duties are assessed in three different ways:

1. *Ad valorem* is the rate most frequently applied. It is a percentage of the appraised value of the merchandise (usually the price on the commercial invoice—the price the importer paid for the goods).

Marketing Considerations

Import Opportunities for U.S. Companies

*(SIC 01) *Ornamental Plants* Humberto Gonzalez, President; Incomer, S.A.; Apartado 8012; 1000 San Jose, COSTA RICA. Phone: (506) 25-5652. Telex: 2411 AA. U. C. R.

*(SIC 01) *Fresh Flowers—Roses, Carnations, Chrysanthemums* Mr. Enrique Soler G.; Exporflor De Cartago, S.A.; Apartado 7-0930; 1000 San Jose, COSTA RICA. Phone: (506) 23-4455, 51-3171. Telex: 8039 AGFLOR.

(SIC 01) *Ornamental Plants, Medicinal Plants* Mr. Billy Finger; Ultramar Exportaciones Biologicas; P.O. Box 257-2120; San Francisco Guadalupe; San Jose, COSTA RICA. Phone: (506) 33-1561. Telex: 2913 CE CQ TEX.

*(SIC 20) *Dried Bananas* Can supply 10 tons per month. In May available supply will increase to 35 tons per month. Edgar Golcher, General Manager; Banavit Dried Fruit Co., Ltd.; P.O. Box 5212; 1000 San Jose, COSTA RICA. Phone: (506) 23-13-04. Cable: BANAVIT.

*(SIC 20) *Sesame Seed* Pablo Ernesto Aviles; Aviles Vela, S.A. De C.V.; 23 Calle Oriente No. 119; Apartado Postal 767; San Salvador, EL SALVADOR, C.A. Phone: (503) 26-5000. Telex: 23334.

*(SIC 20) *Fresh Fruits and Vegetables* Seeks U.S. importers especially in New York and Miami. Chester Grant, Managing Director; Golden Edge Farm Co.; Golden Spring; Stony Hill P.O.; St. Andrew, JAMAICA, W.I.

*(SIC 20) *Fruits—Honey Dew Melons, Strawberries* Plans to expand and produce cauliflower, broccoli and asparagus for export during 1986. Ilse Eichler G.; Corporacion Agricola Ganadera; Del Guanacaste, S.A.; Apartado 1917; 1000 San Jose, COSTA RICA. Phone: (506) 33-5444. Telex: 3293 ADCOSA.

*(SIC 20) *Pre-Cooked Corn Flour, Corn Meal* Sammy Abufele, Manager; Industrias Molineras, S.A.; Apartado Postal No. 683; San Pedro Sula, Cortes, HONDURAS. Phone: (504) 531038. Cable: IMSA. Telex: 5564 HO.

*(SIC 20) *Dried Herbs and Spices* Company has available for immediate delivery 1500 pounds of basil. J. O'Hannes Adriaanes; Agrosol, S.A.; Edificio Antonio Barletta, 3ER Piso; Ave. J.F. Kennedy; Santo Domingo, DOMINICAN REPUBLIC. Phone: (809) 565-5240. Cable: ANBAR.

(SIC 20) *Spices and Herbs* Mr. Billy Finger; Ultramar Exportaciones Biologicas; P.O. Box 257-2120; San Francisco Guadalupe; San Jose, COSTA RICA. Phone: (506) 33-1561. Telex: 2913 CE CO TEX.

(SIC 20) *Spices—Achiote, Turmeric, Oregano and Citronella Oil* Federico Alvarez; P.O. Box 1255; Tegucigalpa, D.C. HONDURAS. Phone: (504) 32-7785, 22-3100. Telex: 1103 BANCADIE.

(SIC 20) *Rum and Vodka* Current production is 10,000 cases per week. Can increase production. Norma Isabel Martinez, General Manager; Destileria Sula; 10 Avenida 18-19 Calle S.E.; Barrio Las Palmas; San Pedro Sula Cortes, HONDURAS. Phone: (504) 53-1296.

*(SIC 21) *Cigars* Company has been producing fine cigars since 1909. Tabaqueria Carbonell; Roberto Pastoriza No. 204; Santo Domingo, DOMINICAN REPUBLIC. Phone: (809) 566-3193. Telex: RCA 3264399/ITT 3460632.

Figure 15.1

2. *Specific* rates are specified per unit or weight or other quantity such as dozen.

3. *Compound* rates combine both the ad val. and specific rates, for example, $.05/pound + 11% ad val.

Other duties may be placed on the import as well. The U.S. applies *countervailing* and *antidumping* duties under certain circumstances. If it is believed the foreign manufacturer receives subsidies of any kind (grants, free land, tax holidays, low-interest loans) and the U.S. International Trade Commission determines that American manufacturers are "materially injured, or threatened with material injury," the U.S. Department of Commerce issues a countervailing duty order. The Commerce Department estimates what the price of the foreign import would have been if it hadn't received an unfair subsidy from its government. The countervailing duty will be the difference between the price without subsidies and the price with subsidies. As one can imagine, it isn't an easy amount to determine. The countervailing duty is often higher than the actual subsidy benefits.

Antidumping duties are placed on imports in much the same way as countervailing duties. To determine if the merchandise is less than "fair value," the net, F.O.B. factory price to the U.S. importer is compared with the net, F.O.B. factory price to the purchaser in the home market.

An import *quota* is a quantity control on imported merchandise. Quotas are applied for specific periods of time. "Tariff-rate quotas" allow a specified amount of the product to enter at a lower duty for a given period. Quantities entered in *excess* of that quota can still be entered, but face a higher duty. "Absolute quotas" aren't tied to duty rates. After the specified amount of goods have entered, no more imports are permitted.

Finding Information about Quotas and Tariffs

If you import a wide range of products, it is a good idea to buy *Tariff Schedules of the United States Annotated* (TSUSA). The price (1987) is $46 for first class mailing. This volume is used to classify imported merchandise for rates of duty and statistical purposes. The price includes supplements for the subscription year. The TSUSA is made available for sale through the Superintendent of Documents, Government Printing Office, Washington, D.C. 20402. A local library, if it is a government depository, should have the current TSUSA. The privately published *Customhouse Guide* also contains the TSUSA as well as customs regulations and addresses of brokers and other members of the trading community. Let's review how the TSUSA works:

1. Look through the contents at the beginning of the TSUSA to find the product. (Contents from the 1987 TSUSA is shown in Figure 15.2).
2. Let's assume that we would like to import some tapestries. Textile products appear in Schedule 3, while "Tapestries, lines, and other furnishings" can be found in Part 5, Section C.
3. Figure 15.3 contains tapestry rates from the TSUSA. There are three columns: 1, Special, and 2. These columns represent special country groupings. The "General Headnotes and Rules of Interpretation," (Figure 15.4) which follows the sample tapestry page shown in Figure 15.3, explains how to ascertain which column the country from which you are importing belongs. Let's review this information, with the caveat that these headnotes are subject to change and should be checked annually. The rationale behind these three columns falls under the *Most Favored Nations* (MFN) provisions of the General Agreement on Tariffs and Trade as well as the *Generalized System of Preferences* (GSP) and similar provisions (Caribbean Basin Initiative and U.S.-Israel Free Trade Area).

Column 1:   These rates are applied to countries with MFN status, that is, Canada, the other advanced industrial democracies, and all other countries that are signatories to the GATT.

Column 2:   Column 2 rates are applied to imports from communist countries. The 1986 headnotes on page 186 indicates that the following countries are classified under Column 2: Albania, Bulgaria, Cuba, Czechoslovakia, Estonia, German Democratic Republic and East Berlin, Indochina, North Korea, Kurile Islands, Latvia, Lithuania, Outer Mongolia, Poland, Southern Sakhalin, Tanna Tuva, and the U.S.S.R.

Note: Not all communist countries get the unfavorable tariff treatment of Column 2. Conspicuous absences are China, Romania, Yugoslavia, and Hungary. China and Hungary fall under MFN, Column 1 status, while Romania and Yugoslavia are classified in the special column. Customs doesn't decide in which category a country will be placed. It merely enforces these foreign policy decisions made by the President through the Commerce and State Departments.

Special: In the "General Headnotes" on page 186, the four-way classification of the special column appears: GSP (A), LDDC (D), Caribbean Basin (E), and the U.S.-Israel Free Trade Area (I). If the Special column is blank, the rate of duty is Column 1 applies.

**TARIFF SCHEDULES OF THE UNITED STATES
ANNOTATED (1987)**

VII

Figure 15.2

Figure 15.2   (*cont.*)

The GSP was provided for in the Trade Act of 1974 and was extended to July 4, 1993 in the Trade and Tariff Act of 1984. It was first legislated as a recognition of the legitimacy of demands by poor countries for more favorable access to American markets than those enjoyed by advanced economies. Figure 15.5 contains some data on GSP imports in 1983. GSP countries are listed under "A" on pages 189 and 190 of the headnotes.

The GSP countries are further subdivided by "A" and "A*." Pages 191–193 of the headnotes list countries and products that are placed under "A*," which is an indication that they are not eligible for special treatment for the particular commodity listed. A brief look at the list illustrates the rationale behind "A*." These countries enjoy large markets for many of their products in the United States and no longer need special treatment, that is, many of their exports are competitive with American products.

One important change in the GSP legislated by the Trade and Tariff Act of 1984 drops a country from GSP eligibility if its GNP per capita income exceeds $8500 (over a two-year phase-out period), therefore the importer must monitor GSP changes.

Item	Stat. Suffix	Articles	Units of Quantity	Rates of Duty			
				1	Special		2
		Subpart C.—Tapestries, Linens, and Other Furnishings					
		Subpart C headnote:					
		1. For the purposes of this subpart, the term "furnishings" means curtains and drapes, including panels and valances; towels, napkins, tablecloths, mats, scarves, runners, doilies, centerpieces, antimacassars, and furniture slipcovers; and like furnishings; all the foregoing, of textile materials, and not specially provided for.					
		Tapestries, including hand-worked petit-point and other needle-point tapestries, all the foregoing of textile materials:					
364.05	00	Gobelin and other hand-woven tapestries fit only for use as wall hangings, and valued over $20 per square foot	Sq. yd..	Free			Free
		Other:					
		Of vegetable fibers:					
		Jacquard-figured:					
		Not pile construction:					
364.07	00	Of cotton..............(320)	Sq. yd.v Lb.	7.2% ad val.	4.3% ad val.(l)		55% ad val.

Item		Description	Unit			
364.09	00	Of vegetable fibers, except cotton	Sq. yd..	7.2% ad val.	Free (A,E*). 4.3% ad val.(I)	55% ad val.
		Pile construction:				
364.13	00	Of cotton................(369)	Sq. yd.v Lb.	7.2% ad val.	4.3% ad val.(I)	40% ad val.
364.14	00	Of vegetable fibers, except cotton................	Sq. yd..	7.2% ad val.	Free (A,E*) 4.3% ad val.(I)	40% ad val.
		Other:				
364.16	00	Certified hand-loomed and folklore products and articles of cotton................(369)	Sq. yd..	7.2% ad val.	Free (E*) 4.3% ad val.(I)	40% ad val.
364.18	00	Other................	Sq. yd..	7.2% ad val.	Free (A,E*) 4.3% ad val.(I)	40% ad val.
		Of wool:				
		Valued not over $2 per				
364.20	00	pound ....(411)	Sq. yd.v Lb.	5¢ per lb. + 9% ad val.	3¢ per lb. + 5.4% ad val.(I)	50¢ per lb. + 50% ad val.
		Valued over $2 per pound:				
364.21	00	Certified hand-loomed and folklore products	Sq. yd.v Lb.	3.5% ad val.	Free (A,E*) 2.1% ad val.(I)	64.5% ad val.
364.23	00	Other................(411)	Sq. yd.v Lb.	3.5% ad val.	Free (I)	64.5% ad val.

Figure 15.3

1. Tariff Treatment of Imported Articles. All articles imported into the customs territory of the United States from outside thereof are subject to duty or exempt therefrom as prescribed in general headnote 3.

2. Customs Territory of the United States. The term "customs territory of the United States," as used in the schedules, includes only the States, the District of Columbia, and Puerto Rico.

3. Rates of Duty. The rates of duty in the "Rates of Duty" columns numbered 1 and 2 and the column designated Special of the schedules apply to articles imported into the customs territory of the United States as hereinafter provided in this headnote:

(a) Products of Insular Possessions.
(i) Except as provided in headnote 6 of subpart E of part 2 of schedule 7, and except as provided in headnote 3 of subpart A of part 7 of schedule 7, articles imported from insular possessions of the United States which are outside the customs territory of the United States are subject to the rates of duty set forth in column numbered 1 of the schedules, except that all such articles the growth or product of any such possession, or manufactured or produced in any such possession from materials the growth, product, or manufacture of any such possession or of the customs territory of the United States, or of both, which do not contain foreign materials

United States shall receive duty treatment no less favorable than the treatment afforded such articles imported from a beneficiary developing country under title V of such Act.

(iv) Subject to the provisions in section 213 of the Caribbean Basin Economic Recovery Act, articles which are imported from insular possessions of the United States shall receive duty treatment no less favorable than the treatment afforded such articles when they are imported from a beneficiary country under such Act.

(b) Products of Cuba. Products of Cuba imported into the customs territory of the United States, whether imported directly or indirectly, are subject to the rates of duty set forth in column numbered 1 of the schedules. Preferential rates of duty for such products apply only as shown in the said column 1.[a]

(c) Products of Canada
(i) Products of Canada imported into the customs territory of the United States, whether imported directly or indirectly, are subject to the rates of duty set forth in column numbered 1 of the schedules. The rates of duty for a Canadian article, as defined in subdivision (e)(ii) of this headnote, apply only as shown in the said column numbered 1.

(ii) The term "Canadian article," as used in the schedules, means an article which is the product of Canada, but does not include any article produced with the use of materials imported into Canada which are to the value of more than 70 percent of their total value (or more than 50 percent of their total value with respect to articles described in section 213(b) of the Caribbean Basin Economic Recovery Act), coming to the customs territory of the United States directly from any such possession, and all articles previously imported into the customs territory of the United States with payment of all applicable duties and taxes imposed upon or by reason of importation whch were shipped from the United States, without remission, refund, or drawback of such duties or taxes, directly to the possession from which they are being returned by direct shipment, are exempt from duty.

(ii) In determining whether an article produced or manufactured in any such insular possession contains foreign materials to the value of more than 70 percent, no material shall be considered foreign which either—

(A) at the time such article is entered, or

(B) at the time such material is imported into the insular possession,

may be imported into the customs territory from a foreign country, other than Cuba or the Philippine Republic, and entered free of duty; except that no article containing material to which (B) of this subdivision applies shall be exempt from duty under subdivision (i) unless adequate documentation is supplied to show that the material has been incorporated into such article during the 18-month period after the date on which such material is imported into the insular possession.

(iii) Subject to the limitations imposed under section 503(b) and 504(c) of the Trade Act of 1974, articles designated eligible articles under section 503 of such Act which are imported from an insular possession of the

products of any foreign country (except materials produced within the customs territory of the United States), if the aggregate value of such imported materials when landed at the Canadian port of entry (that is, the actual purchase price, or, if not purchased, the export value, of such materials, plus, if not included therein, the cost of transporting such materials to Canada but exclusive of any landing cost and Canadian duty) was—

(A) with regard to any motor vehicle or automobile truck tractor entered on or before December 31, 1967, more than 60 percent of the appraised value of the article imported into the customs territory of the United States; and

(B) with regard to any other article (including any motor vehicle or automobile truck tractor entered after December 31, 1967), more than 50 percent of the appraised value of the article imported into the customs territory of the United States.

(d) Products of Communist Countries. Notwithstanding any of the foregoing provisions of this headnote, the rates of duty shown in column numbered 2 shall apply to products, whether imported directly or indirectly, of the following countries and areas pursuant to section 401 of the Tariff Classification Act of 1962, to section 231 or 257(e)(2) of the Trade Expansion Act of 1962, or to action

ªBy virtue of section 401 of the Tariff Classification Act of 1962, the application to products of Cuba of either a preferential or other reduced rate of duty in column 1 is suspended. See general headnote 3(f), infra.

Figure 15.4

185

taken by the President thereunder or pursuant to Presidential Proclamation 4991, dated October 27, 1982:[a]

Afghanistan
Albania
Bulgaria
Cuba[b]
Czechoslovakia
Estonia
German Democratic Republic and East Berlin
Indochina (any part of Cambodia, Laos, or Vietnam which may be under Communist domination or control)
Korea (any part of which may be under Communist domination or control)
Kurile Islands
Latvia
Lithuania
Outer Mongolia
Polish People's Republic
Southern Sakhalin
Tanna Tuva
Union of Soviet Socialist Republics and the area in East Prussia under the provisional administration of the Union of Soviet Socialist Republics.

(e) Products Eligible for Special Tariff Treatment.

(i) The "Special" column reflects rates of duty available under one or more special tariff treatment

(2) which is otherwise eligible for column 1 rates of duty; and

(C) it has satisfied all other requirements for eligibility for such program or programs.

(ii) Programs under which special tariff treatment may be provided to imported articles, and the corresponding symbols for such programs as they are indicated in the "Special" column, are as follows:

Generalized System of
Preferences .... A or A*
Least Developed Developing
Countries .... D
Caribbean Basin Economic Recovery
Act .... E or E*
United States-Israel Free Trade Area
Implementation Act of 1985 I

(iii)(A) Articles which are eligible for the special tariff treatment provided for in subdivision (e) of this headnote and which are subject to temporary modification under any provision of part 1 of the Appendix to these schedules shall be subject, for the period indicated in the "Effective Period" column in the Appendix, to rates of duty as follows:

(1) if the "Special" column in the Appendix is blank, the rate of duty in column numbered 1 therein shall apply;

(2) if a rate of duty for which the article may be eligible is set forth in the "Special" column in the

Appendix followed by one or more symbols described above, such rate shall apply in lieu of the rate followed by the corresponding symbol(s) set forth for such article in the "Special" column in schedules 1 to 8; or

(3) if "No change" followed by one or more symbols described above appears in the "Special" column in the Appendix and subdivision (iii)(A)(2) above does not apply, the rate of duty in column numbered 1 in the Appendix or the applicable rate(s) of duty set forth in the "Special" column in schedules 1 to 8, whichever is lower, shall apply.

(B) Unless the context requires otherwise, articles which are eligible for the special tariff treatment provided for in subdivision (e) of this headnote and which are subject to temporary modification under any provision of parts 2 or 3 of the Appendix to these schedules shall be subject, for the period indicated in the Appendix, to the rates of duty in column numbered 1 therein.

(iv) Whenever any rate of duty set forth in the "Special" column in schedules 1 to 8 is equal to, or higher than, the corresponding rate of duty provided in column numbered 1 in such schedules, such rate of duty in the "Special" column shall be deleted; except that, if the rate of duty in the "Special" column is an intermediate stage in a series of staged rate reductions for that item, such rate shall be treated as a suspended rate and shall be set forth in the "Special" column followed by one or more symbols described above, and followed by an "s" in parentheses. If no rate of duty for which the article may be eligible is provided in the "Special" column for a

programs which are provided for in subdivision (e) of this headnote and which are identified in parentheses immediately following the rate(s) of duty set out in such column. Upon application in proper form by a person who possesses the right to make entry for the imported article, a special rate shall be applied to such article only if—

(A) it is classified in an item for which a special rate (or rates) is set out in the "Special" column opposite such item;

(B) it is imported from a country—

(1) which is designated as an eligible country with respect to such item under a program designated in the "Special" column opposite such item, and

aIn Proclamation 4697, dated October 23, 1979, the President, acting under authority of section 404(a) of the Trade Act of 1974 (88 Stat. 1978) amended general headnote 3(f) by deleting "China (any part of which may be under Communist domination or control)" and "Tibet," effective February 1, 1980, the date on which written notices of acceptance were exchanged, following adoption on January 24, 1980 by the Congress of a concurrent resolution of approval extending nondiscriminatory treatment to the products of the People's Republic of China.

bIn Proclamation 3447, dated February 3, 1962, the President, acting under authority of section 620(a) of the Foreign Assistance Act of 1961 (75 Stat. 445), as amended, prohibited the importation into the United States of all goods of Cuban origin and all goods imported from or through Cuba, subject to such exceptions as the Secretary of the Treasury determines to be consistent with the effective operation of the embargo.

Figure 15.4 (cont.)

TARIFF SCHEDULES OF THE UNITED STATES ANNOTATED (1987)
GENERAL HEADNOTES AND RULES OF INTERPRETATION (continued)

particular item in schedules 1 to 8, the rate of duty provided in column numbered 1 shall apply.

(v) Products of Countries Designated Beneficiary Developing Countries for Purposes of the Generalized System of Preferences (GSP).

(A) The following countries, territories, and associations of countries eligible for treatment as one country (pursuant to section 502(a)(3) of the Trade Act of 1974 (19 U.S.C. 2462(a)(3)) are designated beneficiary developing countries for the purposes of the Generalized System of Preferences, provided for in Title V of the Trade Act of 1974, as amended (19 U.S.C. 2461 et seq.):

Independent Countries[a]

Angola	Fiji	Papua New Guinea	Taiwan
Antigua and	Gambia	Paraguay	Tanzania
Barbuda	Ghana	Peru	Thailand
Argentina	Grenada	Philippines	Togo
Aruba	Guatemala	Romania	Tonga
Bahamas	Guinea	Rwanda	Trinidad and Tobago
Bahrain	Guinea Bissau	Saint Lucia	Tunisia
Bangladesh	Guyana	Saint Vincent and	Turkey
Barbados	Haiti	the Grenadines	Tuvalu
Belize	Honduras	Sao Tome and Principe	Uganda
Benin	India	Senegal	Uruguay
Bhutan	Indonesia	Seychelles	Vanuatu
Bolivia	Israel	Sierra Leone	Venezuela
		Singapore	Western Samoa
		Solomon Islands	Yemen Arab Republic
		Somalia	(Sanáa)
		Sri Lanka	Yugoslavia
		Sudan	Zaire
		Suriname	Zambia
		Swaziland	Zimbabwe
		Syria	

Non-Independent Countries & Territories

Anguilla	Montserrat
Bermuda	Netherlands Antilles
British Indian Ocean	New Caledonia
Territory	Niue
Cayman Islands	Norfolk Island

Botswana	Ivory Coast
Brazil	Jamaica
Brunei Darussalam	Jordan
Burkina Faso	Kenya
Burma	Kiribati
Burundi	Korea, Republic of
Cameroon	Lebanon
Cape Verde	Lesotho
Central African Republic	Liberia
Chad	Madagascar
Chile	Malawi
Colombia	Malaysia
Comoros	Maldives
Congo	Mali
Costa Rica	Malta
Cyprus	Mauritania
Djibouti	Mauritius
Dominica	Mexico
Dominican Republic	Morocco
Ecuador	Mozambique
Egypt	Nauru
El Salvador	Nepal
Equatorial Guinea	Nicaragua
	Niger
	Oman
	Pakistan
	Panama

Christmas Island (Australia)	Pitcairn Islands
Cocos (Keeling) Islands	Saint Christopher-Nevis
Cook Islands	Saint Helena
Falkland Islands (Islas Malvinas)	Tokelau
French Polynesia	Trust Territory of the Pacific Islands
Gibraltar	Turks and Caicos Islands
Heard Island and McDonald Islands	Virgin Islands, British
Hong Kong	Wallis and Futuna
Macau	Western Sahara

Associations of Countries (treated as one country)

Member Countries of the Cartagena Agreement (Andean Group) Consisting of:	Association of South East Asian Nations (ASEAN) Consisting of:
Bolivia	Brunei
Colombia	Indonesia
Ecuador	Malaysia
Peru	Philippines
Venezuela	Singapore
	Thailand

aPursuant to section 4(b)(1) of the Taiwan Relations Act (22 U.S.C. 3303(b)(1)) the reference to countries includes Taiwan.

Figure 15.4 (cont.)

eligible article is imported into the customs territory of the United States directly from a country or territory listed in subdivision (e)(v)(A) of this headnote, it shall be eligible for duty-free treatment as set forth in the "Special" column, unless excluded from such treatment by subdivision (e)(v)(D) of this headnote; provided that, in accordance with regulations promulgated by the Secretary of the Treasury the sum of (1) the cost or value of the materials produced in the beneficiary developing country or any 2 or more countries which are members of the same association of countries which is treated as one country under section 502(a)(3) of the Trade Act of 1974, plus (2) the direct costs of processing operations performed in such beneficiary developing country or such member countries is not less than 35 percent of the appraised value of such article at the time of its entry into the customs territory of the United States.

(D) Articles provided for in an item for which a rate of duty appears in the "Special" column followed by the symbol "A*" in parentheses, if imported from a beneficiary developing country set opposite the TSUS item numbers listed below, are not eligible for the duty-free treatment provided in subdivision (e)(v)(C) of this headnote:

Member Countries of the Caribbean Common Market (CARICOM)

Consisting of:

Antigua and Barbuda	Jamaica
Bahamas	Montserrat
Barbados	Saint Christopher-Nevis
Belize	Saint Lucia
Dominica	Saint Vincent and the
Grenada	Grenadines
Guyana	Trinidad and Tobago

(B) The following beneficiary countries are designated as least-developed beneficiary developing countries pursuant to section 504(c)(6) of the Trade Act of 1974, as amended:

Bangladesh	Malawi
Benin	Maldives
Bhutan	Mali
Botswana	Nepal
Burkina Faso	Niger
Burundi	Rwanda
Cape Verde	Sao Tome and
Central African	Principe
Republic	Sierra Leone
Chad	Somalia

Comoros
Djibouti
Equatorial Guinea
Gambia
Guinea
Guinea-Bissau
Haiti
Lesotho
Sudan
Tanzania
Togo
Uganda
Western Samoa
Yemen Arab
Republic (Sanâa)

Whenever an eligible article is imported into the customs territory of the United States directly from one of the countries designated as a least-developed beneficiary developing country, it shall be entitled to receive the duty-free treatment provided for in subdivision (e)(v)(C) of this headnote without regard to the limitations on preferential treatment of eligible articles in section 504(c) of the Trade Act, as amended (19 U.S.C. 2464(c)).

(C) Articles provided for in an item for which a rate of duty appears in the "Special" column followed by the symbols "A" or "A*" in parentheses are those designated by the President to be eligible articles for purposes of the GSP pursuant to section 503 of the Trade Act of 1974. The symbol "A" indicates that all beneficiary developing countries are eligible for preferential treatment with respect to all articles provided for in the designated TSUS item. The symbol "A*" indicates that certain beneficiary developing countries, specifically enumerated in subdivision (e)(v)(D) of this headnote, are not eligible for such preferential treatment with regard to any article provided for in the designated TSUS item. Whenever an

TSUS item Number	Country or territory[a]	TSUS item Number	Country or territory[a]
121.61	Argentina	148.72	Chile
121.62	India		Brazil
121.65	Argentina	155.20	Dominican Republic
130.37	Argentina		Philippines
135.51	Mexico	167.05	Mexico
135.90	Mexico	192.17	Colombia
135.95	Mexico	192.21	Colombia
136.00	Dominican Republic	202.62	Mexico
136.20	Mexico	204.40	Taiwan
136.22	Mexico	206.60	Mexico
136.30	Mexico	206.98	Taiwan
136.61	Mexico	207.00	Taiwan
136.80	Mexico	222.50	Taiwan
137.10	Mexico	245.20	Brazil
137.50	Mexico	245.30	Brazil
137.63	Mexico	256.60	Republic of Korea
137.71	Mexico	256.87	Mexico
138.05	Mexico	319.05	India
141.77	Mexico	337.40	Hong Kong
146.22	Turkey		Republic of Korea
146.76	Mexico	355.81	Taiwan
148.03	Mexico	386.13	Taiwan
148.12	Mexico	389.61	Hong Kong
148.17	Mexico		Taiwan

[a]Pursuant to section 4(b)(1) of the Taiwan Relations Act (22 U.S.C. 3303(b)(1)) the reference to countries includes Taiwan.

Figure 15.4 (cont.)

TARIFF SCHEDULES OF THE UNITED STATES ANNOTATED (1987)
GENERAL HEADNOTES AND RULES OF INTERPRETATION (continued)

TSUS item Number	Country or territory[a]	TSUS item Number	Country or territory[a]	TSUS item Number	Country or territory[a]	TSUS item Number	Country or territory[a]
406.20	Israel	651.37	Taiwan	682.35	Mexico	688.30	Costa Rica
407.19	{ Mexico / Romania	651.46	{ Republic of Korea / Taiwan	682.60	{ Hong Kong / Mexico / Taiwan	688.41	{ Hong Kong / Taiwan
412.22	Bahamas	651.49	Taiwan	683.01	{ Republic of Korea / Taiwan	688.42	{ Hong Kong / Taiwan
413.24	Republic of Korea	652.03	Republic of Korea	683.15	Mexico	692.32	{ Brazil / Mexico / Taiwan
417.23	Israel	652.70	Republic of Korea	683.70	{ Hong Kong / Taiwan	692.60	Taiwan
418.13	Isreal	652.84	Mexico	683.80	Hong Kong	696.10	Taiwan
419.10	Chile	653.00	Republic of Korea	684.10	Taiwan	696.35	Taiwan
420.82	Israel	653.38	Taiwan	684.15	Singapore	696.40	Taiwan
428.96	Brazil	653.39	Taiwan	684.25	{ Republic of Korea / Singapore	700.90	Mexico
429.49	Israel	653.45	Taiwan	684.48	Hong Kong	703.14	Mexico
437.64	Israel	653.48	Taiwan	684.53	Taiwan	706.61	{ Hong Kong / Taiwan
445.42	Taiwan	653.90	Hong Kong	684.55	Mexico	708.45	Taiwan
452.44	Brazil	653.93	Taiwan	684.58	{ Hong Kong / Republic of Korea / Taiwan	708.47	Hong Kong
465.05	Philippines	653.94	Republic of Korea	684.59	{ Hong Kong / Taiwan	709.09	Mexico
470.85	Mexico	654.08	Taiwan	684.70	{ Republic of Korea / Taiwan	709.40	Hong Kong
473.52	Mexico	654.30	{ Republic of Korea / Taiwan			710.72	Taiwan
511.64	Mexico	654.40	Taiwan			711.38	Mexico
522.21	Mexico	654.50	Taiwan			713.15	Mexico
532.22	Republic of Korea	654.60	Hong Kong				
532.31	Mexico	657.24	Taiwan				
534.84	Taiwan	657.25	Taiwan				
534.91	Taiwan	657.35	Taiwan				
534.94	Taiwan	657.80	Taiwan				
535.31	Mexico						

Code	Country
545.25	Mexico
545.53	Mexico
545.87	Taiwan
606.28	Mexico
606.36	Brazil
606.37	Brazil
606.44	Brazil
610.65	Republic of Korea
610.70	Taiwan
610.74	{ Republic of Korea, Taiwan
610.82	Republic of Korea
610.88	Taiwan
612.03	Chile
612.06	{ Peru, Zambia
613.18	Taiwan
618.15	Venezuela
642.14	Republic of Korea
642.16	Republic of Korea
642.17	Republic of Korea
646.32	Republic of Korea
646.92	Taiwan
649.37	Taiwan
650.87	Hong Kong
650.89	Hong Kong
651.21	Taiwan

Code	Country
660.42	Brazil
660.48	{ Brazil, Mexico
661.06	{ Hong Kong, Taiwan
661.09	Singapore
661.65	Israel
661.94	{ Hong Kong, Taiwan
662.35	Mexico
664.10	Taiwan
672.16	Taiwan
674.31	Taiwan
674.35	Taiwan
676.15	Taiwan
676.20	Taiwan
676.30	{ Republic of Korea, Taiwan
676.56	{ Hong Kong, Malaysia, Mexico, Republic of Korea, Singapore, Taiwan
678.50	{ Hong Kong, Mexico, Republic of Korea, Taiwan
680.14	Taiwan

Code	Country
685.14	{ Hong Kong, Republic of Korea, Singapore, Taiwan
685.16	{ Hong Kong, Republic of Korea, Taiwan
685.18	{ Republic of Korea, Taiwan
685.25	{ Hong Kong, Republic of Korea, Taiwan
685.32	{ Hong Kong, Republic of Korea, Singapore, Taiwan
685.40	{ Republic of Korea, Taiwan
685.70	Singapore
685.90	{ Mexico, Taiwan
686.30	Taiwan
686.60	Mexico
688.10	Taiwan
688.12	{ Mexico, Taiwan
688.17	{ Mexico, Taiwan
688.18	Mexico

Code	Country
722.08	{ Hong Kong, Republic of Korea, Taiwan
722.11	{ Hong Kong, Republic of Korea, Taiwan
724.45	Republic of Korea
725.01	Republic of Korea
725.03	Republic of Korea
725.32	Taiwan
725.50	Taiwan
726.25	Taiwan
727.06	Mexico
727.23	Taiwan
727.29	Taiwan
727.35	Taiwan
727.40	Taiwan
727.70	Taiwan
728.22	Taiwan
730.94	Republic of Korea
732.60	Taiwan
734.15	Taiwan
734.25	Hong Kong
734.70	Republic of Korea
734.86	Taiwan
734.87	Taiwan
734.90	Taiwan
735.07	Republic of Korea
735.09	Taiwan

Figure 15.4 (*cont.*)

TARIFF SCHEDULES OF THE UNITED STATES ANNOTATED (1987)
GENERAL HEADNOTES AND RULES OF INTERPRETATION (continued)

(B) Products of such countries imported into the customs territory of the United States, whether imported directly or indirectly, and entered under an item for which a rate of duty appears in the "Special" column followed by the symbol "D" in parentheses are eligible for full tariff reductions without staging, as set forth in the "Special" column, in accordance with section 503(a)(2)(A) of the Trade Agreements Act of 1979 (93 Stat. 251).

(vii) Products of Countries Designated as Beneficiary Countries for Purposes of the Caribbean Basin Economic Recovery Act (CBERA).

(A) The following countries and territories or successor political entities are designated beneficiary countries for the purposes of the CBERA, pursuant to section 212 of that Act (19 U.S.C. 2702):

Antigua and Barbuda	Honduras
Bahamas	Jamaica
Barbados	Montserrat
Belize	Netherlands Antilles
Costa Rica	Panama
Dominica	Saint Christopher-Nevis
Dominican Republic	Saint Lucia
El Salvador	Saint Vincent and the
Grenada	Grenadines
Guatemala	Trinidad and Tobago
Haiti	Virgin Islands, British

TSUS item Number	Country or territory[a]	TSUS item Number	Country or territory[a]
735.12	Taiwan	741.25	Hong Kong
735.20	Taiwan	745.70	Taiwan
737.07	Hong Kong	748.20	Taiwan
737.15	Hong Kong	748.21	Taiwan
737.21	Hong Kong	750.20	Taiwan
737.23	{ Hong Kong / Taiwan	750.40	Hong Kong
737.28	{ Republic of Korea / Taiwan	750.45	Republic of Korea
737.30	{ Republic of Korea / Taiwan	751.05	Taiwan
737.40	{ Hong Kong / Republic of Korea	755.25	Hong Kong
737.42	Republic of Korea	770.07	Mexico
737.47	Republic of Korea	771.41	Taiwan
737.49	{ Hong Kong / Taiwan	771.43	Taiwan
737.51	Republic of Korea	771.45	Taiwan
737.60	Hong Kong	772.15	Taiwan
737.80	Hong Kong	772.35	Taiwan
737.95	{ Hong Kong / Taiwan	772.51	{ Brazil / Republic of Korea
740.11	{ Hong Kong / Israel	772.60	Republic of Korea
		773.05	Taiwan
		774.45	Hong Kong
		774.55	Taiwan
		790.03	Taiwan
		790.10	Taiwan
		790.39	Taiwan

(B)(1) Unless otherwise excluded from eligibility by the provisions of subdivisions (e)(vii)(D) or (e)(vii)(E) of this headnote, any article which is the growth, product, or manufacture of a beneficiary country shall be eligible for duty-free treatment if that article is provided for in an item for which a rate of duty appears in the "Special" column followed by the symbols "E" or "E*" in parentheses, and if—

(i) that article is imported directly from a beneficiary country into the customs territory of the United States; and

(ii) the sum of (A) the cost or value of the materials produced in a beneficiary country or two or more beneficiary countries, plus (B) the direct costs of processing operations performed in a beneficiary country or countries is not less than 35 per centum of the appraised value of such article at the time it is entered. For purposes of determining the percentage referred to in (ii)(B) above, the term "beneficiary country" includes the Commonwealth of Puerto Rico and the United States Virgin Islands. If the cost or value of materials produced in the customs territory of the United States (other than the Commonwealth of Puerto Rico) is included with respect to an article to which subdivision (e)(vii) of this headnote applies, an amount not to exceed 15 per centum of the appraised value of the article at the time it is entered that is attributed to such United States cost or value may be applied toward determining the percentage referred to in (ii)(B) above.

(2) Pursuant to subsection 213(a)(2) of the CBERA, the Secretary of the Treasury shall prescribe such regulations as may be necessary to carry out subdivision

740.12......Hong Kong		790.70......Republic of Korea	
740.13......Hong Kong		791.15. {	Hong Kong
740.14......Hong Kong			Republic of Korea
740.15......Hong Kong		791.28......Mexico	
740.38 {	Hong Kong		
	Taiwan		

(vi) Products of Least Developed Developing Countries.

(A) The following countries are designated least developed developing countries (LDDC's):

Bangladesh	Lesotho
Benin	Malawi
Bhutan	Maldives
Botswana	Mali
Burkina Faso	Nepal
Burundi	Niger
Cape Verde	Rwanda
Central African	Somalia
Republic	Sudan
Chad	Tanzania
Comoros	Uganda
Gambia	Western Samoa
Guinea	Yemen Arab Republic
Haiti	(Sanaá)

ᵃPursuant to section 4(b)(1) of the Taiwan Relations Act (22 U.S.C. 3303(b)(1)) the reference to countries includes Taiwan.

Figure 15.4 (cont.)

(e)(vii) of this headnote including, but not limited to, regulations providing that, in order to be eligible for duty-free treatment under the CBERA, an article must be wholly the growth, product, or manufacture of a beneficiary country, or must be a new or different article of commerce which has been grown, produced, or manufactured in the beneficiary country, and must be stated as such in a declaration by the appropriate party; but no article or material of a beneficiary country shall be eligible for such treatment by virtue of having merely undergone—

(i) simple combining or packaging operations, or

(ii) mere dilution with water or mere dilution with another substance that does not materially alter the characteristics of the article.

(3) As used in subdivision (e)(vii)(B) of this headnote, the phrase "direct costs of processing operations" includes, but is not limited to—

(i) all actual labor costs involved in the growth, production, manufacture, or assembly of the specific merchandise, including fringe benefits, on-the-job training and the cost of engineering, supervisory, quality control, and similar personnel; and

(ii) dies, molds, tooling, and depreciation on machinery and equipment which are allocable to the specific merchandise.

(D) Articles provided for in an item for which a rate of duty appears in the "Special" column followed by the symbol "E*" in parentheses shall be eligible for the duty-free treatment provided for in subdivision (e)(vii) of this headnote, except—

(1) articles of beef or veal, however provided for in subpart B of part 2 of schedule 1, and sugars, sirups, and molasses, provided for in items 155.20 or 155.30, if a product of the following countries, pursuant to section 213(c) of the CBERA:

Antigua and Barbuda   Saint Lucia
Montserrat   Saint Vincent and
Netherlands Antilles   the Grenadines

(2) sugars, sirups, and molasses, provided for in items 155.20 or 155.30, to the extent that importation and duty-free treatment of such articles are limited by headnote 4, subpart A, part 10, schedule 1, pursuant to section 213(d) of the CBERA; or

(3) textile and apparel articles—

(i) in chief value of cotton, wool, man-made fibers, or blends thereof in which those fibers, in the aggregate, exceed in value each other single component fiber thereof; or

Such phrase does not include costs which are not directly attributable to the merchandise concerned or are not costs of manufacturing the product, such as (i) profit, and (ii) general expenses of doing business which are either not allocable to the specific merchandise or are not related to the growth, production, manufacture, or assembly of the merchandise, such as administrative salaries, casualty and liability insurance, advertising, and salesmen's salaries, commissions or expenses.

(C) Articles provided for in an item for which a rate of duty appears in the "Special" column followed by the symbols "E" or "E*" in parentheses are those designated by the President to be eligible articles for purposes of the CBERA pursuant to section 213 of that Act. The symbol "E" indicates that all articles provided for in the designated TSUS item are eligible for preferential treatment. The symbol "E*" indicates that some articles provided for in the designated TSUS item are not eligible for preferential treatment, as further described in subdivision (e)(vii)(D) of this headnote. Whenever an eligible article is imported into the customs territory of the United States in accordance with the provisions of subdivision (e)(vii)(B) of this headnote from a country or territory listed in subdivision (e)(vii)(A) of this headnote, it shall be eligible for duty-free treatment as set forth in the "Special" column, unless excluded from such treatment by subdivisions (e)(vii)(D) or (e)(vii)(E) of this headnote.

(ii) in which either the cotton content or the man-made fiber content equals or exceeds 50 percent by weight of all component fibers thereof; or

(iii) in which the wool content exceeds 17 percent by weight of all component fibers thereof; or

(iv) containing blends of cotton, wool, or man-made fibers, which fibers, in the aggregate, amount to 50 percent or more by weight of all component fibers thereof; provided, that beneficiary country exports of handloom fabrics of the cottage industry, or handmade cottage industry products made of such handloom fabrics, or traditional folklore handicraft textiles products, if such products are properly certified under an arrangement established between the United States and such beneficiary country, are eligible for the duty-free treatment provided for in subdivision (e)(vii) of this headnote.

(E) The duty-free treatment provided under the CBERA shall not apply to watches, and watch parts (including cases, bracelets, and straps), of whatever type including, but not limited to, mechanical, quartz digital, or quartz analog, if such watches or watch parts contain any material which is the product of any country with respect to which column 2 rates of duty apply.

Figure 15.4 (*cont.*)

(viii) United States-Israel Free Trade Area Implementation Act of 1985.

(A) The products of Israel described in Annex 1 of the Agreement on the Establishment of a Free Trade Area between the Government of the United States of America and the Government of Israel, entered into on April 22, 1985, are subject to duty as provided herein. Products of Israel, as defined in subdivision (e)(viii)(B) of this headnote, imported into the customs territory of the United States and entered under an item for which a rate of duty appears in the "Special" column followed by the symbol "I" in parentheses are eligible for tariff treatment, as set forth in the "Special" column, in accordance with Section 4(a) of the United States-Israel Free Trade Area Implementation Act of 1985 (99 Stat. 82).

(B) For purposes of subdivision (e)(viii) of this headnote, articles imported into the customs territory of the United States are eligible for treatment as "products of Israel" only if—

(1) that article is the growth, product, or manufacture of Israel or is a new or different article of commerce that has been grown, produced, or manufactured in Israel;

(2) that article is imported directly from Israel into the customs territory of the United States; and

(3) the sum of—

(2) mere dilution with water or mere dilution with another substance that does not materially alter the characteristics of the article.

(D) As used in subdivision (e)(viii) of this headnote, the phrase "direct costs of processing operations" includes, but is not limited to—

(1) all actual labor costs involved in the growth, production, manufacture, or assembly of the specific merchandise, including fringe benefits, on-the-job training and the cost of engineering, supervisory, quality control, and similar personnel; and

(2) dies, molds, tooling, and depreciation on machinery and equipment which are allocable to the specific merchandise.

Such phrase does not include costs which are not directly attributable to the merchandise concerned, or are not costs of manufacturing the product, such as (i) profit, and (ii) general expenses of doing business which are either not allocable to the specific merchandise or are not related to the growth, production, manufacture, or assembly of the merchandise, such as administrative salaries, casualty and liability insurance, advertising, and salesmen's salaries, commissions or expenses.

(E) The Secretary of the Treasury, after consultation with the United States Trade Representative, shall prescribe such regulations as may be necessary to carry out subdivision (e)(viii) of this headnote.

(i) the cost or value of the materials produced in Israel, plus

(ii) the direct costs of processing operations performed in Israel, is not less than 35 percent of the appraised value of such article at the time it is entered. If the cost or value of materials produced in the customs territory of the United States is included with respect to an article to which subdivision (e)(viii) of this headnote applies, an amount not to exceed 15 percent of the appraised value of the article at the time it is entered that is attributable to such United States cost or value may be applied toward determining the percentage referred to in subdivision (e)(viii)(B)(3) of this headnote.

(C) No article may be considered to meet the requirements of subdivision (e)(viii)(B)(1) of this headnote by virtue of having merely undergone—

(1) simple combining or packaging operations;

or

(f) Products of All Other Countries. Products of all countries not previously mentioned in this headnote imported into the customs territory of the United States are subject to the rates of duty set forth in column numbered 1 of the schedules.

4. Modification or Amendment of Rates of Duty. Except as otherwise provided in general headnote 3(e) or in the Appendix to the Tariff Schedules—

(a) a statutory rate of duty supersedes and terminates the existing rates of duty in both column numbered 1 and column numbered 2 unless otherwise specified in the amending statute;

(b) a rate of duty proclaimed pursuant to a concession granted in a trade agreement shall be reflected in column numbered 1 and, if higher than the then existing rate in column numbered 2, also in the latter column, and shall supersede but not terminate the then existing rate (or rates) in such column (or columns);

Figure 15.4 (*cont.*)

U.S. Total and GSP Imports in 1983 and 1982 GNP Per Capita

	U.S. Imports[1] ($ Millions)			Country Share of U.S. GSP Imports	1982 GNP Per Capita
	Total	GSP	GSP % of Total		
Total—All GSP Beneficiaries	63,789	10,765	17.0	100.0	
Subtotal— 15 Leading Beneficiaries:	63,358	9,383	14.8	87.2	
Taiwan	11,204	2,981	26.6	27.7	2,640
Korea	7,148	1,524	21.3	14.2	1,910
Hong Kong	6,394	1,102	17.2	10.2	5,340
Mexico	16,776	725	4.3	6.7	2,270
Brazil	4,946	633	12.8	5.9	2,240
Singapore	2,868	512	17.9	4.8	5,910
Israel	1,255	474	37.8	4.4	5,090
Philippines	2,001	258	12.9	2.4	820
Venezuela	4,938	239	4.8	2.2	4,140
Argentina	853	225	26.4	2.1	2,520
India	2,191	181	8.3	1.7	260
Yugoslavia	386	162	42.0	1.5	2,800
Peru	1,151	142	12.3	1.3	1,310
Thailand	967	118	12.2	1.1	790
Portugal	280	107	38.2	1.0	2,450

[1]General imports, customs basis, excluding petroleum imports.
Sources: U.S. Department of Commerce
The World Bank

Business America, November 26, 1984

Figure 15.5

If a "D" appears in the Special column, then the LDDCs (extremely poor countries (that are listed on page 195 of the headnotes will receive special reductions. "Staging" refers to the Customs' practice of assessing duties on only that portion of the labor on the product that occurred outside of the United States. The labor performed in "D" countries on staged goods may not be subject to tariffs.

Countries covered under the Caribbean Basin Recovery Act of 1983 are listed on page 194 of the headnotes. (This program will expire on September 30, 1995 unless Congress extends it.) The CBI is a one-way free trade area providing duty-free access to the U.S. market. Imports with an

"E" or "E*" under the Special column are eligible. (E* indicates that some articles provided for in the designated TSUSA item are not eligible for preferential treatment.) Articles that don't enjoy duty-free status under the CBI are listed on pages 196–197 of the headnotes.

The U.S.–Israel Free Trade Area agreement was legislated by the Tariff and Trade Act of 1984. It provides for free or reduced rates of duty for goods from Israel. There is no termination date on this agreement. In fact, on January 1, 1995, all currently eligible reduced rate importations from Israel will enter duty free. This provision is designated by an "I" in the Special column. To obtain information concerning additions or deletions of merchandise that is eligible under "I" write to Chairperson, Trade Policy Staff Subcommittee, Office of U.S. Trade Representative, 600 17th Street, N.W., Washington, D.C. 20506.

Important: As an importer, you should obtain confirmation of the dutiable status of the import even if you are using the TSUSA. Contact the director of the port or district where the merchandise will be entered. Their evaluations, however, are not binding, but advisory. For a binding classification on a prospective import write to one of the following:

Regional Commissioner of Customs
Region II, New York, N.Y. 10048

Commissioner of Customs
Attention: Office of Regulations and Rulings
Washington, D.C. 20229

Customs recommends that a request for a tariff classification decision should include the following information:[1]

1. A complete description of the goods. Send samples of practical sketches, diagrams, or other illustrative material that will be useful in supplementing the written description.
2. Cost breakdowns of component materials and their respective quantities shown in percentages, if possible.
3. A description of the chief use of the goods, as a class or kind of merchandise, in the United States.
4. Information as to commercial, scientific, or common designations which may be applicable.

---

[1]*Importing into the United States*, Department of the Treasury, U.S. Customs Service (Washington, D.C.: U.S. Government Printing Office, 1984), p. 19.

5. Any other information that may be pertinent or required for the purpose of tariff classification.

This list is only a guide. Disregard any of the above five steps if they are not applicable. The key is to be as detailed as possible.

UPCOMING CHANGES

A new coding system may soon be adopted and called the Harmonized Commodity Description and Coding System (HC). The HC will be used by manufacturers, exporters, importers, Customs, Commerce, statisticians, and anyone classifying goods moving in international trade in the sixty countries, fourteen government-sponsored international organizations, nine private international organizations, and two national trade facilitation organizations.[2] It will be organized the same way as the TSUSA, SIC, SITC, and Schedule B and E numbers as discussed in Chapter Seven. That is, it will begin with agricultural products and progress to manufactured goods. The basic code contains four-digit headings and six-digit subheadings. (Countries will add digits for tariff and statistical purposes as suffixes.) For more information about the HC and its impact on imports write to Director, Office of Regulations and Rulings, U.S. Customs Service, 1301 Constitution Avenue, N.W., Washington, D.C. 20229.

Now that we have considered the impact of tariffs on the product's price, we're ready to consider shipping and other costs involved in getting the product to the United States. Figure 15.6 shows a worksheet of "laid-down landed costs." You might check the American Foreign Trade Definitions in the appendix and the detailed explanation of American Foreign Trade Definitions in Chapter Eight. The importer should insist on a "C.I.F." quote, unless the importer or freight forwarder is very familiar with overseas inland transportation, terminal costs, and government regulations, and can obtain better rates than the exporter can offer.

Special Price Considerations for Importers
Who Intend to Use Imports
in the Manufacturing Process

If the product or material imported will be used in the manufacture of a product, the manufacturer can get 99 percent of the duty back or *draw-*

---

[2]"Harmonized Commodity Description and Coding System," Department of the Treasury, U.S. Customs Service, Customs Publication No. 576, 1986.

DEVELOPMENT OF LAID-DOWN LANDED COSTS

Product   *Unit Price*   *Number of Units*

$_____
(Ex Factory)

Export Packing Charges.. _____
(F.O.B. Plant)

Number of Shipping Containers:_____

WEIGHTS: Gross _____ Tare _____ Legal _____ Net _____

Dimensions: Length   Width   Height

Total Cubic Feet: _____

Inland Freight (Plant to Seaboard)................................. _____
(F.O.B. Truck/Rail, Seaboard)

Freight Forwarding Charges... _____

Pier Unloading Charges .... _____
(F.A.S. Vessel, Port of Export)

Wharfage .... _____

Heavy Lift Charges .... _____

Other from Dock to On-board Vessel .... _____
(F.O.B. Vessel, Port of Export)

Estimated Ocean Freight:

$ per metric/short/long/measurement ton

W/M   tons at $ ton .... _____
(C & F Port of Destination)

INSURANCE: Insured value $

Marine $ per $100 insured value

   War $ per $100 insured value

                         Total Insurance _____
(C.I.F. Port of Destination)

DUTY: Ad valorem: Specific:

        Compound: _____

Duty Insurance: Insurance Rate

                    × Duty   _____

Bank Charges (Letter of Credit,

                Draft Collection, etc.)   _____

Postage, Sundries, Cables....................................... _____

Entry Expenses (Include Custom House Brokerage Fees
and any other charges associated with customs entry not
included in above)   _____

        TOTAL LANDED COST EX DOCK

        PORT OF IMPORTATION   _____

Figure 15.6

PLUS:

Inland Freight, Port of importation/Customer,
   Wholesaler, Retailer, Factory ....   _____

Demurrage or other storage charges while on dock in port of
   importation ....   _____

Transfer and miscellaneous charges from dock to
   destination...   _____

   TOTAL LAID DOWN, LANDED COSTS $_____

Figure 15.6   (*cont.*)

back on the imported parts or material, provided the finished product is exported within a year. Your company is entitled to a full refund on duties paid if the imported goods are exported from a bonded Customs warehouse.

Promotion

This job is easier than that of the exporter because you are selling in the familiar home market. Look over the section on promotion in Chapter Eight. The big job ahead of the importer is to establish distribution channels.

Distribution

This is the most important link for importers attempting to build distributorships. The section on distribution in Chapter Eight is helpful. The decision to organize as an agent or merchant depends on your ability to assume risk, the product itself, and the foreign supplier's terms:

1. Import Agent (Broker). An agent doesn't take title to the goods. He or she acts as a middleman, that is, he or she works for a commission to find export markets for the foreign supplier.
2. Import Merchant. A merchant always takes title to the merchandise, that is, he or she buys the imports and assumes the risk of finding a market.

If the supplier authorizes an importer to distribute his or her product, the next step is to draw up a contract. Both sides of the negotiation will need attorneys. The foreign supplier may wish to amend the contract periodically. An attorney who has experience with international sales contracts is better able to determine what is fair and the pitfalls to avoid.

The importer should obtain domestic orders for the foreign product before purchasing shipments from the foreign supplier. The search can begin by identifying American distributors who handle related products.

Information on wholesalers and jobbers who specialize in the product as well as retailers to whom you can sell direct can be found in directories, many of which are available at your local public or university library. See the suggested readings at the end of this chapter.

SUGGESTED READINGS

Directories

Custom House Guide
North American Publishing Company
401 N. Broad St., Philadelphia, PA 19108
(215) 574-9600. Firms serving U.S. ports. Complete tariff schedule.

Directory of Drug Store Chains
425 Park Avenue, New York, N.Y. 10022
(212) 371-9400. Annual.

Directory of General Merchandise, Mail Order Firms, and Family Centers
424 Park Avenue, New York, N.Y. 10022. Annual.

The Directory of United States Importers
Journal of Commerce
110 Wall Street, New York, N.Y. 10005
(212) 425-1616. Biennial.

Electronic Yellow Pages Retailers Directory
Market Data Retrieval, Inc. P.O. Box 510
Westport, CT 06880 (202) 226-8941, inquire about on-line costs and availability.

Mail Order Business Directory
B. Klein Publications
P.O. Box 8503
Coral Springs, Florida 33065
(305) 752-1708
U.S. and world mail order houses

Major Mass Market Merchandisers, Salesman's Guide
  1140 Broadway, New York, N.Y. 10001
  (212) 684-2985 Annual.

Sheldon's Jobbing and Wholesale Trade
  Phelon, Sheldon, and Massar, Inc.
  15 Industrial Avenue, Fairview, N.J. 07022
  (201) 941-8804 Annual.

Sheldon's Retail Stores
  Annual.

Statistics

Schedule A based (derived from TSUSA):

Bureau of Census. FT 135: *U.S. General Imports and Imports for Consumption*. Customs and CIF value 1 through a 4-digit and 7-digit Schedule A Commodity Descriptions by country of origin. Monthly and year-to-date.

————. FT 900: *Summary of U.S. Export and Import Merchandise Trade*. 1 to 4-digit Schedule A. Monthly and year-to-date.

American Import/Export Bulletin monthly magazine.

Custom House Guide. North American Publishing Company. Annual.

16

CUSTOMS CLEARANCE

This chapter is designed as an overview of Customs regulations. For in-depth treatment of customs regulations, two major sources are available:

> *Customs Regulations of the United States*, U.S. Treasury Department, U.S. Customs Service. Annual loose-leaf volume, 1986 price $55.
>
> *Customs House Guide*

A novice shouldn't attempt handling shipment without the assistance of a customhouse broker unless he or she is importing through the mail.

Arrival Process

When shipping by air, it is easier to determine when the shipment arrives. Ocean transportation is much less punctual. The steamship company notifies the importer or the importer's customhouse broker once it is determined when the ship will dock. When the ship arrives, an *arrival notice* is sent to the importer or customhouse broker. It details the number of packages and their weight, and indicates how long the goods can stay at the terminal without storage charges accruing to the importer.

ALL imports coming into the United States must be cleared through Customs. Customs clearance is a five-step process:

1. Entry
2. Inspection
3. Valuation and Appraisement
4. Classification
5. Liquidation

Entry

Customs requires the importer or customhouse broker to file the following documents with the district or port director within five days of the date of arrival of a shipment at a U.S. port of entry:

1. An *ocean bill of lading, airway bill,* or *carrier's certificate* is used by Customs as "evidence of the right to make entry." The carrier's certificate indicates ownership of goods and port of lading. The carrier names and certifies the importer as owner of the goods. (Chapter Eleven contains an in-depth treatment of the bill of lading and airway bill.)

2. Special Customs documents, depending on how the importer wants the goods entered. Goods may be entered for *consumption,* entered for *warehouse* at the port of arrival, or *transported "in-bond" to another port of entry* and entered there under the same conditions as at the port of arrival. (Chapter Seventeen examines Foreign Trade Zone regulations.)

ENTRY FOR CONSUMPTION

Entry manifest (Customs Form 7533) or *application and special permit for immediate delivery* (Customs Form 3461) or other form of merchandise release is required by the district director.

The exporter must provide the importer with a *commercial invoice* to present to Customs. A pro forma invoice is acceptable if the commercial invoice can't be produced. (Chapters Seven and Eleven explain the information these invoices should contain.)

Immediate delivery or release of the shipment is not permitted in all cases. Release under immediate delivery is limited to the following merchandise:[1]

a. Merchandise arriving from Canada or Mexico, if it is approved by the district director and an appropriate bond is on file.

b. Fresh fruits and vegetables for human consumption arriving from Canada and Mexico and removed from the area immediately contiguous to the border to the importer's premises within the port of importation.

c. Shipments consigned to or for the account of any agency or officer of the U.S. government.

---

[1] *Importing into the United States,* 1986 edition, p. 8.

d. Articles for a trade fair.

e. Tariff-rate quota merchandise and under certain circumstances merchandise subject to absolute quota.

f. In very limited circumstances, merchandise released from a warehouse followed within 10 working days by a warehouse withdrawal for consumption.

g. Merchandise specifically authorized by Customs Headquarters to be entitled to release for immediate delivery.

To obtain release of the goods before customs duties are paid, evidence of "surety" is required. A customhouse broker will permit use of his or her bond to provide the duty coverage. (You can also post the surety in cash.)

Inspection/Examination

After entry, Customs may waive examination of the goods or it may examine the goods to determine the value and dutiable status (classification) of the import. Goods may be checked for compliance with regulations requiring that the country of origin be clearly marked. Customs searches for prohibited articles and also determines if requirements of other government agencies are satisfied.

If the quantity marked on the sealed container is shown by a Customs inspection to be incorrect and it is determined that the omission was intended or fraudulent, the contents of the *entire* package are subject to seizure and forfeiture. If Customs determines that there wasn't fraudulent intent, it will go ahead and collect the duties payable on the excess goods. In the opposite case (less goods are found than are listed on the invoice) there will be an appropriate reduction in duties.

Valuation

The product is assessed at its transaction value, defined as the price the importer paid for the products imported. This value includes export packing and domestic transportation, but excludes expenses related to international shipment, such as wharfage, marine insurance, and ocean freight.

Specific duties (those duties assessed on weight) are dutiable on net weight. A deduction is made from gross weight for the tare. Tares are provided by Customs on apple boxes, china clay in half-ton casks, figs in skeleton cases, fresh tomatoes, lemons, oranges, ocher, pimentos, and to-bacco leaves. Otherwise Customs uses the tare stated on the invoice.

Classification

The Tariff Schedule of the U.S. Annotated (TSUSA) is used in determining the duty. Chapter Fifteen examines the use of this tariff schedule.

Liquidation

When a final determination of duty is made and it is paid to Customs, the import entry is "liquidated," that is, it is released from Customs. Duties must be paid within ten working days after release of the merchandise. Entry summary documentation is filed after release of the goods from the customhouse. Entry summary documentation includes the entry package documents that are returned to the importer or broker, an *entry summary* (Customs Form 7501), and other invoices as necessary.

ENTRY FOR WAREHOUSE

The importer may enter the merchandise into a "customs-bonded ware-house" under a *warehouse entry*. This warehouse is a building or other secured area such as a tank in which dutiable goods can be stored, ma-nipulated, or undergo manufacturing (under Customs supervision) with-out the payment of duties until the goods leave the warehouse. A company can own its own customs-bonded warehouse (by application to District Director of Customs) or can store its goods in a public customs-bonded warehouse. Perishable goods, explosive substances, or prohibited mer-chandise can't be stored in a customs-bonded warehouse. Certain re-stricted articles (for instance merchandise subject to quotas, which can't be released for consumption) can be stored in a customs-bonded ware-house until the quota is lifted.

Importers enter goods into a bonded warehouse to postpone payment of duties until the goods leave the warehouse and a consumption entry is filed. In this way the company can avoid paying duties until such time as the good is sold. The limit for storage is five years. The duty effective on the date of *withdrawal* will be assessed.

Warehoused goods may also be reexported without the payment of duties. If the goods are destroyed under Customs supervision, no duty is payable.

ENTRY AT A PORT OTHER THAN THE PORT OF ARRIVAL

Filing an *Immediate Transportation Entry* allows imports to be transported from the port of arrival to an inland destination via a "bonded" carrier without paying duties or completing customs filing regulations at the port of arrival.

Unentered Goods

If an import isn't entered within five working days after arrival, Customs can place the merchandise in a *General Order* warehouse. The importer is responsible for storage charges as well as the risk to the cargo while in storage. Goods unentered for one year can be sold at a public auction, but if your product is perishable, subject to depreciation, or an explosive substance, Customs may sell the import immediately.

Mail Entries

Merchandise can be imported through the mail. Duties on parcels not exceeding $1000 in value are collected by the letter carrier. (Articles classified in Schedule 3, parts 1, 4A, 7B, 12A, 12D, and 13B of Schedule 7; and parts 2 and 3 of the Appendix to the Tariff Schedules of the United States are subject to duty collection by Customs if the parcel exceeds $250 in value.)

A *commercial invoice* must accompany commercial shipments. The invoice should be enclosed in the package or securely attached to the parcel. The address side should be marked "Invoice Enclosed."

A *Customs Declaration* that contains a clear and complete description and the value of the contents must be securely attached to the parcel. This form is available at post offices. U.S. Customs Declarations are also available at foreign post offices. The appendix lists the location and telephone numbers of Customs International Mail Branches.

If the parcel exceeds $1000 in value, the addressee is notified to prepare and file a CONSUMPTION ENTRY at the nearest Customs port of entry. A commercial invoice is required.

Protesting Dutiable Status

If the importer disagrees with the dutiable status of imported merchandise, he or she can file a protest of a Customs' decision within 90 days after the date of liquidation. This protest must be accompanied by *Customs Form 19.*

Notice of the denial of a protest will be mailed to the importer. If the importer decides to litigate the decision, he or she can file a summons in the Court of International Trade (located in New York City).

Special Licensing Requirements and Prohibitions

No license is required to import merchandise. But certain commodities are regulated by other government agencies. A license or permit is required to import:

> alcoholic beverages
> animals and animal products
> certain drugs
> firearms and ammunition
> fruits and nuts
> meat and meat products
> milk, dairy, and cheese products
> plants and plant products
> poultry and poultry products
> petroleum and petroleum products
> trademarked articles
> vegetables

The table at the end of this chapter contains information about restrictions and prohibitions for importing the products listed above.

Marking Country of Origin

Every article of foreign origin entering the United States must be legibly marked in a conspicuous place with the English name of the country of origin unless an exception from marking is provided in the law. This mark must be permanent, that is, affixed through processes such as stenciling, stamping, branding, printing, and molding. If a foreign supplier has not shipped to the United States before, the importer should send the foreign supplier a copy of U.S. guidelines which can be found in any of the following Customs publications: *Customs Regulations* manual, *Importing into the United States,* or a special pamphlet provided by Customs entitled "Marking of Country of Origin on U.S. Imports." U.S. Customs Attachés or Representatives stationed abroad and American consular offices can also provide exporters with appropriate guidelines.

Temporary Free Importations

A good imported under bond can be exported within one year without duties. Fifteen classes of goods are permitted under temporary importation bond:[2]

1. Merchandise to be repaired, altered, or processed.
2. Models of women's wearing apparel.
3. Articles imported by illustrators and photographers for use as models to illustrate catalogs, pamphlets, or advertising matter.
4. Samples for use in taking orders for merchandise.
5. Articles for examination with a view to reproduction or for examination and reproduction.
6. Articles intended for testing, experimental, or review purposes.
7. Automobiles, motorcycles, bicycles, airplanes, and the like brought in by nonresidents for purpose of taking part in a specific contest.
8. Locomotives and other railroad equipment brought for use in emergency work.
9. Containers for compressed gas or other articles for holding merchandise.
10. Professional or camping equipment for nonresident's use.
11. Articles of special design for temporary use exclusively in connection with the manufacture or production of articles for export.
12. Animals and poultry brought into the United States for the purpose of breeding, exhibition, or competition for prizes.
13. Theatrical scenery, apparel.
14. Works of fine arts for exhibition.
15. Automobiles, automobile chassis, or parts intended for show purposes.

---

[2]*Importing into the U.S.,* 1986 edition, p. 21.

ATA Carnet

"Admission Temporaire-Temporary Admission" allows for temporary duty-free importation of certain goods without customs declarations. It's valid for a year and covers the temporary admission of professional equipment, commercial samples, and advertising material. The ATA Carnet is often used by foreign sales representatives.

Shipping under GSP, CBI, and FTA Agreements

The special rates associated with these groups was covered in Chapter Fifteen.

GSP REGS: The exporter must include an *UNCTAD Certificate of Origin Form A* in order to be eligible for GSP status. This form must be signed by the exporter and certified by the designated governmental authority of the GSP country. It should be filed with the entry or furnished before liquidation.

GSP countries are responsible for supplying this form. It is not available for sale in the United States. If this form is not available from the government certifying authority, the exporter can contact the Director, Technical Assistant Project/GSP, UNCTAD, 1211 Geneva 10, Switzerland.

CBI REGS: *UNCTAD Certificate of Origin Form A*. The words "Generalized System of Preferences" appearing on the front of the Form A must be replaced by the words "Caribbean Basin Initiative."

U.S.-ISRAEL (FTA) REGs: UNCTAD Certificate of Origin Form A.

Restrictions, Prohibitions, Other Agency Requirements

The importation of certain classes of merchandise may be prohibited or restricted to protect the economy and security of the United States, to safeguard consumer health and well-being, and to preserve domestic plant and animal life. Some commodities are also subject to an import quota or a restraint under bilateral trade agreements and arrangements.

Many of these prohibitions and restrictions on importations are subject, in addition to Customs requirements, to the laws and regulations administered by other United States Government agencies with which Customs cooperates in enforcement. These laws and regulations may, for example, prohibit entry; limit entry to certain ports; restrict routing, storage, or use; or require treatment, labeling, or processing as a condition of release. Customs clearance is given only if these various additional requirements are met. This applies to all types of importations, including those made by mail and those placed in foreign-trade zones.

The foreign exporter should make certain that the United States importer has provided proper information to (1) permit the submission of necessary information concerning packing, labeling, etc., and (2) that necessary arrangements have been made by the importer for entry of the merchandise into the United States.

It is impracticable to list all articles specifically; however, various classes of articles are discussed below. Foreign exporters and U.S. importers should consult the agency mentioned for detailed information and guidance, as well as for any changes to the laws and regulations under which the commodities are controlled.

Agricultural Commodities

1. Cheese, Milk, and Dairy Products. Cheese and cheese products are subject to requirements of the Food and Drug Administration and the Department of Agriculture. Most importations of cheese require an import license and are subject to quotas administered by the Department of Agriculture, Foreign Agricultural Service, Washington, D.C. 20250 (see chapter 27).

The importation of milk and cream is subject to requirements of the Food, Drug and Cosmetic Act and the Import Milk Act. These products may be imported only by holders of permits from the Department of Health and Human Services, Food and Drug Administration, Rockville, Md. 20857, and the Department of Agriculture.

2. Fruits, Vegetables, and Nuts. Certain agricultural commodities (including fresh tomatoes, avocadoes, mangoes, limes, oranges, grapefruit, green peppers, Irish potatoes, cucumbers, eggplants, dry onions, walnuts and filberts, processed dates, prunes, raisins, and olives in tins) must meet United States import requirements relating to grade, size, quality, and maturity (7 U.S.C. 608(e)). These commodities are inspected and an inspection certificate must be issued by the Food Safety and Quality Service of the Department of Agriculture to indicate import compliance. Inquiries on general requirements should be made to the Agricultural Marketing Service of the Department of Agriculture, Washington, D.C. 20250. Additional restrictions may be imposed by the Animal and Plant Health Inspection Service of that department, Washington, D.C. 20782, under the Plant Quarantine Act and by the Food and Drug Administration under the Federal Food, Drug and Cosmetic Act.

3. Insects. Insects in a live state which are injurious to cultivated crops (including vegetables, field crops, bush

(cont.)

fruit, and orchard, forest, or shade trees) and the eggs, pupae, or larvae of such insects are prohibited importation, except for scientific purposes under regulations prescribed by the Secretary of Agriculture.

All packages containing live insects or their eggs, pupae, or larvae, which are not injurious to crops or trees, are permitted entry into the United States only if covered by a permit issued by the Animal and Plant Health Inspection Service of the Department of Agriculture and are not prohibited by the U.S. Fish and Wildlife Service.

4. Livestock and Animals. Inspection and quarantine requirements of the Animal and Plant Health Inspection Service must be met for the importation of (1) all cloven-hoofed animals (ruminants), such as cattle, sheep, deer, antelope, camels, giraffes; (2) swine including the various varieties of wild hogs and the meat from such animals; (3) horses, asses, mules, and zebras; (4) animal by-products, such as untanned hides, wool, hair, bones, bone meal, blood meal, animal casings, glands, organs, extracts or secretions of ruminants and swine; and (5) hay and straw. A permit for importation must be obtained from that agency before shipping from the country of origin. An exception is made in the case of Canada and certain northern states of Mexico. Importations from any country where rinderpest or foot-and-mouth disease exists are prohibited; also, hay and straw packing materials from these countries are not eligible for entry into the United States. Entry of animals is restricted to certain ports which are designated as quarantine stations.

5. Meat and Meat Products. All commercial shipments of meat and meat food products offered for entry into the United States are subject to the regulations of the Department of Agriculture and must be inspected by the Animal and Plant Health Inspection Service and the Food Safety and Quality Service of that department prior to release by U.S. Customs.

6. Plant and Plant Products. The importation of plants and plant products is subject to regulations of the Department of Agriculture and may be restricted or prohibited. Plants and plant products include fruits, vegetables, plants, nursery stock, bulbs, roots, seeds, certain fibers including cotton and broomcorn, cut flowers, sugarcane, certain cereals, elm logs and elm lumber with bark attached. Import permits are required. Further information should be obtained from the Animal and Plant Health Inspection Service. Also certain endangered species of plants may be prohibited or require permits or certificates (see section 31).

7. Poultry and Poultry Products. Poultry, live, dressed, or canned; eggs, including eggs for hatching; and egg products are subject to the requirements and regulations of the Animal and Plant Health Inspection Service and the Food Safety and Quality Service of the Department of Agriculture. Permits are required, as well as special marking and labeling; and, in some cases, foreign inspection certification. The term poultry includes chickens, turkeys, swans, pheasants, grouse, partridges, quail, guinea fowl, pea fowl, and the non-migratory types of ducks, geese, pigeons, and doves. Inquiry should also be made to the Food and Drug Administration and the U.S. Fish and Wildlife Service about their requirements, restrictions, or prohibitions.

8. Seeds. The importation into the United States of agricultural and vegetable seeds and screenings is governed by the provisions of the Federal Seed Act of 1939 and regulations of the Agricultural Marketing Service, Department of Agriculture. Shipments are detained pending the drawing and testing of samples.

Arms, Ammunition
Radioactive Materials

9. Arms, Ammunition, Explosives, and Implements of War. These items are prohibited importation except when a license is issued by the Bureau of Alcohol, Tobacco and Firearms of the Department of the Treasury, Washington, D.C. 20226, or the importation is in compliance with the regulations of that department. The temporary importation, in-transit movement, and exportation of arms and ammunition is prohibited unless a license is issued by the Office of Munitions Control, Department of State, Washington, D.C. 20520. Importations of surplus arms, ammunition, and implements of war are also subject to the Foreign Excess Property regulations of the International Trade Administration, Department of Commerce, Washington, D.C. 20230. Importations of foreign excess property must be accompanied by an import authorization from that agency.

10. Radioactive Materials and Nuclear Reactors. Many radioisotopes, all forms of uranium, thorium, and plutonium, and all nuclear reactors imported into the United States are subject to the regulations of the Nuclear Regulatory Commission in addition to import regulations imposed by any other agency of the United States. Authority to import these commodities or articles containing these commodities is granted by the Nuclear Regulatory Commission, Washington, D.C. 20545.

In order to comply with the Nuclear Regulatory Commission requirements, the importer must be aware of the identity and amount of any NRC-controlled radioisotopes, of uranium, thorium, and plutonium, and of any nuclear reactor being imported into the United States. To assure passage through customs, the importer must demonstrate to U.S. Customs the Nuclear Regulatory Commission au-

(cont.)

thority under which the controlled commodity is being imported. The authority which is cited may be the number of a specific or general license, or the specific section of the Nuclear Regulatory Commission regulations which establishes a general license or grants an exemption to the regulations. The foreign exporter may save time for the prospective importer by furnishing him complete information concerning the presence of NRC-controlled commodities in U.S. importations.

Consumer Products—
Energy Conservation

11. Household Appliances. The Energy Policy and Conservation Act, as amended, calls for energy efficiency standards for household consumer appliances and for labeling them to indicate expected energy consumption. The Department of Energy, Consumer Products Efficiency Branch, Washington, D.C. 20585, is responsible for test procedures and energy performance standards. The Federal Trade Commission, Division of Energy and Product Information, Washington, D.C. 20580, regulates the labeling of these appliances. The Act covers the following consumer products: (1) refrigerators and refrigerator-freezers; (2) freezers; (3) dishwashers; (4) clothes dryers; (5) water heaters; (6) room air conditioners; (7) home heating equipment, not including furnaces; (8) television sets; (9) kitchen ranges and ovens; (10) clothes washers; (11) humidifiers and dehumidifiers; (12) central air conditioners; (13) furnaces; (14) certain other types of household consumer appliances, as appropriate.

Importations of these products must comply with the applicable Department of Energy and Federal Trade Commission requirements. Importers should contact these agencies for requirements which will be in effect at the time of anticipated shipment. It should be noted that not all appliances are covered by requirements of both agencies.

Consumer Products—
Safety

Any consumer product offered for importation will be refused admission if the product fails to comply with an applicable consumer product safety rule, specified labeling or certification requirements, or is determined to be a hazardous product or contain a product defect which constitutes a substantial product hazard.

12. Flammable Fabrics. Any article of wearing apparel or interior furnishing, or any fabric or related material which is intended for use or which may be used in wearing apparel or interior furnishings cannot be imported into the United States if it fails to conform to an applicable flammability standard issued under section 4 of the Flammable Fabrics Act. This Act is administered by the U.S. Consumer Product Safety Commission, Washington,

D.C. 20207. Certain products can be imported into the United States as provided in Section 11(c) of the Act for the purpose of finishing or processing to render such products not so highly flammable as to be dangerous when worn by individuals, provided that the exporter states on the invoice or other paper relating to the shipment that the shipment is being made for that purpose. The provisions of the Flammable Fabrics Act apply to products manufactured in the United States, as well as to imported products.

Electronic Products

13. Radiation Producing Products. Television receivers, cold-cathode gas discharge tubes, microwave ovens, cabinet and diagnostic X-ray equipment and devices, laser products, and other electronic products for which there are radiation performance standards are subject to the Radiation Control for Health and Safety Act of 1968. An electronic product imported for sale or use in the United States for which there is a radiation performance standard may be imported only if there is filed with each importation an importer's entry notice (Form FD 701) and an electronic product declaration (Form FD 2877) which are issued by the Food and Drug Administration, Bureau of Radiological Health, Rockville, Md. 20857.

The declaration must describe the compliance status of the product. The importer must affirm that the product either was (1) manufactured prior to the effective date of the applicable Federal standard; or (2) complies with the standard and has a label affixed by the manufacturer certifying compliance; or (3) does not comply with the standard but is being imported only for purposes of research, investigation, study, demonstration, or training; or (4) does not now comply with the standard but will be brought into compliance. The provisions of the Radiation Control for Health and Safety Act apply to electronic products manufactured in the United States, as well as to imported products.

14. Radio Frequency Devices. Radios, tape recorders, stereos, televisions, citizen band radios or combinations thereof, and other radio frequency devices are subject to radio emission standards of the Federal Communications Commission, Washington, D.C. 20554, under the Communications Act of 1934, as amended. Importations of such products must be accompanied by an FCC declaration (FCC 740) certifying that the imported model or device is in conformity with, will be brought into conformity, or is exempt from the Federal Communications Commission requirements.

Foods, Drugs,
Cosmetics, and
Medical Devices

15. Foods, Cosmetics, etc. The importation into the United States of food, beverages, drugs, devices, and cosmetics is governed by the provisions of the Federal Food,

(cont.)

221

Drug, and Cosmetic Act which is administered by the Food and Drug Administration of the Department of Health and Human Services, Rockville, Md. 20857. That Act prohibits the importation of articles that are adulterated or misbranded including products that are defective, unsafe, filthy, or produced under unsanitary conditions. The term "misbranded" includes statements, designs, or pictures in labeling that are false or misleading and failure to provide required information in labeling.

Imported products regulated by the Food and Drug Administration are subject to inspection at the time of entry. Shipments found not to comply with the laws and regulations are subject to detention. They must be brought into compliance, destroyed, or re-exported. At the discretion of the Food and Drug Administration, an importer may be permitted to bring a nonconforming importation into compliance if it is possible to do so. Any sorting, reprocessing, or relabeling must be supervised by the Food and Drug Administration at the expense of the importer.

Various imported foods such as confectionery, dairy products, poultry, eggs and egg products, meats, fruits, nuts, and vegetables are also subject to requirements of other agencies as discussed in this booklet. Seafoods are also subject to the requirements of the National Marine Fisheries Service of the Department of Commerce, Washington, D.C. 20852.

16. Biological Drugs. The manufacture and importation of biological products for human consumption are regulated under the Public Health Service Act. Domestic and foreign manufacturers of such products must obtain a license for both the manufacturing establishment and the product intended to be produced or imported. Additional information may be obtained from the Food and Drug Administration, Department of Health and Human Services, Rockville, Md. 20857.

Biological drugs for animals are regulated under the Virus Serum Toxin Act administered by the Department of Agriculture. The importation of viruses, serums, toxins and analogous products, and organisms and vectors for use in the treatment of domestic animals is prohibited unless the importer holds a permit from the Department of Agriculture covering the specific product. These importations are also subject to special labeling requirements.

17. Biological Materials and Vectors. The importation into the United States for sale, barter, or exchange of any virus, therapeutic serum, toxin, antitoxin, or analogous products, or arsphenamine or its derivatives (or any other trivalent organic arsenic compound), except materials to be used in research experiments, applicable to the prevention, treatment, or cure of diseases or injuries of man is prohibited unless these products have been propagated or prepared at an establishment holding an unsuspended and unrevoked license for such manufacturing issued by the Secretary, Department of Health and Human Services. Samples of the licensed product must accompany each importation for forwarding by the port director of Customs at the port of entry to the Director, Bureau of Biologics, Food and Drug Administration, Bethesda, Maryland 20014.

A permit from the U.S. Public Health Service, Atlanta, Georgia 30333, is required for shipments of any etiological agent or insect, animal or plant vector of human disease or any exotic living insect, animal, or plant capable of being a vector of human disease.

18. Narcotic Drugs and Derivatives. The importation of controlled substances including narcotics, marihuana and other dangerous drugs is prohibited except when imported in compliance with regulations of the Drug Enforcement Administration of the Department of Justice, Washington, D.C. 20537. Examples of some of the prohibited controlled substances are amphetamines; barbiturates; coca leaves and derivatives such as cocaine; hallucinogenic substances such as LSD, mescaline, peyote, marihuana and other forms of Cannabis; opiates including methadone; opium including opium derivatives, such as morphine and heroin; synthetic substitutes for narcotic drugs.

Gold, Silver, Currency, Stamps

19. Gold and Silver. The provisions of the National Stamping Act, as amended (15 U.S.C. 291-300) are enforced by the Department of Justice, Washington, D.C. 20530. Articles made of gold or alloys thereof are prohibited importation into the United States if the gold content is one-half carat divergence below the indicated fineness. In the case of articles made of gold or gold alloys, including the solder and alloy of inferior fineness, a one carat divergence below the indicated fineness is permitted. Articles marked "sterling" or "sterling silver" must assay at least 0.925 of pure silver with a 0.004 divergence allowed. Other articles of silver or silver alloys must assay not less than 0.004 part below the indicated fineness thereof. Articles marked "coin" or "coin silver" must contain at least 0.900 part pure silver with an allowable divergence therefrom of 0.004 part.

A person placing articles of gold or silver bearing a fineness or quality mark such as 14K, sterling, etc., in the mail or in interstate commerce must place his name or registered trademark next to the fineness mark in letters the same size as the fineness mark. The trademark or name is not required at the time of importation; therefore, Customs has no direct responsibility for enforcement

(cont.)

of the law. Persons making inquiry or seeking advice or interpretation of the law should consult the Department of Justice.

Articles bearing the words "United States Assay" are prohibited importations. Articles which are made wholly or in part of inferior metal and are plated or filled with gold or silver or alloys thereof and are marked with the degree of fineness must also be marked to indicate the plated or filled content, and in such cases the use of the words "sterling" or "coin" is prohibited.

All restrictions on the purchase, holding, selling, or otherwise dealing with gold were removed effective December 31, 1974, and gold may be imported subject to the usual Customs entry requirements. Under the Hobby Protection Act, any imitation numismatic item must be plainly and permanently marked "copy"; those that do not comply are subject to seizure and forfeiture. Unofficial gold coin restrikes must be marked with the country of origin. It is advisable to obtain a copy of the legal proclamation under which the coins are issued or an affidavit of government sanction of coins should be secured from a responsible banking official if the proclamation is unavailable.

20. Counterfeit Articles. Articles bearing facsimiles or replicas of coins or securities of the United States or of any foreign country are prohibited importation. Counterfeits of coins in circulation in the United States; counterfeited, forged, or altered obligations or other securities of the United States or of any foreign government; plates, dies, or other apparatus which may be used in making any of the foregoing are prohibited importations.

21. Monetary Instruments. Under the Currency and Foreign Transactions Reporting Act, 31 USC 1101 et seq., if more than $5,000 in monetary instruments is transported or caused to be transported (including by mail or other means) on any occasion into or out of the United States, or if a person in the United States receives more than that amount, a report of the transaction, Customs Form 4790, must be filed with U.S. Customs. Monetary instruments include U.S. or foreign coin, currency, travelers checks, money orders, and negotiable instruments or investment securities in bearer form but do not include bank checks, travelers checks, or money orders made payable to the order of a named person which have not been endorsed or which bear restrictive endorsement.

22. Postage stamps. Facsimiles of United States postage stamps are prohibited except those for philatelic, educational, historical, or newsworthy purposes. Further information should be obtained from the United States Secret

Service, Department of the Treasury, Washington, D.C. 20223.

23. Pesticides. The importation into the United States of economic poisons and devices, including insecticides, Paris greens, lead arsenates, fungicides, herbicides, and rodenticides, is governed by the provisions of the Insecticide, Fungicide, and Rodenticide Act of 1947, as amended by the Federal Environmental Pesticide Control Act of 1972. All imported pesticides are required to be registered in accordance with the criteria established by the Environmental Protection Agency, Office of Pesticides and Toxic Substances, Washington, D.C. 20460. Devices, although not required to be registered, must not bear any statement, design, or graphic representation that is false or misleading in any particular. Importations of pesticides and devices will not be released from Customs custody unless a Notice of Arrival approved by the Office of Pesticides and Toxic Substances is presented to Customs.

24. Toxic Substances. The Toxic Substances Control Act, effective January 1, 1977, regulates the manufacturing, processing, distribution in commerce, use or disposal of any chemical substance or mixture that may present an unreasonable risk of injury to health and the environment. This includes importation of such substances into the United States. Inquiries should be directed to the Office of Pesticides and Toxic Substances, Environmental Protection Agency, Washington, D.C. 20460.

25. Hazardous Substances. The importation into the United States of dangerous caustic or corrosive substances in packages suitable for household use and of hazardous substances is regulated by the Hazardous Substances Act; the Caustic Poison Act; the Food, Drug and Cosmetic Act; and the Consumer Product Safety Act. The marking, labeling, packaging, and transportation of hazardous materials, substances, wastes, and their containers is regulated by the Materials Transportation Bureau of the Department of Transportation, Washington, D.C. 20590.

26. Textile Products. All textile fiber products imported into the United States shall be stamped, tagged, labeled, or otherwise marked with the following information as required by the Textile Fiber Products Identification Act, unless exempted from marking under section 12 of the Act.

a. The generic names and percentages by weight of the constitutent fibers present in the textile fiber product, exclusive of permissive ornamentation, in amounts of more than 5 percent in order of predominance by weight, with any percentage of fiber or fibers required to be designated as "other fiber" or "other fibers" appearing last. Fibers

(cont.)

225

present in amounts of 5 percent or less must be designated as "other fibers."

b. The name of the manufacturer or the name or registered identification number issued by the Federal Trade Commission of one or more persons marketing or handling the textile fiber product. A word trademark, used as a house mark, registered in the United States Patent Office, may be used on labels in lieu of the name otherwise required, if the owner of such trademark furnishes a copy of the registration to the Federal Trade Commission prior to use.

c. The name of the country where processed or manufactured.

For the purpose of the enforcement of the Textile Fiber Products Identification Act, a commercial invoice covering a shipment of textile fiber products exceeding $500 in value and subject to the labeling requirements of the Act is required to show the information noted in chapter 6, in addition to that ordinarily required on the invoices.

Regulations and pamphlets containing the text of the Textile Fiber Products Identification Act may be obtained from the Federal Trade Commission, Washington, D.C. 20580.

27. **Wool.** Any product containing woolen fiber imported into the United States, with the exception of carpets, rugs, mats, upholsteries, and articles made more than 20 years prior to importation, shall be tagged, labeled, or otherwise clearly marked with the following information as required by the Wool Products Labeling Act of 1939:

a. The percentage of the total fiber weight of the wool product, exclusive of ornamentation not exceeding 5 percent of the total fiber weight of (1) wool, (2) recycled wool, (3) each fiber other than wool if the percent by weight of such fiber is 5 percent or more, and (4) the aggregate of all other fibers.

b. The maximum percent of the total weight of the wool product, of any nonfibrous loading, filling, or adulterating matter.

c. The name of the manufacturer or person introducing the product in commerce in the United States; i.e., the importer. If the importer has a registered identification number issued by the Federal Trade Commission, that number may be used instead of the individual's name.

For the purpose of the enforcement of the Wool Products Labeling Act, a commercial invoice covering a shipment of wool products exceeding $500 in value and subject to the labeling requirements of the act is required to show the information noted in chapter 6.

Customs Clearance

The provisions of the Wool Products Labeling Act apply to products manufactured in the United States as well as to imported products.

Pamphlets containing the text of the Wool Products Labeling Act and the regulations may be obtained from the Federal Trade Commission, Washington, D.C. 20580.

28. Fur. Any article of wearing apparel made in whole or in part of fur or used fur, with the exception of articles that are made of new fur of which the cost or manufacturer's selling price does not exceed $7, imported into the United States shall be tagged, labeled, or otherwise clearly marked to show the following information as required by the Fur Products Labeling Act:

a. The name of the manufacturer or person introducing the product in commerce in the United States; i.e., the importer. If the importer has a registered identification number, that number may be used instead of the individual's name.

b. The name or names of the animal or animals that produced the fur as set forth in the Fur Products Name Guide and as permitted under the rules and regulations.

c. That the fur product contains used or damaged fur when such is the fact.

d. That the fur product is bleached, dyed, or otherwise artificially colored when such is the fact.

e. That the fur product is composed in whole or in substantial part of paws, tails, bellies, or waste fur when such is the fact.

f. The name of the country of origin of any imported furs contained in a fur product.

The entry or withdrawal from warehouse for consumption of raw or not dressed, or dressed ermine, fox, kolinsky, marten, mink, muskrat, and weasel furs and skins which are products of the Union of Soviet Socialist Republics (Russia) or any part of China, which at the time of entry or withdrawal from warehouse for consumption is under Communist domination or control, is prohibited.

For the purpose of enforcement of the Fur Products Labeling Act, a commercial invoice covering a shipment exceeding $500 in value of furs or fur products is required to show the information noted in chapter 6.

The provisions of the Fur Products Labeling Act apply to fur and fur products in the United States as well as to imported furs and fur products. Regulations and pamphlets containing the text of the Fur Products Labeling Act may be obtained from the Federal Trade Commission, Washington, D.C. 20580.

Trademarks, Trade Names, and Copyrights

29. Trademarks and Trade Names. Articles bearing counterfeit trademarks, or marks which copy or simulate a registered trademark of a United States or foreign corpo-

(cont.)

ration are prohibited importation, provided a copy of the U.S. trademark registration is filed with the Commissioner of Customs and recorded in the manner provided by regulations (19 CFR 133.1–133.7). The U.S. Customs Service also affords similar protection against unauthorized shipments bearing trade names which are recorded with Customs pursuant to regulations (19 CFT Part 133, Subpart B). It is also unlawful to import articles bearing genuine trademarks owned by a U.S. citizen or corporation without permission of the U.S. trademark owner, if the foreign and domestic trademark owners are not parent and subsidiary companies or otherwise under common ownership and control, provided the trademark has been recorded with Customs and the U.S. trademark owner has not authorized the distribution of trademarked articles abroad.

The Customs Reform and Simplification Act of 1978 strengthened the protection afforded trademark owners against the importation of articles bearing a counterfeit mark. A "counterfeit trademark" is defined as a spurious trademark which is identical with, or substantially indistinguishable from, a registered trademark. Articles bearing a counterfeit trademark which are seized by Customs and forfeited to the government may be (1) given to any Federal, state, or local government agency which has established a need for the article; (2) given to a charitable institution; or (3) sold at public auction if more than 1 year has passed since forfeiture and no eligible organization has established a need for the article. The law also provides an exemption from trademark restrictions for certain articles accompanying a person arriving in the United States when the articles are for personal use and not for sale.

30. Copyrights. Section 602(a) of the Copyright Revision Act of 1976 (17 U.S.C. 602(a)) provides that the importation into the United States of copies of a work acquired outside the United States without authorization of the copyright owner is an infringement of the copyright. Articles imported in violation of the import prohibitions are subject to seizure and forfeiture. Forfeited articles shall be destroyed; however, the articles may be returned to the country of export whenever Customs is satisfied that there was no intentional violation. The substantial similarity test is employed to determine if a design has been copied. Copyright owners seeking import protection from the U.S. Customs Service must register their claim to copyright with the U.S. Copyright Office and record their registration with Customs in accordance with applicable regulations (19 CFR Part 133, Subpart D).

The U.S. Customs Service also enforces the "manufacturing clause" of the Copyright Revision Act of 1976 (17 U.S.C. 601). In general, the "manufacturing clause" prohibits the importation of works authored by a U.S. national or domiciliary consisting preponderantly of nondramatic literary material that is in the English language and protected by copyright, unless the portions consisting of such material have been manufactured in the United States or Canada. The manufacturing requirements do not extend to dramatic, musical, pictorial or graphic works; foreign language works; bilingual or multilingual dictionaries; or public domain material. The manufacturing restrictions will terminate on July 1, 1986, unless extended by Congress.

Wildlife and Pets

31. Wildlife and Pets. The importation of live wild or game animals, birds, and other wildlife, or any part or product made therefrom, and the eggs of wild or game birds, is subject to certain prohibitions, restrictions, permit and quarantine requirements of several Government agencies. Importations of wildlife, parts, or their products must be entered at certain designated Customs ports of entry unless an exception is granted by the U.S. Fish and Wildlife Service, Department of the Interior, Washington, D.C. 20240.

On or after January 1, 1981, most firms (with some significant exceptions) importing or exporting wildlife must obtain a license from the Fish and Wildlife Service. Applications and further information may be obtained from the Fish and Wildlife Special Agent in Charge for the state in which the importer or exporter is located.

Endangered species of wildlife and certain species of animals and birds are generally prohibited entry into the United States and may be imported only under a permit granted by the U.S. Fish and Wildlife Service. Specific information concerning import requirements should be obtained from that agency.

Antique articles which would otherwise be prohibited under the Endangered Species Act may be admitted provided certain conditions are met. These articles must be entered at certain designated antique ports.

The taking and importation of marine mammals and their products are subject to the requirements of the Marine Mammal Protection Act of 1972 and cannot be imported without a permit from the National Marine Fisheries Service, National Oceanic and Atmospheric Administration, Washington, D.C. 20235, or the U.S. Fish and Wildlife Service.

Regulations to implement the Convention on International Trade in Endangered Species of Wild Fauna and Flora became effective on May 23, 1977. Certain animals, mammals, birds, reptiles, amphibians, fish, snails, clams,

(cont.)

229

and insects may be prohibited or require permits or certification which may be obtained from the U.S. Fish and Wildlife Service.

The importation into the United States of any wild animal or bird is prohibited if the animal or bird was captured, taken, shipped, possessed, or exported contrary to the law of the foreign country or subdivision thereof. In addition, no wild animal or bird from any foreign country may be taken, purchased, sold or possessed contrary to the laws of any State, territory, or possession of the United States.

The importation of the feathers or skin of any wild bird, except for scientific and educational purposes, is prohibited. This prohibition does not apply to fully manufactured artificial flies used for fishing. The feathers of certain birds for use in the manufacture of artificial flies used for fishing or for millinery purposes may be imported under permit issued by the U.S. Fish and Wildlife Service.

Live birds protected under the Migratory Bird Treaty Act may be imported into the United States from foreign countries for scientific or propagating purposes only under permits issued by the U.S. Fish and Wildlife Service. These migratory birds and any game animals (e.g., antelope, mountain sheep, deer, bears, peccaries, squirrels, rabbits, and hares) imported from Mexico, must be accompanied by Mexican export permits.

Importations in this class are also subject to the quarantine requirements of the Department of Agriculture and the United States Public Health Service. Appropriate inquiries in this respect should be directed to those agencies.

The importation of birds, cats, dogs, monkeys, and turtles is subject to the requirements of U.S. Public Health Service, Center for Disease Control, Quarantine Division, located in Atlanta, Georgia 30333, and the Veterinary Services of the Animal and Plant Health Inspection Service, Department of Agriculture, Hyattsville, Maryland 20782.

Other Miscellaneous Prohibited or Restricted Merchandise

White or yellow phosphorus matches, fireworks banned under federal or state restrictions, pepper shells, switchblade knives, and lottery tickets are prohibited.

32. Foreign Assets Control Restrictions. The Foreign Assets Control Regulations (31 CFR, part 500) prohibit unlicensed importations of merchandise of mainland Chinese, North Korean, Cambodian, or Vietnamese origin, including articles grown, produced, or manufactured therein. The unlicensed importation of goods of Cuban origin, articles containing Cuban components, and all goods imported from or through Cuba are prohibited.

Importations of merchandise of Zimbabwe origin, as well as ferrochrome and certain alloyed steel mill products from other countries are now authorized. Goods of mainland Chinese origin are now authorized to be imported under general license contained in the regulations.

Specific inquiries should be made to Foreign Assets, Control Department of the Treasury, Washington, D.C. 20220, or to the Foreign Assets Control Division, Federal Reserve Bank of New York, New York 10045.

33. Foreign Excess Property. Importation of surplus materials, products, or equipment is subject to Foreign Excess Property Regulations. Importations must be accompanied by an import authorization issued by the International Trade Administration, Department of Commerce, Washington, D.C. 20230.

34. Obscene, Immoral, and Seditious Matter. Section 305, Tariff Act of 1930, as amended, prohibits the importation of any book, writing, advertisement, circular, or picture containing any matter advocating or urging treason or insurrection against the United States, or forcible resistance to any law of the United States, or containing any threat to take the life of or inflict bodily harm upon any person in the United States, or any obscene book, writing, advertisement circular, picture or other representation, figure, or image on or of paper or other material, or any case, instrument, or other article which is obscene or immoral, or any drug or medicine for causing unlawful abortion.

35. Petroleum and Petroleum Products. Importation of petroleum and petroleum products is subject to the requirements of the Department of Energy. Most products require an import license from the Office of Oil Imports, Department of Energy, Washington, D.C. 20461, before Customs will authorize the importations. These importations may also be subject to an oil import license fee collected and administered by the Department of Energy.

36. Products of Convict or Forced Labor. Merchandise produced, mined, or manufactured by means of the use of convict labor, forced labor, or indentured labor under penal sanctions is prohibited importation.

37. Unfair Competition. Section 337 of the Tariff Act, as amended, prohibits the importation of merchandise if the President finds that unfair methods of competition or unfair acts exist. This section is most commonly invoked in the case of patent violations, although a patent need not be at issue. Prohibition of entries of the merchandise in question generally is for the term of the patent, although a different term may be specified.

Following a section 337 investigation, the International Trade Commission may find that unfair methods of com-

231

(cont.)

petition or unfair acts exist with respect to the importation of certain merchandise. After the International Trade Commission has issued an order, the President is allowed 60 days to take action; should the 60 days expire without presidential action, the order becomes final. During the 60-day period or until the President acts, importation of the merchandise is allowed under a special bond but it must be recalled by Customs if appropriate under the conditions of the order when it becomes final. If the President determines that entry of the merchandise is not in violation of section 337, the bond is canceled.

Alcoholic Beverages

Any person or firm wishing to engage in the business of importing distilled spirits, wines, or malt beverages into the United States must first obtain an importer's basic permit from the Bureau of Alcohol, Tobacco and Firearms, Department of the Treasury, Washington, D.C. 20226. That agency is responsible for administering the Federal Alcohol Administration Act.

Distilled spirits imported in bulk containers of a capacity of more than one gallon may be withdrawn from Customs custody only by persons to whom it is lawful to sell or otherwise dispose of distilled spirits in bulk. Bulk or bottled shipments of imported spirits or distilled or intoxicating liquors must at the time of importation be accompanied by a copy of a bill of lading or other documents, such as an invoice showing the name of the consignee, the nature of its contents, and the quantity contained therein (18 U.S.C. 1263).

U.S. Customs will not release alcoholic beverages destined to any State for use in violation of its laws, and the importation of alcoholic beverages in the mails is prohibited.

The United States adopted the metric system of measure with the enactment of the Metric Conversion Act of 1975. In general, imported wine must conform with the metric standards of fill if bottled or packed on or after January 1, 1979. Imported distilled spirits, with some exceptions, must conform with the metric standards of fill if bottled or packed on or after January 1, 1980. Distilled spirits and wines bottled or packed prior to the respective dates must be accompanied by a statement to that effect signed by a duly authorized official of the appropriate foreign country. This statement may be a separate document or be shown on the invoice. Malt beverages including beer are not subject to metric standards of fill.

Marking

If distilled spirits are bottled abroad in containers having a capacity of 200 milliliters or more, these containers must be legibly and permanently marked with (1) the words "Liquor Bottle" and (2) the city or country address of the manufacturer of the spirits or of the exporter abroad, or the city of address of the importer in the United States. Empty liquor bottles imported to be filled in the United States shall be marked with the words "Liquor Bottle" and the city or country of address of the bottle manufacturer. Empty or filled distinctive liquor bottles not bearing such indicia may be imported only with the approval of the Bureau of Alcohol, Tobacco and Firearms.

Imported wines in bottles and other containers are required to be packaged, marked, branded, and labeled in accordance with the regulations in 27 CFR Part 4. Imported malt beverages are also required to be labeled in conformance with the regulations in 27 CFR Part 7.

Each bottle, cask or other immediate container of imported distilled spirits, wines, or malt beverages must be marked for customs purposes to indicate the country of origin of the alcoholic beverage contained therein, unless the shipment comes within one of the exceptions outlined in chapter 21 of this booklet.

Certificate of Label Approval

Labels affixed to bottles of imported distilled spirits and wine must be covered by certificates of label approval issued to the importer by the Bureau of Alcohol, Tobacco and Firearms. Certificates of label approval or photostatic copies must be filed with Customs before the goods may be released for sale in the United States. Certificate of label approval requirements must also be met for fermented malt beverages if for delivery into a State which has adopted Federal labeling requirements or has labeling requirements similar to the Federal requirements (27 CFR Parts 4, 5, and 7).

Red Strip Stamps

A red strip stamp indicating the payment of internal revenue taxes must be affixed to each bottle of imported distilled spirits subject to tax before it can be released from Customs custody. An alternate device, if approved by the Bureau of Alcohol, Tobacco and Firearms, may be used in lieu of the strip stamp. The name and address of the importer must be indelibly overprinted in plain and legible letters on each stamp or device. The importer may send these stamps or devices abroad to be affixed by the bottler or exporter, or they may be affixed to the containers under Customs supervision in a bonded warehouse before release from Customs custody.

Foreign Documentation

Importers of wines and distilled spirits should consult the Bureau of Alcohol, Tobacco and Firearms about foreign documentation required; for example, certificates of origin, age, etc.

(cont.)

*Requirements
of Other Agencies*

In addition, importation of alcoholic beverages is subject to the specific requirements of the Food and Drug Administration. Certain plant materials when used for bottle jackets for wine or other liquids are subject to special restrictions under plant quarantine regulations of the Animal and Plant Health Inspection Service. All bottle jackets made of dried or unmanufactured plant materials are subject to inspection upon arrival and are referred to the Department of Agriculture.

*Confectionery
Containing Alcohol*

Confectionery which contains any alcohol is considered an adulterated article and as such is generally prohibited under the Food, Drug, and Cosmetic Act. This prohibition does not apply to any confectionery which contains less than one-half percent by volume of alcohol which is derived solely from the use of flavoring extracts.

Motor Vehicles and Boats

*Automobiles, Vehicles,
and Vehicle
Equipment*

Safety Standards. All imported automobiles or automobile equipment, whether new or used, manufactured after December 31, 1967 (except those designed for competition, show, test, or experimental purposes), will be refused entry into the United States unless they are in conformity with applicable Federal motor vehicle safety standards. An automobile or automobile equipment imported solely with the intention of exportation and so labeled is exempt from these safety standards. Motorcyles and mopeds are also required to conform with certain safety standards. The best evidence of conformance to the safety standards is the original manufacturer's certification label attached to the car, which must include the date of manufacture and vehicle identification number. A declaration, NHTSA Form HS-7, is required to be filed at the time of entry for all subject importations.

If the vehicle or equipment was manufactured in conformity with the applicable safety standards and lacks the required certificate, the importer's declaration should be accompanied by a statement of the original manufacturer as evidence of compliance. If the vehicle or equipment was not manufactured in conformity with the applicable safety standards but has since been brought into conformity, the declaration must be accompanied by a statement of the manufacturer, contractor, or other persons who have brought the vehicle or equipment into conformity which describes the nature and extent of the work performed. Bond is required in both cases until claim of conformity is approved by NHTSA.

A nonconforming automobile or automobile equipment may be admitted under bond. It must be brought into conformity within 120 days or such additional time as may be allowed by the Administrator of the National Highway Traffic Safety Administration, if good cause is known. Note: the maximum time authorized for bringing into conformity is 180 days after entry.

For complete information, write to the U.S. Department of Transportation, Office of Enforcement, Motor Vehicle Program, National Highway Traffic Safety Administration, Washington, D.C. 20590.

Emissions Standards. The Clean Air Act, as amended, prohibits the importation into the United States of any motor vehicle or motor vehicle engine not in conformity with emission standards prescribed by the U.S. Environmental Protection Agency. For imported vehicles, these standards apply whether the vehicle is new or used. Vehicles imported for display, competition, or testing are allowed entry provided they are not sold or licensed for use on the public roads.

In addition to passenger cars, certain trucks, multipurpose vehicles (e.g., campers), motorcycles, etc., are subject to EPA standards. Model years covered by EPA go back to 1968. All complying 1971 and later models are required to have a label in a readily visible position in the engine compartment stating that the vehicle conforms to U.S. standards. This label will read "Vehicle Emission Control Information" and include the full corporate name and trademark of the manufacturer. If this label is not present, the importer should verify conformity with the manufacturer.

A declaration, EPA Form 3520-1, is required to be filed at the time of entry for all nonconforming importations. A nonconforming vehicle or engine may be admitted under bond provided it is brought into conformity within the time period specified by EPA.

For further information, including details of anticipated requirements and procedures, contact: Environmental Protection Agency, Public Information Center (PM-215), Washington, D.C. 20460.

Word of Caution. Modifications necessary to bring a nonconforming vehicle into conformity with the safety standards and/or emission standards may require extensive engineering, be impractical or impossible, or the labor and materials may be unduly expensive.

Boat Safety Standards   Imported boats and associated equipment are subject to U.S. Coast Guard safety regulations or standards under the Federal Boat Safety Act of 1971. Products subject to standards must have a compliance certification label affixed. Certain hulls also require a hull identification number to be affixed. A U.S. Coast Guard import declaration is required to be filed with entries of nonconforming

(cont.)

235

boats. Further information may be obtained from the Commandant, U.S. Coast Guard, Washington, D.C. 20593.

Dutiability

Vessels that are brought into the United States for use in trade or commerce are not dutiable. Yachts or pleasure boats brought into the United States by nonresidents for their own use in pleasure cruising are also not dutiable. Yachts or pleasure boats owned by a resident or brought into the United States for sale or charter to a resident are dutiable. Yachts or pleasure boats owned by a resident or brought into the United States for sale or charter to a resident are dutiable. Further information may be obtained in U.S. Customs pamphlet "Pleasure Boats."

Restrictions on Use

Vessels that are foreign-built or of foreign registry may be used in the United States for pleasure purposes and in the foreign trade of the United States. However, Federal law prohibits the use of such vessels in the coastwise trade, i.e., the transportation of passengers or merchandise between points in the United States, including carrying fishing parties for hire. Questions concerning the use of foreign-built or foreign-flag vessels should be addressed to Chief, Carrier Rulings Branch, U.S. Customs Service, 1301 Constitution Ave., N.W., Washington, D.C. 20229.

Source: Reprinted from Department of the Treasury, U.S. Customs Service, *Importing into the United States.*

17

FOREIGN TRADE ZONES

A foreign trade zone (free trade zone in other countries) is an industrial park that operates under U.S. Customs regulations but is considered legally outside U.S. Customs jurisdiction. The Foreign Trade Zones Act of 1934 (amended in 1950) created foreign trade zones (FTZ) in the United States.

An FTZ can be operated by a state, local community, or corporation. FTZs are often, but not always, located near lakeports, seaports, and airports. "Subzones" are authorized for companies that have special manufacturing requirements.

In 1982 there were 107 FTZs operating in the United States. The value of the goods received totaled $3.4 billion with $2.02 billion admitted to subzones for manufacturing and assembly operations.[1] About 53 percent of the goods were reexported from FTZs, 30 percent from subzones. Some 1500 firms use zones, including small and large manufacturers. Employment in FTZs and subzones reached approximately 14,900 in 1982. Yet this figure doesn't take into account the additional employment generated outside the zone in service industries such as banking, legal counsel, insurance, marketing, consulting, and education.

Merchandise brought into an FTZ or subzone can be stored, sold, exhibited, broken up, repacked, assembled, distributed, sorted, graded, cleaned, or mixed with foreign or domestic merchandise. There is no time limit placed on merchandise imported into an FTZ.

When a product enters a FTZ it is checked by a customs official and placed in one of five statuses. The importer must apply for the status com-

[1]*44th Annual Report of the Foreign Trade Zones Board to the Congress of the United States.* (Washington, D.C.: U.S. Government Printing Office, 1985.)

patible with his or her intentions for the product when the product is entered into the FTZ.

1. With "Privileged Foreign Status" products are classified and *appraised* as of the date of entry. This classification will hold when the products are shipped from the FTZ, and are subject to duties, even if they have been manipulated or manufactured.

2. "Privileged Domestic Status" is the classification used for products made in the United States, for previously imported products on which duties have already been paid, and goods previously admitted to the United States duty-free. If the goods have this status, the importer won't be charged customs duties when the product is readmitted to customs territory.

3. Products that enter that zone under "Nonprivileged Status Foreign and Domestic" are appraised according to their condition at time of *entry for consumption* into customs territory.

4. "Articles of Mixed Status" are appraised according to their privileged (domestic/foreign) and nonprivileged components.

5. "Zone Restricted Status" is used for merchandise transferred from the customs territory for storage or for satisfying a legal requirement for exportation or destruction. Products entering under this category can't be returned to customs territory nor can they be manipulated or manufactured.

Benefits for Importers

1. The importer doesn't pay a customs duty until the goods leave the zone. While in the zone the product can be manipulated or manufactured. A new Custom's Classification will reflect the product change. For instance, duties are higher for assembled goods than for parts. Higher rates are designed to encourage American assembly. Instead of paying the higher rates for the imported assembled product, manufacturers can mix foreign parts with domestic parts in zone assembly and ship the finished product out of the zone under a lower duty status.

A company can realize cost savings by entering bulk products into an FTZ. Waste can be removed. The shipment will be lighter when it leaves the territory and subject to lower duties. Damaged packages or broken bottles can also be discarded before duty assessment.

2. If there is a quota on the good, the good can be shipped into the

zone and stored until the quota is removed, or the product can be manip-ulated or manufactured within the zone into a product that is not subject to a quota.

3. No customs bond is necessary as long as the goods are in the zone.

Benefits for Exporters

Goods may be reexported from the zone free of duty and tax. If a man-ufacturer requires foreign parts to produce a product it intends to export, the manufacturer can import the product duty free by using an FTZ. When the manufacturer reexports, Customs doesn't assess a duty.

Restrictions

Products subject to internal revenue tax can't be manufactured in an FTZ. These include alcoholic beverages, products containing alcoholic bever-ages, perfumes containing alcohol, tobacco products, white phosphorus material, firearms, and sugar. Clocks and watch movements can't be man-ufactured in a zone, either. Retail trade can't be conducted in an FTZ. If it is illegal to import a product into the United States, it cannot be im-ported into an FTZ.

Additional information is available through the director of the local foreign trade zone or district customs director. Or write to the Foreign-Trade Zones Board, Department of Commerce, Washington, D.C. 20230.

GLOSSARY OF INTERNATIONAL TRADE TERMS

Ad Valorem Duty: U.S. Customs duty calculated as a percentage of the value of the goods.

Air Waybill: Analogous to the straight or nonnegotiable ocean bill of lading, the air waybill provides evidence of contract of carriage, receipt of goods, and transfer of ownership to the consignee. In addition, the air waybill serves as a document for customs declaration.

ATA Carnet: An international customs document that is recognized as an internationally valid guarantee and may be used in lieu of national customs documents and as security for import duties and taxes to cover the temporary admission of goods and sometimes the transit of goods. ATA Carnets are issued by National Chambers of Commerce affiliated with the International Chambers of Commerce, which also guarantees payment of duties in the event of failure to reexport. The ATA Carnet simplifies procedures for salespeople bringing equipment into the United States.

Balance of Payments: A tabulation of a country's credit and debit transactions with other countries and international institutions. These transactions are divided into two broad groups: Current Account and Capital Account. The Current Account includes exports and imports of goods, services (including investment income), and unilateral transfers. The Capital Account includes financial flows related to international direct investment, investment in government and private securities, international bank transactions, and changes in official gold holdings and foreign exchange reserves.

Balance of Trade: A component of balance of payments, or the surplus or deficit that results from comparing a country's expenditures on merchandise imports and receipts derived from its merchandise exports.

Barter: The direct exchange of goods for other goods, without the use of money as a medium of exchange.

Beggar-Thy-Neighbor Policy: A course of action through which a country tries to reduce unemployment and increase domestic output by raising tariffs and instituting nontariff barriers that impede imports, or by accomplishing the same objective through competitive devaluation in currency. Countries that pursued such policies in the early 1930s found that other countries retaliated by raising their own barriers against imports, which by reducing export markets tended to exacerbate the economic difficulties that precipitated the initial protectionist action. The U.S. Smoot-Hawley Tariff Act of 1930 is often cited as an example of this approach.

Bilateral Trade Agreement: A formal or informal agreement involving commerce between two countries. Such agreements sometimes list the quantities of specific goods that may be exchanged between participating countries within a given period.

(Ocean) Bill of Lading: The bill of lading serves three vital functions in international trade. It is evidence of a contract of carriage or the final receipt from the ocean carrier for the goods shipped. Second, it is a receipt for the cargo. Third, it is a document of title with which the consignee can claim the goods. It contains information such as the notify party, port of loading and discharge, destination, number of packages, marks, description of cargo, gross weight, condition of the goods. Types of bills of lading:

Clean: Such a B/L is issued when the shipment is received by the carrier in good order. Actually, "clean" is the only acceptable bill of lading, especially for draft and letter of credit shipments.

On Board: When the B/L is stamped "On Board," the carrier is certifying that the cargo has been placed aboard the named vessel. This B/L requires the signature of the captain or the captain's representative. The cargo *cannot* be along the side of the ship, in a warehouse or any other place except on board the named vessel. On draft or letter of credit transactions an On Board B/L is usually required for the bank to release funds to the shipper.

Stale: A B/L is termed "stale" when the exporter or his or her agent does not present the B/L to the issuing bank under a letter of credit transaction within a reasonable time after its date. The requirement is such that the B/L arrives at the port of importation *before* the steamer arrives.

Straight: A nonnegotiable B/L that provides for the delivery of goods to the person named in the B/L and to *no one else*.

(Shipper's) *Order:* This B/L is negotiable because it provides for the delivery of goods to a named person *or* to anyone he or she may designate, but only on proper endorsement and surrender of the B/L to the carrier or carrier's agents. Used with sight draft or letter of credit shipments. Shipper endorses original copy of B/L before presenting to bank for collection.

Through: Also termed a "combined transport document," when more than one carrier is handling the shipment (railroad, truck, and steamship) the same B/L can be used by all parties involved. One set of bills prevents the confusion and errors that may result when each carrier makes out a new set of bills at each transfer. This document shows, in addition to the information already contained in the ocean B/L, the place of delivery and evidence that the shipment is taken in charge.

C&F (port of import): Price quote covers the cost of the product, export packing, forwarder's fees, consular fees, inland freight, pier delivery, wharfage, and any other pier charges, and ocean or air freight.

C.I.F.: Quote is C&F terms plus cost of marine and war insurance. Exporters are commonly expected to deliver a C.I.F. quote.

Certificate of Origin: Signed statement providing evidence of the origin of the goods. For countries requiring a certificate of origin, the U.S. shipper needs to obtain the official seal or stamp from the district office of the U.S. Department of Commerce or the Chamber of Commerce. A certificate of origin is required for all imports into the United States.

Code of Conduct: International instruments that indicate standards of behavior by nation, states or multinational corporations deemed desirable by the international community. Several codes of conduct were negotiated during the Tokyo Round that liberalized and harmonized domestic measures that might impede trade, and these are considered legally binding for the countries that choose to adhere to them. Each of these codes is monitored by a special committee that meets under the auspices of GATT and encourages consulations and the settlement of disputes arising under the code. Countries that are not Contracting Parties to GATT may adhere to these codes. GATT Articles III through XXIII also contain commercial policy provisions that have been described as GATT's code of good conduct in trade matters. The United Nations has also encouraged the negotiation of several "voluntary" codes of conduct, including one that seeks to specify the rights and obligations of multinational corporations and of governments.

Commercial Invoice: Contains addresses of buyer and seller, shipment details, unit and total price, date, order number, quantity, weight, number of packages, shipping marks. Required in letter of credit transactions. Used for customs declarations and for the preparation of ocean bill of lading. Some countries require a certified commercial invoice. Check with Commerce Department for country regulations.

Commodity: Broadly defined, any article exchanged in trade, but most commonly used to refer to raw materials, including such minerals as tin, copper, and manganese, and bulk-produced agricultural products such as coffee, tea, and rubber.

Common External Tariff: A tariff rate uniformly applied by a common market or customs union, such as the European Community, to imports from countries outside the union.

Comparative Advantage: A central concept in international trade theory which holds that a country or a region should specialize in the production and export of those goods and services that it can produce relatively more efficiently than other goods and services, and import those goods and services in which it has a comparative disadvantage. This theory was first propounded by David Ricardo in his *Principles of Political Economy,* 1817, as a basis for increasing the economic welfare of a population through international trade. The comparative advantage theory normally favors specialized production in a country based on intensive utilization of those factors of production in which the country is relatively well-endowed (land, labor, capital, entrepreneurship) or "relative factor intensity" as advanced by the "Heckscher-Ohlin Theory of Factor Endowments."

Compound Duty: A combination of ad valorem (percentage) and specific duty.

Consignee: Importer (Buyer)

Consignor: Exporter (Shipper, Seller)

Consul: A government official residing in a foreign country who represents the interests of his or her country and its nationals.

Consular Invoice: Some countries require this form which is prepared in the language of the consignee's country. Obtain at consulate.

Countertrade: A reciprocal trading arrangement. Countertrade transactions include:

a) Counterpurchase agreements require the foreign supplier to purchase from the buyer goods and services unrelated to the goods and services sold, usually with a one- to five-year period.

b) Reverse countertrade contracts require the importer to export goods equivalent in value to a specified percentage of the value of the imported goods—an obligation that can be sold to an exporter in a third country.

c) Buyback arrangements obligate the foreign supplier of plant, machinery, or technology to buy from the importer a portion of the resultant production during a 5–25 year period.

d) Clearing agreements between two countries that agree to purchase specific amounts of each other's products over a specified period of time, using a designated "clearing currency" in transactions;

e) "Switch" arrangements that permit the sale of unpaid balances in a clearing account to be sold to a third party, usually at a discount, that may be used for producing goods in the country holding the balance;

f) Swap schemes through which products from different locations are traded to save transportation costs (for example, Soviet oil may be "swapped" for oil from a Latin American producer, so the Soviet oil is shipped to a country in South Asia, while the Latin American oil is shipped to Cuba);

g) Barter arrangements through which two parties directly exchange goods deemed to be of approximately equivalent value without any flow of money taking place.

Countervailing Duties: Special duties imposed on imports to offset the benefits of subsidies to producers or exporters in the exporting country. GATT Article VI permits the use of such duties. The Executive Branch of the U.S. Government has been legally empowered since the 1890s to impose countervailing duties in amounts equal to any bounties or grants reflected in products imported into the United States. Under U.S. law and the Tokyo Round Agreement on Subsidies and Countervailing Duties, a wide range of practices are recognized as constituting subsidies that may be offset through the imposition of countervailing duties.

Current Account: That portion of a country's balance of payments that records current (as opposed to capital) transactions, including visible trade (exports and imports), invisible trade (income and expenditures for services), profits earned from foreign operations, interest and transfer payments.

Customs Entries:

a) Consumption entry—a U.S. Customs form used for entering goods into the U.S. Estimated duties must be paid when the entry is filed.

b) Immediate delivery entry—used to expedite the clearance of cargo. It allows up to ten days for the payment of estimated duty and processing of the consumption entry. It permits the delivery of cargo prior to payment of the estimated duty and allows subsequent filing of the consumption entry and duty.

c) Immediate transportation entry—allows the cargo to be moved from the pier to an inland destination via a bonded carrier without the payment of duties or finalization of the entry at the port of arrival.

d) Transportation and exportation entry—allows goods coming from or going to a third country, such as Canada or Mexico, to enter the United States for the purpose of transshipment.

e) Warehouse entry—allows goods to be placed in a customs-bonded warehouse.

Customhouse Broker: A person or firm licensed by the Treasury Department. The broker enters and clears goods through Customs. He or she prepares customs documents, handles duty payment, and arranges inland transportation.

Customs-Bonded Warehouse: A warehouse where imported goods may be stored for a total of five years without the payment of duty or taxes.

Customs Classification: The particular category in a tariff nomenclature in which a product is classified for tariff purposes, or the procedure for determining the appropriate tariff category in a country's nomenclature system used for the classification, coding, and description of internationally traded goods. The major trading nations—except Canada, the Soviet Union, and the United States—classify imported goods in conformity with the Customs Cooperation Council Nomenclature (CCCN), formerly known as Brussels Tariff Nomenclature (BTN).

Customs Cooperation Council Nomenclature (CCCN): A system for classifying goods for customs purposes, formerly known as the Brussels Tariff Nomenclature (BTN).

Customs Harmonization: International efforts to increase the uniformity of customs nomenclatures and procedures in cooperating countries. The Customs Cooperation Council has been seeking since 1970 to develop an up-to-date and internationally accepted "Harmonized Commodity Coding and Description System" for classifying goods for customs, statistical, and other purposes.

Delivery Instructions: Provides specific information to the inland carrier concerning the arrangement made by the forwarder to deliver the merchandise to a particular ocean pier or airport. Used in the export trade.

Delivery Order: Issued by the consignee or customs broker to the ocean or air carrier as authority to release the cargo to the inland carrier. Used in the import trade.

Devaluation: The lowering of the value of a national currency in terms of the currency of another nation. Devaluation tends to reduce domestic demand for imports in a country by raising their prices in terms of the devalued currency and to raise foreign demand for the country's exports by reducing their prices in terms of foreign currencies. Devaluation can therefore help to correct a balance of payments deficit and sometimes provide a short-term basis for economic adjustment of a national economy.

Developed Countries: A term used to distinguish the advanced industrial countries. It includes OECD countries, the Soviet Union, and most of Eastern Europe. Sometimes referred to as the "North" because most of these advanced economies are located in the Northern Hemisphere.

Developing Countries or Lesser Developed Countries (LDCs):   A broad range of countries that generally lack a high degree of industrialization, infrastructure and other capital investment, sophisticated technology, widespread literacy, and advanced living standards among their populations. All of the countries of Africa (except South Africa), Asia and Oceania (except Australia, Japan, and New Zealand), Latin America, and the Middle East are generally considered "developing countries," as are a few European countries (Cyprus, Malta, Turkey, and Yugoslavia). Developing countries are further subdivided: 1) the wealthy OPEC countries advocate a financially sound international economy and open capital markets; 2) Newly Industrializing Countries (NICs) have a growing stake in an open international trading system; 3) A number of middle income countries—particularly commodity exporters—advocate commodity price stabilization schemes; 4) "Least Developed Countries" are predominantly agricultural and are heavily dependent on development assistance.

Dock Receipt: A receipt issued to verify that the cargo has arrived at the dock.

Documents Against Acceptance (D/A):   Used with a time draft, the draft and documents are sent to the overseas bank with instructions to "deliver against acceptance only." The title is released to the importer only when he or she signs an acceptance, stamped on a draft, guaranteeing payment on the draft.

Documents Against Payment (D/P):   Used with a sight draft, the exporter delivers all the necessary shipping documents together with the draft drawn at sight on the importer to the advising bank. The title is not released until payment is made on the shipment.

Dumping: Selling goods overseas at a price lower than the fair market value. Dumping is considered an unfair trade practice that can disrupt markets and injure producers of competitive products in the importing countries. If an American manufacturer suspects dumping, he or she can petition the International Trade Commission to investigate.

Drawback: Refund of duties because merchandise is manufactured and then exported. Importing into a foreign trade zone would avoid duty if reconstituted goods are exported.

Embargo: Sometimes called "sanctions," a prohibition on exports and imports, either with respect to specific products or specific countries.

Escape Clause: A provision in a bilateral or multilateral commercial agreement permitting a signatory nation to suspend tariff or other concessions when imports threaten serious harm to the producers of competitive domestic goods.

Exchange Controls: The rationing of foreign currencies, bank drafts, and other instruments for settling international financial obligations by countries seeking to ameliorate acute balance of payments difficulties. When such measures are imposed, importers must apply for prior authorization from the government to obtain the foreign currency required to bring in designated amounts and types of goods. Because such measures have the effect of restricting imports, they are considered nontariff barriers to trade.

Exchange Rate: The price at which one currency is exchanged for another currency, for gold, or for Special Drawing Rights.

Excise Tax: A selective tax—sometimes called a consumption tax—on certain goods produced within or imported into a country.

Ex-Dock: Price quote includes that of C.I.F. plus all costs associated with the export trade—unloading the vessel or aircraft, import duties, inland freight, and import broker's fees. Not recommended as a quote for exporters because many costs on the import side are difficult to assess.

Ex-Factory (Ex-Plant, Ex-Mill, Ex-Warehouse, Ex-Mine): Price quote only includes the cost of the product put out on the loading dock. Doesn't include the cost of export packing.

Export Trading Company: A business set up principally for the purpose of exporting, covered by The Export Trading Act of 1982, which allows banks to own ETCs and exempts ETCs from certain antitrust provisions.

Export Quota: Restrictions imposed by an exporting country on the value or volume of certain imports. Used for many different reasons—to alleviate temporary shortages, keep down inflation, bolster prices in world markets.

F.A.S. Vessel: (Free along side)—Price quote includes all costs of delivering the goods alongside the ocean vessel (or plane) and within reach of its loading tackle.

F.O.B. Plant: (Free on Board)—Price quote includes the cost of export packing.

F.O.B. Port: Price quote includes the costs of export packing, forwarder's fees, consular fees, and inland freight.

F.O.B. Vessel: Price quote includes all delivery costs up to and including the loading of the goods on the ocean vessel or aircraft.

Foreign Freight Forwarder: Acts as the exporter's agent—schedules, routes, and consolidates shipments, prepares documents, provides marine and war insurance.

Foreign Sales Corporation: A firm incorporated in areas designated by the Treasury Department where U.S. exports to sales offices enjoy tax exemptions.

Foreign Trade Zone: Analogous to the "free trade zone," an area outside U.S. custom territory. The FTZ can be administered through state, local, or corporate authority.

General License: No formal application required for "G-Dest" shipments. Check with Commerce Department for correct General License symbol for insertion in the Shipper's Export Declaration.

Generalized System of Preferences (GSP): Tariff preferences given to LDCs to encourage the exportation of manufactured goods from developing countries.

Graduation: The presumption that individual developing countries are capable of assuming greater responsibilities and obligations in the international community as their economies advance. Countries may remove the more advanced developing countries from eligibility for all or some products under the Generalized System of Preferences. The World Bank graduation moves a country from dependence on concessional grants to non-concessional loans from international financial institutions and private banks.

Gross Weight: Entire weight of goods, packing, and container ready for export shipment.

Import Substitution: An attempt by a country to reduce imports by encouraging the development of domestic industries.

Import Quota: Limitations on the quantity of imports that can be brought into a country.

Infant Industry Argument: The idea that new industries or firms should be protected from world competition until they are fully competitive.

Invisible Trade: Items such as freight, insurance, and financial services that are included in a country's balance of payments accounts even though they are not recorded as physically visible imports and exports.

Legal Weight: Weight of the goods plus any immediate wrappings. This weight doesn't include export crating.

Marine Insurance Terms: "Average" in marine law is the "loss" arising by damage to a ship or cargo.

"Perils of the Sea" are those causes of loss of goods for which the carrier is not legally liable, the elemental risks of ocean transport—the seas, fire, assailing thieves, jettison, and barratry—the basic perils that marine insurance policies cover.

a) General Average—a deliberate loss or damage to goods in the face of peril, which sacrifice is made for the preservation of the vessel and other goods.

b) Free of Particular Average (F.P.A.)—A marine insurance clause providing that partial loss or damage is not insured. F.P.A. American conditions—Free of particular average (partial loss not insured) unless caused by the vessel being stranded, sunk, burned, on fire, or in collision. F.P.A. English conditions—Free of particular average unless the vessel be stranded, sunk, burned, on fire, or in collision.

c) With Average (or With Particular Average)—Partial loss or damage to goods is insured. There may be a minimum percentage of damage, usually three percent, required before payment claim will be honored. These terms are usually used for damage caused by sea water, but can be extended to cover loss by theft, pilferage, delivery, leakage, and breakage. In addition, each case or shipping package is separately insured.

d) Average irrespective of percentage (named perils)—subject to particular average irrespective of percentage, including the risks of theft, pilferage, non-delivery, fresh water damage, sweat and steam of steamer's hold, bale hook damage, contact with fuel oil and other cargo.

e) Free of Capture and Seizure (F.C.&S.)—an insurance clause providing that loss is not insured if due to capture, seizure, confiscation and like actions, whether legal or not, or from such acts as piracy, civil war, rebellion, and civil strife.

f) Strikes, Riots, and Civil Commotions (S.R.&C.C.)—a term referring to an insurance clause excluding insurance of loss caused by labor disturbances, riots, and civil commotions.

g) All Risks—an insurance policy that covers against all risks of physical loss or damage from any external cause irrespective of percentage, but excluding the risks of war, strikes, riots, seizure, detention, and other risks excluded by the F.C.&S. and S.R.&C.C., unless coverage is extended to such risks specifically by endorsement.

h) War Risk—separate insurance coverage for loss of goods that results from any act of war

Mini Landbridge: Carrier will offer a through bill of lading from East Coast to West Coast. Ocean rate will be affixed from the original point. The ocean carrier will apply a division of rates with the inland carrier.

Mixed Credits: Exceptionally liberal financing terms for an export sale.

Most Favored Nation Treatment (MFN):   The policy of nondiscrimination in trade policy that provides to all trading partners the same customs and tariff treatment given to the so-called "Most Favored Nation." The MFN principle has provided the foundation of the world trading system in the post WWII era. All contracting parties to GATT apply MFN treatment to one another under Article I of GATT.

Multilateral Agreement: An international compact involving three or more parties.

Multilateral Trade Negotiations (MTN):   The "Rounds" held under the auspices of GATT since 1947, e.g., "Kennedy Round" 1963–1967 and "Tokyo Round" 1973–1979, and the "Uruguay Round" 1986–present. Each Round becomes the new GATT commitment.

Net Weight: Weight of the goods alone without any immediate wrappings. For instance the weight of the sardines in a tin can, *without* the weight of the can. (Opposite of tare)

Newly Industrializing Countries (NICs):   Relatively advanced developing countries whose industrial production and exports have grown rapidly in recent years. Countries in this category include Brazil, Hong Kong, South Korea, Mexico, Singapore, and Taiwan.

Nontariff Barriers: Government measures other than tariffs that restrict imports.

Open Account: Shipping merchandise to the importer in the foreign country with no guarantee of payment.

Par Value: The official fixed exchange rate between two currencies or between a currency and a specific weight of gold or a basket of currencies.

Pro Forma Invoice: A document containing the exporter's quote to the foreign buyer. The quotation remains valid for the period specified.

Protectionism: The deliberate use or encouragement of restrictions on imports to enable relatively inefficient domestic producers to compete successfully with foreign producers.

Shipper's Export Declaration: Official Commerce Department document required on the exportation of goods valued at or above $1000. It is used to compile U.S. export statistics as well as for enforcing U.S. export control laws.

Shipper's Summary Export Declaration: Shippers who meet certain criteria can use this document (instead of the one listed above) to report on a monthly basis rather than include a SED each time shipment is made.

Special Drawing Rights (SDRs): Created in 1969 by the International Monetary Fund as a supplemental international monetary reserve asset based on a basket of currencies—the U.S. dollar, the German mark, the French franc, the Japanese yen, and the British pound.

Specific Duty: Tariff imposed on imported goods based on weight or number of pieces rather than value.

Tare Weight: The weight of packing and containers without the goods to be shipped. (Opposite of net weight)

Validated License: Special license obtained from Commerce Department before shipment of certain goods, especially high-technology goods thought to be important for national security.

Valuation: The appraisal of the worth of the imported goods by customs officials for the purpose of determining the amount of duty payable in the importing country. The GATT Customs Valuation Code obligates signatory governments to use the "transaction value" of imported goods—or the price actually paid or payable for them—as the principal basis for valuing the goods for customs purposes.

Value Added Tax: An indirect tax on consumption that is levied at each discrete point in the chain of production and distribution, from the raw material stage to final consumption. Each processor or merchant pays a tax proportional to the amount by which he increases the value of the goods purchased for resale. The Value Added Tax is imposed throughout the EEC.

Wharfage: These charges are separate from ocean freight, representing loading and unloading of freight as well as terminal charges.

Appendix B

REVISED AMERICAN FOREIGN TRADE DEFINITIONS—1941*

*Adopted July 30, 1941, by a Joint Committee representing the Chamber of Commerce of the United States of America, the National Council of American Importers, Inc., and the National Foreign Trade Council, Inc.

Foreword

Since the issuance of *American Foreign Trade Definitions* in 1919, many changes in practice have occurred. The 1919 Definitions did much to clarify and simplify foreign trade practice, and received wide recognition and use by buyers and sellers throughout the world. At the Twenty-Seventh National Foreign Trade Convention, 1940, further revisions and clarification of these Definitions was urged as necessary to assist the foreign trader in the handling of his transactions.

The following *Revised American Foreign Trade Definitions—1941* are recommended for general use by both exporters and importers. These revised definitions have no status at law unless there is specific legislation providing for them, or unless they are confirmed by court decisions. Hence, it is suggested that sellers and buyers agree to their acceptance as part of the contract of sale. These revised definitions will then become legally binding upon all parties.

In view of changes in practice and procedure since 1919, certain new responsibilities for sellers and buyers are included in these revised definitions. Also, in many instances, the old responsibilities are more clearly defined than in the 1919 Definitions, and the changes should be beneficial both to sellers and buyers. Widespread acceptance will lead to a greater standardization of foreign trade procedure, and to the avoidance of much misunderstanding.

Adoption by exporters and importers of these revised terms will impress on all parties concerned their respective responsibilities and rights.

General Notes of Caution

1. As foreign trade definitions have been issued by organizations in various parts of the world, and as the courts of countries have interpreted these definitions in different ways, it is important that sellers and buyers agree that their contracts are subject to the *Revised American Foreign Trade Definitions—1941* and that the various points listed are accepted by both parties.

2. In addition to the foreign trade terms listed herein, there are terms that are at times used, such as Free Harbor, C.I.F. & C. (Cost, Insurance, Freight, and Commission), C.I.F.C. & I. (Cost, Insurance, Freight, Commission, and Interest), C.I.F. Landed (Cost, Insurance, Freight, Landed), and others. None of these should be used unless there has first been a definite understanding as to the exact meaning thereof. It is unwise to attempt to interpret other terms in the light of the terms given herein. Hence, whenever possible, one of the terms defined herein should be used.

3. It is unwise to use abbreviations in quotations or in contracts which might be subject to misunderstanding.

4. When making quotations, the familiar terms "hundredweight" or "ton" should be avoided. A hundredweight can be 100 pounds of the short ton, or 112 pounds of the long ton. A ton can be a short ton of 2,000 pounds, or a metric ton of 2,204.6 pounds, or a long ton of 2,240 pounds. Hence, the type of hundredweight or ton should be clearly stated in quotations and in sales confirmations. Also, all terms referring to quantity, weight, volume, length, or surface should be clearly defined and agreed upon.

5. If inspection, or certificate of inspection is required, it should be agreed, in advance, whether the cost thereof is for account of seller or buyer.

6. Unless otherwise agreed upon, all expenses are for the account of seller up to the point at which the buyer must handle the subsequent movement of goods.

7. There are a number of elements in a contract that do not fall within the scope of these foreign trade definitions. Hence, no mention of these is made herein. Seller and buyer should agree to these sepa-

rately when negotiating contracts. This particularly applies to so-called "customary" practices.

Definitions of Quotations

(I) Ex (Point of Origin)

"Ex Factory," "Ex Mill," "Ex Mine," "Ex Plantation," "Ex Ware-house," etc. (named point of origin).

Under this term, the price quoted applies only at the point of origin, and the seller agrees to place the goods at the disposal of the buyer at the agreed place on the date or within the period fixed.

Under this quotation:

Seller must
(1) bear all costs and risks of the goods until such time as the buyer is obliged to make delivery thereof;
(2) render the buyer, at the buyer's request and expense, assistance in obtaining the documents issued in the country of origin, or of ship-ment, or of both, which the buyer may require either for purposes of exportation, or of importation at destination.

Buyer must
(1) take delivery of the goods as soon as they have been placed at his disposal at the agreed place on the date or within the period fixed;
(2) pay export taxes, or other fees or charges, if any, levied because of exportation;
(3) bear all costs and risks of the goods from the time when he is obli-gated to take delivery thereof;
(4) pay all costs and charges incurred in obtaining the documents issued in the country of origin, or of shipment, or of both, which may be required either for purposes of exportation, or of importation at des-tination.

(II) F.O.B. (Free on Board)

Note: *Seller and buyer should consider not only the definitions but also the "Comments on All F.O.B. Terms" given at the end of this section, in order to understand fully their respective responsibilities and rights un-der the several classes of "F.O.B." terms.*

(II-A) "F.O.B. (named inland carrier at named inland point of departure)* Under this term, the price quoted applies only at inland shipping point, and the seller arranges for loading of the goods on, or in, railway cars, trucks, lighters, barges, aircraft, or other conveyance furnished for transportation.

Under this quotation:

Seller must

(1) place goods on, or in, conveyance, or deliver to inland carrier for loading;

(2) provide clean bill of lading or other transportation receipt, freight collect;

(3) be responsible for any loss or damage, or both, until goods have been placed in, or on, conveyance at loading point, and clean bill of lading or other transportation receipt has been furnished by the carrier;

(4) render the buyer, at the buyer's request and expense, assistance in obtaining the documents issued in the country of origin, or of shipment, or of both, which the buyer may require either for purposes of exportation, or of importation at destination.

Buyer must

(1) be responsible for all movement of the goods from inland point of loading, and pay all transportation costs:

(2) pay export taxes, or other fees or charges, if any, levied because of exportation;

(3) be responsible for any loss or damage, or both, incurred after loading at named inland point of departure;

(4) pay all costs and charges incurred in obtaining the documents issued in the country of origin, or of shipment, or of both, which may be required either for purposes of exportation, or of importation at destination.

(II-B) "F.O.B. (named inland carrier at named inland point of departure) Freight Prepaid To (named point of exportation)"* Under this term, the seller quotes a price including transportation charges to the named point of exportation and prepays freight to named point of exportation, without assuming responsibility for the goods after obtaining a clean bill of lading or other transportation receipt at named inland point of departure.

---

*See Note above and Comments on all F.O.B. Terms

Under this quotation:

Seller must

(1) assume the seller's obligations as under II-A, except that under (2) he must provide clean bill of lading or other transportation receipt, freight prepaid to named point of exportation.

Buyer must

(1) assume the same buyer's obligations as under II-A, except that he does not pay freight from loading point to named point of exportation.

(II-C) "F.O.B. (named inland carrier at named inland point of departure) Freight Allowed To (named point)"* Under this term, the seller quotes a price including the transportation charges to the named point, shipping freight collect and deducting the cost of transportation, without assuming responsibility for the goods after obtaining a clean bill of lading or other transportation receipt at named inland point of departure.

Under this quotation:

Seller must

(1) assume the same seller's obligations as under II-A, but deducts from his invoice the transportation cost to named point.

Buyer must

(1) assume the same buyer's obligations as under II-A, including payment of freight from inland loading point to named point, for which seller has made deduction.

(II-D) "F.O.B. (named inland carrier at named point of exportation)"* Under this term, the seller quotes a price including the costs of transportation of the goods to named point of exportation, bearing any loss or damage, or both, incurred up to that point.

Under this quotation:

Seller must

(1) place goods on, or in, conveyance, or deliver to inland carrier for loading;

(2) provide clean bill of lading or other transportation receipt, paying all transportation costs from loading point to named point of exportation;

---

*See Note above and Comments on all F.O.B. Terms

(3) be responsible for any loss or damage, or both, until goods have arrived in, or on, inland conveyance at the named point of exportation;

(4) render the buyer, at the buyer's request and expense, assistance in obtaining the documents issued in the country of origin, or of shipment, or of both, which the buyer may require either for purposes of exportation, or of importation at destination.

Buyer must

(1) be responsible for all movement of the goods from inland conveyance at named point of exportation;

(2) pay export taxes, or other fees or charges, if any, levied because of exportation;

(3) be responsible for any loss or damage, or both, incurred after goods have arrived in, or on, inland conveyance at the named point of exportation;

(4) pay all costs and charges incurred in obtaining the documents issued in the country of origin, or of shipment, or of both, which may be required either for purposes of exportation, or of importation at destination.

(II-E) "F.O.B. Vessel (named port of shipment)"* Under this term, the seller quotes a price covering all expenses up to, and including, delivery of the goods upon the overseas vessel provided by, or for, the buyer at the named port of shipment.

Under this quotation:

Seller must

(1) pay all charges incurred in placing goods actually on board the vessel designated and provided by, or for, the buyer on the date or within the period fixed;

(2) provide clean ship's receipt or on-board bill of lading;

(3) be responsible for any loss or damage, or both, until goods have been placed on board the vessel on the date or within the period fixed;

(4) render the buyer, at the buyer's request and expense, assistance in obtaining the documents issued in the country of origin, or of shipment, or of both, which the buyer may require either for purposes of exportation, or of importation at destination.

---

*See Note above and Comments on all F.O.B. Terms

Buyer must

(1) give seller adequate notice of name, sailing date, loading berth of, and delivery time to, the vessel;

(2) bear the additional costs incurred and all risks of the goods from the time when the seller has placed them at his disposal if the vessel named by him fails to arrive or to load within the designated time;

(3) handle all subsequent movement of the goods to destination:
(a) provide and pay for insurance;
(b) provide and pay for ocean and other transportation;

(4) pay export taxes, or other fees or charges, if any, levied because of exportation;

(5) be responsible for any loss or damage, or both, after goods have been loaded on board the vessel;

(6) pay all costs and charges incurred in obtaining the documents, other than clean ship's receipt or bill of lading, issued in the country of origin, or of shipment, or of both, which may be required either for purposes of exportation, or of importation at destination.

(II-F) "F.O.B. (named inland point in country of importation)"* Under this term, the seller quotes a price including the cost of merchandise and all costs of transportation to the named inland point in the country of importation.

Under this quotation:

Seller must

(1) provide and pay for all transportation to the named inland point in the country of importation;

(2) pay export taxes, or other fees or charges, if any, levied because of exportation;

(3) provide and pay for marine insurance;

(4) provide and pay for war risk insurance, unless otherwise agreed upon between the seller and buyer;

(5) be responsible for any loss or damage, or both, until arrival of goods on conveyance at the named inland point in the country of importation;

(6) pay the costs of certificates of origin, consular invoices, or any other

---

*See Note above and Comments on all F.O.B. Terms

documents issued in the country of origin, or of shipment, or of both, which the buyer may require for the importation of goods into the country of destination and, where necessary, for their passage in transit through another country;

(7) pay all costs of landing, including wharfage, landing charges, and taxes, if any;

(8) pay all costs of customs entry in the country of importation;

(9) pay customs duties and all taxes applicable to imports, if any, in the country of importation.

Note: *The seller under this quotation must realize that he is accepting important responsibilities, costs, and risks, and should therefore be certain to obtain adequate insurance. On the other hand, the importer or buyer may desire such quotations to relieve him of the risks of the voyage and to assure him of his landed costs at inland point in country of importation. When competition is keen, or the buyer is accustomed to such quotations from other sellers, seller may quote such terms, being careful to protect himself in an appropriate manner.*

Buyer must

(1) take prompt delivery of goods from conveyance upon arrival at destination;

(2) bear any costs and be responsible for all loss or damage, or both, after arrival at destination.

Comments On All F.O.B. Terms

In connection with F.O.B. terms, the following points of caution are recommended:

1. The method of inland transportation, such as trucks, railroad cars, lighters, barges, or aircraft should be specified.

2. If any switching charges are involved during the inland transportation, it should be agreed, in advance, whether these charges are for account of the seller or the buyer.

3. The term "F.O.B. (named port)", without designating the exact point at which the liability of the seller terminates and the liability of the buyer begins, should be avoided. The use of the term gives rise to disputes as to the liability of the seller or the buyer in the event of

loss or damage arising while the goods are in port, and before delivery to or on board the ocean carrier. Misunderstandings may be avoided by naming the specific point of delivery.

4. If lighterage or trucking is required in the transfer of goods from the inland conveyance to ship's side, and there is a cost therefor, it should be understood, in advance, whether this cost is for account of the seller or the buyer.

5. The seller should be certain to notify the buyer of the minimum quantity required to obtain a carload, a truckload, or a barge-load freight rate.

6. Under F.O.B. terms, excepting "F.O.B. (named inland point in country of importation)", the obligation to obtain ocean freight space, and marine and war risk insurance, rests with the buyer. Despite this obligation on the part of the buyer, in many trades the seller obtains the ocean freight space, and marine and war risk insurance, and provides for shipment on behalf of the buyer. Hence, seller and buyer must have an understanding as to whether the buyer will obtain the ocean freight space, and marine and war risk insurance, as is his obligation, or whether the seller agrees to do this for the buyer.

7. For the seller's protection, he should provide in his contract of sale that marine insurance obtained by the buyer include standard warehouse to warehouse coverage.

(III) F.A.S. (Free Along Side)

Note: *Seller and buyer should consider not only the definition but also the "Comments" given at the end of this section, in order to understand fully their respective responsibilities and rights under "F.A.S." terms.*

"F.A.S. VESSEL (named port of shipment)"

Under this term, the seller quotes a price including delivery of the goods along side overseas vessel and within reach of its loading tackle.

Under this quotation:

Seller must

(1) place goods along side vessel or on dock designated and provided by, or for, buyer on the date or within the period fixed; pay any heavy lift charges, where necessary, up to this point;

(2) provide clean dock or ship's receipt;

(3) be responsible for any loss or damage, or both, until goods have been delivered along side the vessel or on the dock;

(4) render the buyer, at the buyer's request and expense, assistance in obtaining the documents issued in the country of origin, or of shipment, or of both, which the buyer may require either for purposes of exportation, or of importation at destination.

Buyer must

(1) give seller adequate notice of name, sailing date, loading berth of, and delivery time to, the vessel;

(2) handle all subsequent movement of the goods from along side the vessel;

    (a) arrange and pay for demurrage or storage charges, or both, in warehouse or on wharf, where necessary;

    (b) provide and pay for insurance;

    (c) provide and pay for ocean and other transportation;

(3) pay export taxes, or other fees or charges, if any, levied because of exportation;

(4) be responsible for any loss or damage, or both, while the goods are on a lighter or other conveyance along side vessel within reach of its loading tackle, or on the dock awaiting loading, or until actually loaded on board the vessel, and subsequent thereto;

(5) pay all costs and charges incurred in obtaining the documents, other than clean dock or ship's receipt, issued in the country of origin, or of shipment, or of both, which may be required either for purposes of exportation, or of importation at destination.

F.A.S. Comments

1. Under F.A.S. terms, the obligation to obtain ocean freight space, and marine and war risk insurance, rests with the buyer. Despite this obligation on the part of the buyer, in many trades the seller obtains ocean freight space, and marine and war risk insurance, and provides for shipment on behalf of the buyer. In others, the buyer notifies the seller to make delivery along side a vessel designated by the buyer and the buyer provides his own marine and war risk insurance. Hence, seller and buyer must have an understanding as to whether the buyer will obtain the ocean freight space, and marine and war risk insurance, as is his obligation, or whether the seller agrees to do this for the buyer.

2. For the seller's protection, he should provide in his contract of sale

that marine insurance obtained by the buyer include standard warehouse to warehouse coverage.

(IV) C. & F. (Cost and Freight)

Note: *Seller and buyer should consider not only the definitions but also the "C. & F. Comments" and the "C. & F. and C.I.F. Comments", in order to understand fully their respective responsibilities and rights under "C. & F." terms.*

"C. & F. (named point of destination)"   Under this term, the seller quotes a price including the cost of transportation to the named point of destination.

Under this quotation:

Seller must
(1) provide and pay for transportation to named point of destination;
(2) pay export taxes, or other fees or charges, if any, levied because of exportation;
(3) obtain and dispatch promptly to buyer, or his agent, clean bill of lading to named point of destination;
(4) where received-for-shipment ocean bill of lading may be tendered, be responsible for any loss or damage, or both, until the goods have been delivered into the custody of the ocean carrier;
(5) where on-board ocean bill of lading is required, be responsible for any loss or damage, or both, until the goods have been delivered on board the vessel;
(6) provide, at the buyer's request and expense, certificates of origin, consular invoices, or any other documents issued in the country of origin, or of shipment, or of both, which the buyer may require for importation of goods into country of destination and, where necessary, for their passage in transit through another country.

Buyer must
(1) accept the documents when presented;
(2) receive the goods upon arrival, handle and pay for all subsequent movement of the goods, including taking delivery from vessel in accordance with bill of lading clauses and terms; pay all costs of landing, including any duties, taxes, and other expenses at named point of destination;

(3) provide and pay for insurance;

(4) be responsible for loss of or damage to goods, or both, from time and place at which seller's obligations under (4) or (5) above have ceased;

(5) pay the costs of certificates of origin, consular invoices, or any other documents issued in the country of origin, or of shipment, or of both, which may be required for the importation of goods into the country of destination and, where necessary, for their passage in transit through another country.

C. & F. Comments

1. For the seller's protection, he should provide in his contract of sale that marine insurance obtained by the buyer include standard warehouse to warehouse coverage.

2. The comments listed under the following C.I.F. terms in many cases apply to C. & F. terms as well, and should be read and understood by the C. & F. seller and buyer.

(V) C.I.F. (Cost, Insurance, Freight)

Note: *Seller and buyer should consider not only the definitions but also the "Comments", at the end of this section, in order to understand fully their respective responsibilities and rights under "C.I.F." terms.*

"C.I.F. (named point of destination)"   Under this term, the seller quotes a price including the cost of the goods, the marine insurance, and all transportation charges to the named point of destination.

Under this quotation:

Seller must

(1) provide and pay for transportation to named point of destination;

(2) pay export taxes, or other fees or charges, if any, levied because of exportation;

(3) provide and pay for marine insurance;

(4) provide war risk insurance as obtainable in seller's market at time of shipment at buyer's expense, unless seller has agreed that buyer provide for war risk coverage (See Comment 10 (c));

(5) obtain and dispatch promptly to buyer, or his agent, clean bill of lading to named point of destination, and also insurance policy or negotiable insurance-certificate;

(6) where received-for-shipment ocean bill of lading may be tendered, be responsible for any loss or damage, or both, until the goods have been delivered into the custody of the ocean carrier;

(7) where on-board ocean bill of lading is required, be responsible for any loss or damage, or both, until the goods have been delivered on board the vessel;

(8) provide, at the buyer's request and expense, certificates of origin, consular invoices, or any other documents issued in the country of origin, or of shipment, or both, which the buyer may require for importation of goods into country of destination and, where necessary, for their passage in transit through another country.

Buyer must

(1) accept the documents when presented;

(2) receive the goods upon arrival, handle and pay for all subsequent movement of the goods, including taking delivery from vessel in accordance with bill of lading clauses and terms; pay all costs of landing, including any duties, taxes, and other expenses at named point of destination;

(3) pay for war risk insurance provided by seller;

(4) be responsible for loss of or damage to goods, or both, from time and place at which seller's obligations under (6) or (7) above have ceased;

(5) pay the cost of certificates of origin, consular invoices, or any other documents issued in the country of origin, or of shipment, or both, which may be required for importation of the goods into the country of destination and, where necessary, for their passage in transit through another country.

C. & F. and C.I.F. Comments

Under C. & F. and C.I.F. contracts there are the following points on which the seller and the buyer should be in complete agreement at the time that the contract is concluded:

1. It should be agreed upon, in advance, who is to pay for miscellaneous expenses, such as weighing or inspection charges.

2. The quantity to be shipped on any one vessel should be agreed upon, in advance, with a view to the buyer's capacity to take delivery upon arrival and discharge of the vessel; within the free time allowed at the port of importation.

3. Although the terms C. & F. and C.I.F. are generally interpreted

to provide that charges for consular invoices and certificates of origin are for the account of the buyer, and are charged separately, in many trades these charges are included by the seller in his price. Hence, seller and buyer should agree, in advance, whether these charges are part of the selling price, or will be invoiced separately.

4. The point of final destination should be definitely known in the event the vessel discharges at a port other than the actual destination of the goods.

5. When ocean freight space is difficult to obtain, or forward freight contracts cannot be made at firm rates, it is advisable that sales contracts, as an exception to regular C. & F. or C.I.F. terms, should provide that shipment within the contract period be subject to ocean freight space being available to the seller, and should also provide that changes in the cost of ocean transportation between the time of sale and the time of shipment be for account of the buyer.

6. Normally, the seller is obligated to prepay the ocean freight. In some instances, shipments are made freight collect and the amount of the freight is deducted from the invoice rendered by the seller. It is necessary to be in agreement on this, in advance, in order to avoid misunderstanding which arises from foreign exchange fluctuations which might affect the actual cost of transportation, and from interest charges which might accrue under letter of credit financing. Hence, the seller should always prepay the ocean freight unless he has a specific agreement with the buyer, in advance, that goods can be shipped freight collect.

7. The buyer should recognize that he does not have the right to insist on inspection of goods prior to accepting the documents. The buyer should not refuse to take delivery of goods on account of delay in the receipt of documents, provided the seller has used due diligence in their dispatch through the regular channels.

8. Sellers and buyers are advised against including in a C.I.F. contract any indefinite clause at variance with the obligations of a C.I.F. contract as specified in these Definitions. There have been numerous court decisions in the United States and other countries invalidating C.I.F. contracts because of the inclusion of indefinite clauses.

9. Interest charges should be included in cost computations and should not be charged as a separate item in C.I.F. contracts, unless otherwise agreed upon, in advance, between the seller and buyer; in which case, however, the term C.I.F. and I (Cost, Insurance, Freight and Interest) should be used.

10. In connection with insurance under C.I.F. sales, it is necessary that seller and buyer be definitely in accord upon the following points:

(a) The character of the marine insurance should be agreed upon insofar as being W.A. (With Average) or F.P.A. (Free of Particular Average), as well as any other special risks that are covered in specific trades, or against which the buyer may wish individual protection. Among the special risks that should be considered and agreed upon between seller and buyer are theft, pilferage, leakage, breakage, sweat, contact with other cargoes, and others peculiar to any particular trade. It is important that contingent or collect freight and customs duty should be insured to cover Particular Average losses, as well as total loss after arrival and entry but before delivery.

(b) The seller is obligated to exercise ordinary care and diligence in selecting an underwriter that is in good financial standing. However, the risk of obtaining settlement of insurance claims rests with the buyer.

(c) War risk insurance under this term is to be obtained by the seller at the expense and risk of the buyer. It is important that the seller be in definite accord with the buyer on this point, particularly as to the cost. It is desirable that the goods be insured against both marine and war risk with the same underwriter, so that there can be no difficulty arising from the determination of the cause of the loss.

(d) Seller should make certain that in his marine or war risk insurance, there be included the standard protection against strikes, riots and civil commotions.

(e) Seller and buyer should be in accord as to the insured valuation, bearing in mind that merchandise contributes in General Average on certain bases of valuation which differ in various trades. It is desirable that a competent insurance broker be consulted, in order that full value be covered and trouble avoided.

(VI) Ex Dock

(VI) "Ex Dock (named port of importation)"

Note: *Seller and buyer should consider not only the definitions but also the "Ex Dock Comments" at the end of this section, in order to understand fully their respective responsibilities and rights under "Ex Dock" terms.*

Under this term, seller quotes a price including the cost of the goods and all additional costs necessary to place the goods on the dock at the named port of importation, duty paid, if any.

Under this quotation:

Seller must

(1) provide and pay for transportation to named port of importation;

(2) pay export taxes, or other fees or charges, if any, levied because of exportation;

(3) provide and pay for marine insurance;

(4) provide and pay for war risk insurance, unless otherwise agreed upon between the buyer and seller;

(5) be responsible for any loss or damage, or both, until the expiration of the free time allowed on the dock at the named port of importation;

(6) pay the costs of certificates of origin, consular invoices, legalization of bill of lading, or any other documents issued in the country of origin, or of shipment, or of both, which the buyer may require for the importation of goods into the country of destination and, where necessary, for their passage in transit through another country;

(7) pay all costs of landing, including wharfage, landing charges, and taxes, if any;

(8) pay all costs of customs entry in the country of importation;

(9) pay customs duties and all taxes applicable to imports, if any, in the country of importation, unless otherwise agreed upon.

Buyer must

(1) take delivery of the goods on the dock at the named port of importation within the free time allowed;

(2) bear the cost and risk of the goods if delivery is not taken within the free time allowed.

Ex Dock Comments

This term is used principally in United States import trade. It has various modifications, such as "Ex Quay", "Ex Pier", etc., but it is seldom, if ever, used in American export practice. Its use in quotations for export is not recommended.

Appendix C

BUILDING AN
EXPORT LIBRARY

There are many publications geared toward helping the exporter. This list contains the publications that are most helpful. Unless stated otherwise, the following documents can be obtained from the Superintendent of Documents, U.S. Government Printing Office, Washington, D.C. 20402.

Basic Guide to Exporting,   Commerce Department, 1987, $8.50

Business America,   Commerce Department. Biweekly, $57/year for 26 issues. Designed especially for American exporters who want to grow and American businesses who are ready to enter the world of exporting. It contains country-by-country marketing reports, incisive economic analyses, worldwide trade leads, advance notice of planned exhibitions of U.S. products worldwide, and success stories of selected American business firms in the field of exporting.

Overseas Business Reports.   Monthly, $26 annual, single copy price varies. Includes current and detailed marketing information, trade outlooks, statistics, regulations, and marketing profiles.

TOP Bulletin.   A weekly publication of all the trade leads received the previous week for all products from all countries. $175 annual. Office of Information and Product Development Distribution, Room H-1324, International Trade Administration, U.S. DOC Washington, D.C., 20444.

U.S. Export Administration Regulations   is a loose-leaf compilation of regulations with which exporters must familiarize themselves in order to conduct their export business. Annual subscribers receive supplemental *Export Administration Bulletins* which explain recent policy changes and provide replacement pages to keep the set of regulations up-to-date. $86.

Foreign Economic Trends Reports. (FETS) Each report in this series presents business and economic developments and the latest economic indicators for a particular country. $70 annual, single copies available for $1.00 from Publications & Distribution, Roon H-1617, U.S. DOC, Washington, D.C. 20230

Exporter's Encyclopedia. Annual with semimonthly updates. Dun & Bradstreet International, One Exchange Plaza, Suite 715, Jersey City, NJ 07302. Comprehensive country-by-country coverage of 220 world markets. Documents. Transportation data. Government regulations. Business travel. $365

Appendix D

RESOURCE GUIDE

U.S. Department of Commerce District Offices

Northeastern Region I
CONNECTICUT
*Hartford, 06103,
Room 610-B, Fed. Bldg.,
450 Main St.
(203) 722-3530.
MAINE
Augusta, 04330,
1 Memorial Circle,
Casco Bank Bldg.,
(207) 622-8249.
MASSACHUSETTS
Boston, 02210,
World Trade Center Boston,
Commonwealth Pier
(617) 223-2312.
NEW HAMPSHIRE
Serviced by Boston District
  Office
NEW YORK
Buffalo, 14202,
1312 Federal Bldg.,
111 W. Huron St.
(716) 846-4191.

New York, 10278,
Rm. 3718, Federal Office Bldg.,
26 Federal Plaza, Foley Sq.
(212) 264-0634.
Rochester, 14604,
121 East Ave.
(716) 263-6480.

RHODE ISLAND
Providence, 02903,
7 Jackson Walkway
(401) 528-5104.

VERMONT
Serviced by Boston District
  Office

Mid-Atlantic Region II
DELAWARE
Serviced by Philadelphia District
  Office

DISTRICT OF COLUMBIA
Serviced by Baltimore District
  Office

MARYLAND
Baltimore, 21202,
413 U.S. Customhouse,
Gay and Lombard Sts.
(301) 962-3560.
Rockville,
U.S. Department of Commerce,
Herbert C. Hoover
Bldg., Rm. 1066,
14th and E Sts. N.W.,
Washington, D.C. 20230,
(202) 377-3181.

NEW JERSEY
*Trenton, 08608,
240 West State St.,
8th Fl.
(609) 989-2100.

PENNSYLVANIA
Philadelphia, 19106,
9448 Federal Bldg.,
600 Arch St.
(215) 597-2866.
Pittsburgh, 15222,
2002 Fed. Bldg.,
1000 Liberty Ave.
(412) 644-2850.

Appalachian Region III
KENTUCKY
Louisville, 40202,
Rm. 636B,
U.S. Post Office and Courthouse
  Bldg.
(502) 582-5066.

NORTH CAROLINA
*Greensboro, 27402,
203 Federal Bldg.,
324 W. Market St.,
P.O. Box 1950
(919) 333-5345.

SOUTH CAROLINA
Columbia, 29201,
Strom Thurmond Fed. Bldg.,
Suite 172, 1835 Assembly St.
(803) 765-5345.
Charleston, 29401,
17 Lockwood Drive
(803) 724-4361.

TENNESSEE
Nashville, 37219-1505,
1114 Parkway Towers,
404 James Robertson Parkway
(615) 736-5161.
Memphis, 38103,
555 Beale St.
(901) 521-4137

VIRGINIA
Richmond, 23240,
8010 Federal Bldg.,
400 N. 8th St.
(804) 771-2246.

WEST VIRGINIA
Charleston, 25301
3000 New Federal Office Bldg.,
500 Quarrier St.
(304) 347-5123.

Southeastern Region IV
ALABAMA
*Birmingham, 35203,
3rd Floor, Berry Bldg.,
2015 2nd Ave.
(205) 731-1331.

FLORIDA
Clearwater, 33515,
128 N. Osceola Ave.
(813) 461-0011.
Jacksonville, 32202,
3 Independent Dr.
(904) 791-2796.

Miami, 33130,
Suite 224, Federal Bldg.,
51 S.W. First Ave.
(305) 536-5267.
Orlando, 32802,
75 E. Ivanhoe Blvd.
(305) 648-6235.
Tallahassee, 32304,
Collins Bldg., Rm. 401
107 W. Gaines St.
(904) 488-6469.

GEORGIA
Atlanta, 30309,
Suite 600,
1365 Peachtree St., N.E.
(404) 881-7000.
Savannah, 31401,
120 Barnard St., Federal Bldg.
(912) 944-4204.

MISSISSIPPI
Jackson, 39213,
Suite 328,
300 Woodrow Wilson Blvd.
(601) 965-4388.

PUERTO RICO
San Juan, (Hato Rey), 00918,
Room 659 Federal Bldg.
(809) 753-4555.

Great Lakes Region V
ILLINOIS
Chicago, 60603,
Room 1406,
Mid-Continental Plaza Bldg.,
55 E. Monroe St.
(312) 353-4450.
Palatine, 60067,
W.R. Harper College,
Algonquin & Roselle Rd.
(312) 397-3000. Ext. 532.

Rockford, 61110-0247,
515 North Court St.,
P.O. Box 1747
(815) 987-8128.

INDIANA
Indianapolis, 46204,
357 U.S. Courthouse & Federal
    Office Bldg.,
46 E. Ohio St.
(317) 269-6214.

MICHIGAN
Detroit, 48226,
1140 McNamara Bldg.,
477 Mich. Ave.
(313) 226-3650
Grand Rapids, 49503,
300 Monroe N.W.,
Rm. 409
(616) 456-2411.

MINNESOTA
Minneapolis, 55401,
108 Federal Bldg., 110 S. 4th St.
(612) 349-3338.

OHIO
*****Cincinnati,** 45202,
9504 Fed. Office Bldg.,
550 Main St.
(513) 684-2944.
Cleveland, 44114,
Room 600, 666 Euclid Ave.
(216) 522-4750.

WISCONSIN
Milwaukee, 53202,
605 Federal Bldg.,
517 E. Wisconsin Ave.
(414) 291-3473.

Plains Region VI

IOWA
Des Moines, 50309
817 Federal Bldg.,
210 Walnut St.
(515) 284-4222.

KANSAS
Wichita, 67202,
River Park Place,
Suite 565, 727 North Waco
(316) 269-6160.

MISSOURI
Kansas City, 64106,
Rm. 635, 601 E. 12th St.
(816) 374-3142.
*St. Louis, 63105,
120 S. Central Ave.
(314) 425-3302.

NEBRASKA
Omaha, 68102,
Empire State Bldg.,
1st Floor, 300 S. 19th St.
(402) 221-3664.

NORTH DAKOTA
Serviced by Omaha District
   Office

SOUTH DAKOTA
Serviced by Omaha District
   Office

Central Region VII

ARKANSAS
Little Rock, 72201,
Ste. 320, Savers Federal Bldg.,
320 W. Capitol Ave.
(501) 378-5794.

LOUISIANA
New Orleans, 70130,
432 World Trade Center,
2 Canal St.
(504) 589-6546.

NEW MEXICO
Albuquerque, 87102,
517 Gold S.W., Suite 4303
(505) 766-2386.

OKLAHOMA
Oklahoma City, 73116,
5 Broadway Executive Park,
Ste. 200,
6601 Broadway Extension
(405) 231-5302.
Tulsa, 74127,
440 S. Houston St.
(918) 581-7650.

TEXAS
*Dallas, 75242,
Room 7A5, 1100 Commerce St.
(214) 767-0542.
Austin, 78711,
P.O. Box 12728,
Capitol Station
(512) 472-5059.
Houston, 77002
2625 Federal Bldg.,
Courthouse, 515 Rusk St.
(713) 229-2578.

Rocky Mt. Region VIII

ARIZONA
Phoenix, 85025,
Federal Bldg. & U.S.
   Courthouse,
230 N. First Ave.
(602) 261-3285.

COLORADO
*Denver, 80202,
Room 119, U.S. Customhouse,
721 19th St.
(303) 844-3246.

IDAHO
Boise, 83720,
Statehouse, Rm. 113
(208) 334-9254.

MONTANA
Serviced by Denver District
  Office
NEVADA
Reno, 89502,
1755 East Plumb Lane,
Rm. 152
(702) 784-5203.
UTAH
Salt Lake City, 84101,
Rm. 340,
U.S. Post Office Bldg.,
350 S. Main St.
(801) 524-5116.
WYOMING
Serviced by Denver District
  Office

Pacific Region IX
ALASKA
Anchorage, 99513,
P.O. Box 32, 701 C St.
(907) 271-5041.
CALIFORNIA
Los Angeles, 90049
Rm. 800,
11777 San Vicente Blvd.
(213) 209-6707.
San Diego, 92138,
P.O. Box 81404
(619) 293-5395.
Santa Ana, 92701,
116-A W. 4th St.,
Ste. 1
(714) 836-2461.
*San Francisco, 94102,
Federal Bldg.,
Box 36013,
450 Golden Gate Ave.
(415) 556-5860.

---

*Denotes Regional Managing Director

HAWAII
Honolulu, 96850,
4106 Federal Bldg.,
300 Ala Moana Blvd.,
P.O. Box 50026
(808) 546-8694.
OREGON
Portland, 97204,
Room 618,
1220 S.W. 3rd Ave.
(503) 221-3001.
WASHINGTON
Seattle, 98109,
Rm. 706, Lake Union Bldg.,
1700 Westlake Ave. North
(206) 442-5616.
Spokane, 99210,
P.O. Box 2170
(509) 456-4557

FINANCING—CONTACTS/
ADDRESSES

SMALL BUSINESS
ADMINISTRATION

Office of Business Loans
U.S. Small Business
  Administration
1441 L Street, NW
Suite 804
Washington, D.C. 20416
(202) 653-6470

EXIMBANK

Export-Import Bank of the
  United States
811 Vermont Avenue, N.W.
Washington, D.C. 20571
(202) 566-8990
Small Business Hotline:
  (800) 424-5201

PEFCO

Private Export Funding
  Corporation
280 Park Avenue
New York, N.Y. 10017
(212) 557-3100

FCIA

Foreign Credit Insurance
  Association
40 Rector Street
New York, N.Y. 10006
(212) 306-5000

OPIC

Overseas Private Investment
  Corporation
1129 20th Street, N.W.
Washington, D.C. 20527
(202) 653-2800

AID

Agency for International
  Development
for information on loan agree-
  ments, products and firms
  likely to import:
Office of Small Business and
  Disadvantaged Business Utili-
  zation
AID/SDB/C
Agency for International
  Development
Washington, D.C. 20523
(703) 235-1822

For specific information:

AID Country Desk Officer
Agency for International
  Development
Washington, D.C. 20523

For general information:
Assistant Administrator
Bureau for Program and Policy
  Coordination
Agency for International
  Development
Washington, D.C. 20523
(202) 632-0482

IDCA

Trade and Development
  Program
International Development
  Cooperation Agency
Washington, D.C. 20523
(703) 235-3663

U.S. DEPARTMENT
  OF AGRICULTURE
Food for Peace
For information on supplier
  approval (Titles I/III):
Department of Agriculture
Export Credits
Foreign Agricultural Service
U.S. Department of Agriculture
Washington, D.C. 20250
(202) 447-5780

For information on current and
  future Title I Agreements:

Program Development Division
Export Credits
Foreign Agricultural Service
U.S. Department of Agriculture
Washington, D.C. 20250
(202) 382-9221

For information on Title II
  Procurement:
Director
Kansas City ASCS Commodity
  Office

U.S. Department of Agriculture
P.O. Box 205
Kansas City, Mo. 64141
(816) 926-6301

Commodity credit corporation—
Commercial export program
For information on program
operations, sales registrations,
applicable regulations:
CCC Operations Division
Export Credits
Foreign Agricultural Service
U.S. Department of Agriculture
Washington, D.C. 20250
(202) 447-3224

For questions about specific
country programs or market-
ing opportunities:
Program Development Division
Export Credits
Foreign Agricultural Service
U.S. Department of Agriculture
Washington, D.C. 20250
Europe and Africa Area
(202) 382-9219
Asia and Near East Area
(202) 382-9216
Latin America and Caribbean
Area (202) 382-9225

WORLD BANK GROUP

Information for IBRD and IDA:
1818 H St., NW
Washington, D.C. 20433
(202) 477-1234

International Finance
Corporation
1850 I St., NW
Room I 12-109
Washington, D.C. 20433
(202) 477-1234

New York Office:
747 3rd Avenue
26th Floor
New York, N.Y. 10017
(212) 754-6008

DEVELOPMENT BANKS

Inter-American Development
Bank
External Relations Office
808 17th St., NW
Washington, D.C. 20577
(202) 634-8087

Office of the U.S. Director and/or
Chief Information Officer
Asian Development Bank
P.O. Box 789
Manila 2800
Republic of the Philippines

African Development Bank
Group
B.P. No. 1387
Abidjan, Ivory Coast

CUSTOMS ORGANIZATION

Mission

The major responsibility of the U.S. Customs Service is to administer the Tariff Act of 1930, as amended. Primary duties include the assessment and collection of all duties, taxes, and fees on imported merchandise, the enforcement of customs and related laws, and the administration of certain navigation laws and treaties. As a major enforcement organization, the Customs Service combats smuggling and frauds on the revenue and enforces the regulations of numerous other Federal agencies at ports of entry and along the land and sea borders of the United States.

Organization

The customs territory of the United States consists of the 50 states, the District of Columbia, and Puerto Rico. The Customs Service, an agency under the Department of the Treasury, has its headquarters in Washington, D.C., and is headed by a Commissioner of Customs. The field organization consists of seven geographical regions further divided into districts with ports of entry within each district. These organizational elements are headed respectively by regional commissioners, district directors (or area directors in the case of the New York region), and port directors. The Customs Service is also responsible for administering the customs laws of the Virgin Islands of the United States.

Both an alphabetical list of all ports by State and a list of districts by region (including postal ZIP code) are provided. Whenever it is suggested that you write to the district or port director for information, the director referred to is the one at the district or port where your goods will be entered.

Ports of Entry by State (Including Puerto Rico and the U.S. Virgin Islands)

Key: Districts shown in boldface
 • Regional Headquarters

ALABAMA
 Birmingham
 Huntsville
 Mobile

ALASKA
 Alcan
 Anchorage
 Dalton Cache
 Fairbanks
 Juneau
 Ketchikan

Sitka
Skagway
Valdez
Wrangell

ARIZONA
Douglas
Lukeville
Naco
Nogales
Phoenix
San Luis
Sasabe

ARKANSAS
Little Rock-N. Little Rock

CALIFORNIA
Andrade
Calexico
Eureka
Fresno
•**Los Angeles—Long Beach**
Port San Luis
San Diego
San Francisco-Oakland
Tecate
San Ysidro

COLORADO
Denver

CONNECTICUT
Bridgeport
Hartford
New Haven
New London

DELAWARE
Wilmington
(see Philadelphia)

DISTRICT OF COLUMBIA
Washington

FLORIDA
Apalachicola
Boca Grande
Carrabelle
Fernandina Beach
Jacksonville
Key West
•**Miami**
Orlando
Panama City
Pensacola
Port Canaveral
Port Everglades
Port St. Joe
St. Petersburg
Tampa
West Palm Beach

GEORGIA
Atlanta
Brunswick
Savannah

HAWAII
Honolulu
Hilo
Kahului
Nawiliwili-Port Allen

IDAHO
Eastport
Porthill
Boise

ILLINOIS
•**Chicago**
Peoria
Rock Island-Moline*
(see Davenport)

INDIANA
Evansville/
Owensboro, Ky.
Indianapolis

Lawrenceburg/
Cincinnati, Ohio

IOWA
Davenport-Rock
Island-Moline*
Des Moines

KANSAS
Wichita

KENTUCKY
Louisville
Owensboro/
Evansville, Ind.

LOUISIANA
Baton Rouge
Gramercy
Lake Charles
Morgan City
•**New Orleans**
Shreveport/Bossier
City*

MAINE
Bangor
Bar Harbor
Bath
Belfast
Bridgewater
Calais
Eastport
Fort Fairfield
Fort Kent
Houlton
Jackman
Jonesport
Limestone
Madawaska
Portland
Rockland
Van Buren
Vanceboro

MARYLAND
Annapolis
Baltimore
Cambridge

MASSACHUSETTS
•**Boston**
Fall River
Gloucester
Lawrence
New Bedford
Plymouth
Salem
Springfield
Worcester

MICHIGAN
Battle Creek
Detroit
Grand Rapids
Muskegon
Port Huron
Saginaw-Bay City/Flint
Sault Ste. Marie

MINNESOTA
Baudette
Duluth and Superior, Wis.
Grand Portage
International Falls-Ranier
Minneapolis-St. Paul
Noyes
Pinecreek
Roseau
Warroad

MISSISSIPPI
Greenville
Gulfport
Pascagoula
Vicksburg

MISSOURI
Kansas City

St. Joseph
St. Louis
Springfield
(Temporary)

MONTANA
Butte
Del Bonita
Great Falls
Morgan
Opheim
Piegan
Raymond
Roosville
Scobey
Sweetgrass
Turner
Whitetail
Whitlash

NEBRASKA
Omaha

NEVADA
Las Vegas
Reno

NEW HAMPSHIRE
Portsmouth

NEW JERSEY
Perth Amboy (See New York/
  Newark)

NEW MEXICO
Albuquerque
Columbus

NEW YORK
Albany
Alexandria Bay
Buffalo-Niagara Falls
Cape Vincent
Champlain-Rouses Point
Chateaugay

Clayton
Fort Covington
Massena
•**New York**
  Kennedy Airport Area
  Newark Area
  New York Seaport Area
  Ogdensburg
Oswego
Rochester
Sodus Point
Syracuse
Trout River
Utica

NORTH CAROLINA
Beaufort-Morehead City
Charlotte
Durham
Reidsville
Wilmington
Winston-Salem

NORTH DAKOTA
Ambrose
Antler
Carbury
Dunseith
Fortuna
Hannah
Hansboro
Maida
Neche
Noonan
Northgate
Pembina
Portal
Sarles
Sherwood
St. John
Walhalla
Westhope

OHIO
Akron
Ashtabula/Conneaut
Cincinnati/Lawrenceburg,
Ind.
Cleveland
Columbus
Dayton
Toledo/Sandusky

OKLAHOMA
Oklahoma City
Tulsa

OREGON
Coos Bay
Newport
Portland*

PENNSYLVANIA
Chester (see Phila.)
Erie
Harrisburg
**Philadelphia/Chester/
Wilmington**
Pittsburg
Wilkes-Barre/Scranton

PUERTO RICO
Aguadilla
Fajardo
Guanica
Humacao
Jobos
Mayaguez
Ponce
San Juan

RHODE ISLAND
Newport
Providence

SOUTH CAROLINA
Charleston
Georgetown
Greenville-Spartanburg

TENNESSEE
Chattanooga
Knoxville
Memphis
Nashville

TEXAS
Amarillo
Austin
Beaumont*
Brownsville
Corpus Christi
Dallas/Ft. Worth
Del Rio
Eagle Pass
El Paso
Fabens
Freeport
Hidalgo
•Houston/Galveston
Laredo
Lubbock
Orange*
Port Arthur*
Port Lavaca-Point Comfort
Presidio
Progreso
Rio Grande City
Roma
Sabine*
San Antonio

UTAH
Salt Lake City

VERMONT
Beecher Falls
Burlington
Derby Line
Highgate Springs/Alburg
Norton
Richford
St. Albans

VIRGIN ISLANDS
Charlotte Amalie, St. Thomas
Christiansted
Coral Bay
Cruz Bay
Frederiksted

VIRGINIA
Alexandria
Cape Charles City
Norfolk-Newport News
Reedville
Richmond-Petersburg

WASHINGTON
Aberdeen
Anacortes*
Bellingham*
Blaine
Boundary
Danville
Everett*
Ferry
Friday Harbor*
Frontier
Laurier
Longview*
Lynden
Metaline Falls
Neah Bay*

Nighthawk
Olympia*
Oroville
Point Roberts
Port Angeles*
Port Townsend*
Seattle*
Spokane
Sumas
Tacoma*

WEST VIRGINIA
Charleston

WISCONSIN
Ashland
Green Bay
Manitowoc
Marinette
Milwaukee
Racine
Sheboygan

---

*Consolidated Ports:
Columbia River port of entry includes Longview, Washington, and Portland, Oregon.
Beaumont, Orange, Port Arthur, Sabine port of entry includes ports of the same name.
Port of Puget Sound includes Tacoma, Seattle, Port Angeles, Port Townsend, Neah Bay, Friday Harbor, Everett, Bellingham, Anacortes, and Olympia in the State of Washington.
Port of Philadelphia includes Wilmington and Chester.
Port of Rock Island includes Moline and Davenport, Iowa.
Port of Shreveport includes Bossier City, La.
Designated User-fee Airports: Allentown-Bethlehem-Easton, PA, Fargo, ND, Lebanon, NH, Santa Teresa, NM, Wilmington, OH, and Southwest Florida Reginal Airport, Fort Myers, FL.

Customs Regions and Districts

Headquarters
U.S. Customs Service
1301 Constitution Ave., N.W.
Washington, D.C. 20229

Northeast Region—
Boston, Mass. 02110
Districts:
Portland, Maine 04112
St. Albans, Vt. 05478
Boston, Mass. 02109
Providence, R.I. 02903
Buffalo, N.Y. 14202
Ogdensburg, N.Y. 13669
Bridgeport, Conn. 06601
Philadelphia, Pa. 19106
Baltimore, Md. 21202
Norfolk, Va. 23510
Washington, D.C. 20041

New York Region—
New York, N.Y. 10048
New York Seaport Area
New York, N.Y. 10048
Kennedy Airport Area
Jamaica, N.Y. 11430
Newark Area
Newark, N.J. 07114

Southeast Region—
Miami, Fla. 33131
Districts:
Wilmington, N.C. 28401
San Juan, P.R. 00903
Charleston, S.C. 29402
Savannah, Ga. 31401
Tampa, Fla. 33602
Miami, Fla. 33131
St. Thomas, V.I. 00801

South Central Region—
New Oreleans, La. 70130

Districts:
Mobile, Ala. 36601
New Orleans, La. 70130

Southwest Region—
Houston, Tex. 77057
Districts:
Port Arthur, Tex. 77642
Houston/Galveston, Tex.
77052
Laredo, Tex. 78041-3130
El Paso, Tex. 79985
Dallas/Fort Worth, Tex. 75261

Pacific Region—
Los Angeles, Calif. 90012
Districts:
Nogales, Ariz. 85621
San Diego, Calif. 92189
Los Angeles/Long Beach,
Calif. 90731
San Francisco, Calif. 94126
Honolulu, Hawaii 96806
Portland, Oreg. 97209
Seattle, Wash. 98174
Anchorage, Alaska 90501
Great Falls, Mont. 59401

North Central Region—
Chicago, Ill. 60605-5790
Districts:
Chicago, Ill. 60607
Pembina, N. Dak. 58271
Minneapolis-St. Paul, Minn.
55401
Duluth, Minn. 55802
Milwaukee, Wis. 53202
Cleveland, Ohio 44114
St. Louis, Mo. 63105
Detroit, Mich. 48226-2568

U.S. Customs Officers in Foreign Countries

Austria
Customs Attaché
American Embassy
Boltzmanngasse 16, A-1091
Vienna
Tel: 315-5511

Belgium
Customs Attaché
U.S. Mission to the European
 Communities (USEC)
No. 40 Blvd. du Regent
1000 Brussels
Tel: 513-4450 Ext. 2779

Brazil
Customs Attaché
American Embassy
Avenida Das Nocoes, Lote 3
Brasilia
Tel: 223-0120

Canada
Customs Attaché
American Embassy
95 Sparks St.
Suite 1130
Ottawa, Ontario K1P5T1
Tel: (613) 238-5335 X 322

England
Customs Attaché
American Embassy
24/31 Grosvenor Square
London, W. 1
Tel: 1/493-4599

France
Customs Attaché
American Embassy
58 bis Rue la Boetie
Room 210
75008 Paris
Tel: 296-1202 Ext. 2392/2393

Hong Kong, B.B.C.
Senior Customs Representative
American Consulate General
St. John's Building-11th Floor
33 Garden Road
Tel: 5-239011 Ext. 244

Italy
Customs Attaché
American Embassy
Via V. Veneto 119
Rome
Tel: 6/4674 Ext. 475 or 413

Japan
Customs Attaché
American Embassy
Minato-Ku Akasaka 1-chome
13 go, No. 14
Tokyo
Tel: 583-7141 Ext. 7205

Korea
Customs Attaché
82 SeJong Ro
Chongro-Ku
Seoul
Tel: 732-2601 Ext. 4563

Mexico
Customs Attaché
American Embassy
Paseo de la Reforma 305
Colonia Cuahtemoc
Mexico, D.F., Mexico
Tel: (905) 211-0042 Ext. 3687

Pakistan
Senior Customs Rep.
American Consulate General
8 Abdullah Haroon Road
Karachi
Tel: 51-50-81

Panama
Customs Attaché
Calle 38 & Avenida Balboa
Panama, R.P.
Tel: 271777

Thailand
Customs Attaché
American Embassy
95 Wireless Road
Bangkok
Tel: 252-5040

West Germany
Customs Attaché
American Embassy
Mahlemer Avenue 5300
Bonn-Bad Godesberg
Tel: 228/3392207
228/3312853

The location and telephone numbers for Customs International Mail Branches are as follows:

Mail Branch	Location	Telephone No.
Atlanta, Georgia	619 Piedmont Ave., N.E. Atlanta, GA 30308	(404) 881-4956
Boston, Massachusetts	South Postal Annex, Rm. 322 Boston, MA 02203	(617) 223-7853
Buffalo, New York	1200 William Street Buffalo, NY 14206	(716) 846-4319
Charlotte Amalie	P.O. Box 510 St. Thomas, VI 00801	(809) 774-1455
Chicago, Illinois	610 S. Canal St., Rm. 104 Chicago, IL 60607	(312) 353-6140
Dallas, Texas	1100 Commerce St. Dallas, TX 75202	(214) 729-0413
Detroit, Michigan	General P.O. Building Detroit, MI 48232	(313) 226-3137
El Paso, Texas	Bridge of Americas Building B, P.O. Box 9516 El Paso, TX 79985	(915) 572-7836
Honolulu, Hawaii	3599 Nimitz Highway Honolulu, HI 96819	(808) 546-9608
Laredo, Texas	1000 Zaragoza Street Laredo, TX 78040	(512) 734-6207
Los Angeles, California	300 N. Los Angeles St. Los Angeles, CA 90053	(213) 688-2573
Miami, Florida	P.O. Box 523212 Miami, FL 33152	(305) 350-4281
Minneapolis/ St. Paul, Minnesota	180 E. Kellogg Blvd. St. Paul, MN 55101	(612) 725-7861

Resource Guide

Mail Branch	Location	Telephone No.
Newark, New Jersey (NYBFMC) (Surface Mail)	80 County Road Jersey City, NJ 07097	(201) 420-6370
New Orleans, Louisiana	701 Loyola Ave. New Orleans, LA 70113	(504) 589-2205
New York, New York (Air Mail)	201 Varick Street New York, NY 10014	(212) 620-3211
Oakland, California	1675 7th Street Oakland, CA 94615	(415) 273-7560
Philadelphia, Pennsylvania	GPO-30th & Market Streets Philadelphia, PA 19104	(215) 596-5540
San Juan, Puerto Rico	P.O. Box 2112 San Juan, PR 00903	(809) 765-8586
Seattle, Washington (AMF)	Seattle/Tacoma Int'l. Airport Seattle, WA 98158	(206) 442-5382
Washington, D.C.	3180 Bladensburg Rd., N.E. Washington, D.C. 20018	(202) 566-8444

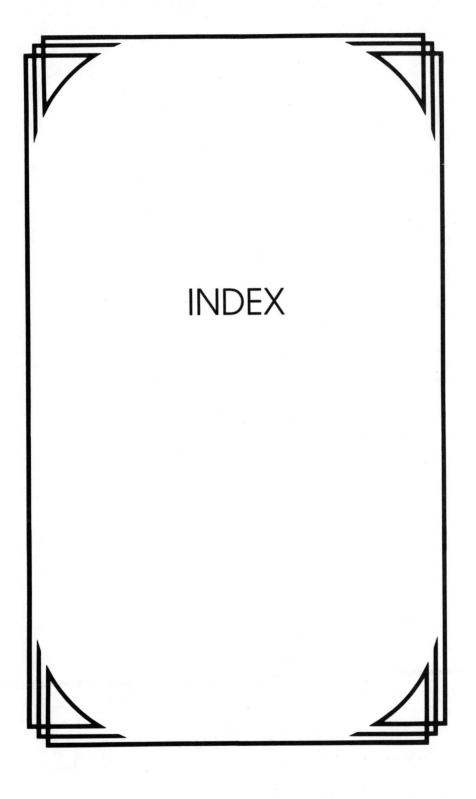

INDEX